Arab background series

Editor: N. A. Ziadeh, Emeritus Professor of History, American University of Beirut

By the same author
Sudan Colloquial Arabic, 1946
The Christian Approach to Islam in the Sudan, 1948
Islam in the Sudan, 1949
The Christian Church in Post-War Sudan, 1949
Church and Mission in Ethiopia, 1950
Islam in Ethiopia, 1952
The Christian Church and Islam in West Africa, 1955
Islam in West Africa, 1959
A History of Islam in West Africa, 1962
Islam in East Africa, 1964
The Sufi Orders in Islam, 1971
Two Worlds are Ours, 1971
Christianity Among the Arabs in Pre-Islamic Times, 1979

The influence of Islam upon Africa

Second edition

J. Spencer Trimingham

Longman London and New York
Librairie du Liban

LONGMAN GROUP LIMITED
London and New York

LIBRAIRIE DU LIBAN
Beirut

Associated companies, branches and representatives throughout the world

First impression 1968, Second edition 1980

ISBN 0 582 78499 9

British Library Cataloguing in Publication Data

Trimingham, John Spencer
The Influence of Islam upon Africa.—2nd ed.
—(Arab background series).
1. Islam—Africa—History 2. Africa—History
I. Title II. Series
960'.3 BP64.A1 79-42873

ISBN 0-582-78499-9

Jacket picture by courtesy of Jil Paul

Printed in Great Britain by Butler and Tanner Ltd, Frome and London

Contents

Maps

Editor's Preface

The Arab World has, for some time, been attracting the attention of a growing public throughout the world. The strategic position of the Arab countries, the oil they produce, their sudden emancipation and emergence as independent states, their revolutions and *coups d'état*, have been the special concern of statesmen, politicians, businessmen, scholars and journalists, and of equal interest to the general public.

An appreciation of the present-day problems of Arab countries and of their immediate neighbours demands a certain knowledge of their geographical and social background; and a knowledge of the main trends of their history—political, cultural and religious—is essential for an understanding of current issues. Arabs had existed long before the advent of Islam in the seventh century AD, but it was with Islam that they became a world power. Arab civilization, which resulted from the contacts the Arabs had with other peoples and cultures, especially after the creation of this world power, and which reached its height in the ninth, tenth and eleventh centuries, was, for a few centuries that followed, the guiding light of a large part of the world. Its rôle cannot, thus, be ignored.

The Arab Background Series provides the English-speaking, educated reader with a series of books which attempt to clarify the historical past of the Arabs and to analyse their present problems. The contributors to the series, who come from many parts of the world, are all specialists in their own fields. This variety of approach and attitude creates for the English-speaking reader a unique picture of the Arab World.

N. A. ZIADEH

Preface

My previous studies of Islam in Africa have been of a regional nature. Here I try to take an overall view, but the limitations indicated in the title should be borne in mind. I have not attempted a study of Islam in Africa, but am concerned with a historical process. My aim is to show the influence of Islam as a religious culture upon Africans, with emphasis upon the more strictly religious aspects. The study begins with an account of Islam's historical penetration, which it has been convenient to treat regionally. Then seeks to show the way in which it has changed African societies, how it has introduced universalist concepts into particularist societies and inculcated a new attitude and outlook on life; how it exerts a constant influence, and what are the forms and institutions through which that influence has been effected. It is necessary to indicate whether developments in one region have affected others, what trends and features are common to all African Muslims and what are regional. But the subject cannot be left there if it is to be kept in touch with the present. A converse phenomenon of change has now to be taken into account, with Islamic societies as the object of the pressure of new forces, and the last chapter is concerned with the impact of Western secular culture.

The attempt to cover a process of change embracing every aspect of life has meant that I have had to be highly selective in illustrative material and to generalize too frequently without making the qualifications which might modify the tones of the picture. But it is difficult to avoid this in a short survey of the revolution which the impulse and diffusion of Islam sets in motion in African life.

Whilst primarily concerned with African societies south of the Sahara, account is taken of the influence of and relationships with Mediterranean Islamic culture. In the wider context of Islamic culture zones the Maghrib and Egypt need relating to their

African context, though no account is given of the structure of Islamic life in these environments. The great difference between the two areas north and south of the Sahara derives from the fact that Mediterranean Africa was Islamized at an early date and an integrated Islamic culture formed. This was the main source of Islamic currents among Negroes and Hamites (though currents from Arabia are also important), but they did not begin to penetrate until the eleventh century, whilst African reaction to their infiltration had peculiar features, and it is only since the theocratic, Islamically legalistic, revolution of the eighteenth and nineteenth centuries that Islam gained a real hold. Even after that until today the position is special in that we are still in a transitionary period and situation. Islam gained adherents with great rapidity during the period of colonial rule, which means that Africans are at all stages of transition and Islamic integration. Hence the studies which follow will pay attention to such aspects as the process of transition into Islam and the changes that ensue.

The main distinction I shall be making is between what I designate as 'Sudan' Islam or Muslims and 'Hamitic' Islam or Muslims. My use of these terms does not imply any racial assumptions. They are used simply because I found it necessary to distinguish two different types of African mentality, culture and outlook on life which affected their respective reactions to Islam and absorption of elements of Islamic culture. One of these was roughly conterminous with those who speak, or at one time spoke, Hamitic languages.

I am often asked the question, 'Is there anything basically different in the Islam believed and practised by African Muslims from the Islam of Muslims elsewhere?' If I answer, 'No, there is no basic difference', the answer is strictly correct but gravely misleading. The Islam of African Muslims is based on the law books and, so far as they are expressing Islam it is unexceptional; but this Islam does not express 'the religion of African Muslims' which is really what I am concerned with. It is a question of their apprehension and expression of Islam, and we have to show in what way this adheres to and differs from patterns developed in the Near East.

J. S. T.

Beirut
July 1966

Preface to the Second Edition (1979)

This book was planned as a religious study. Specifically it was intended to introduce the religious factors that are involved in any study of peoples of Africa who had been influenced by the intrusion of a religion that was alien to the natural religious genius of Africans, and to assess and analyse the way in which they had assimilated it. It was written in a Beirut whose present-day state I would not have predicted at the time, even though I was acutely aware of the factors, historical, religious, and psychological, that have led to the present state of Lebanon. At least, it was a setting that was appropriate for understanding the foundations of what are misleadingly called 'religious conflicts', some of which are touched on in a chapter that has been added to this new edition.

I have not found it necessary to make changes in the body of the text; the principles upon which I worked still hold, but in the new chapter attention has been given to specific changes that have taken place in the last decade or so which affect religion. But the main purpose of the chapter is to draw attention to the ways in which the modern African is thinking. Since the coming of independence there has been a drawing together in sympathy of black and white Africans, significant in itself, but marking a drawing together of the African and the Arab worlds.

Because in this chapter Africa is being considered as a whole in the context of a new awareness of human relationships in spite of difference, I have added an Appendix which brings out the differences between the Maghribi complex and the Egyptian unity that the Nilotic peasant population provides. Accordingly, the Bibliography has been enlarged to give a wider coverage.

J. S. T.

March, 1979

Introduction: Africa marginal to the Islamic world

The Islamic world, in spite of the different peoples in different environments it embraced and the physical difficulties of communication, was formerly one in a way it is no longer. Islam was a religious culture, since religion provided the basis for its existence and unity. Its religious institutions, its morality and law, scholarship and art were one in the sense that all expressed that Islamic spirit animating its members which differentiated them from other cultures. There was, of course, no blank uniformity, no monochrome pattern, even in the Islamic linking elements. The deepest division was the Sunnī-Shī'ī split. There were also great differences in levels of civilization, the contrasts between nomads, peasants and townspeople, as well as other regional differences, local loyalties and so forth.

It is convenient to use here the terms 'civilization' and 'culture' in the way they are used by philosophers and sociologists. Civilization, as the name shows, is concerned with the city and is that aspect of culture which relates to man's equipment to control his environment. In this sense it is the outer or material form of culture. Culture is concerned with life itself and the way it is lived. The two aspects are inseparable (and changes are interrelated movements, for change in material civilization may inaugurate cultural change), but the degree to which life is based upon them varies.

Islam in Africa south of the Sahara was a very marginal region in relation to the wider Islamic world. In African Islam civilization remained at a primitive level. This is a statement which Africans may misinterpret, but they might reflect that, whilst ancient Greek culture was highly developed, Greek civilization was relatively primitive, whereas with the Romans the reverse was the case. The adoption of Islam brought little change in the capacity of Africans to control the conditions of their existence for they were in touch in but a peripheral way with the developed civilizations of other

Islamic peoples. On the other hand, the adoption of Islam led in the course of time to deep cultural change, though even so it was not as great as if Africans had received the full impact of Islamic culture, whilst there were many levels of acceptance of Islamic institutions and consequently the degrees of actual change. Exactly the same sort of thing, of course, occurred elsewhere, the main contrast being between different occupational groups, for example, nomad and townsman.

Though all the resources of Islamic culture were theoretically open to African Muslims, not all these resources were in fact available, and others that were were blocked by the mentality or structure of African society. The actual process of change will be sketched later, but we may say that the result was an amalgam of African and Islamic elements, with the Islamic elements (though even these were characteristic of only certain strata of society) giving the general cultural outlook on life. That is why we may distinguish a Negro-African Islamic subculture. The Maghribi and Nilotic-'Ethiopic' subcultures were distinct from this, and above all the Egyptian which, Islamically, was undifferentiated, belonging wholly to Arab Islam. Consequently, the specifically Egyptian features are mainly seen in the practices and institutions of the *fallāḥīn*.

The Mediterranean zones, therefore, were fully within the Islamic world, whereas the rest of Africa remained on the periphery, quite outside the consciousness of other Muslims to whom Africa, if they thought of it at all, was the unknown region beyond the vast desert from which came black slaves and red gold. The Sahara imposed a cultural as well as a physical barrier. Internally, Africa south of the Sahara was always in what may be called a 'missionary situation'. At the same time, a study of the process by which Islam was assimilated and the subsequent changes which took place in the cultural outlook and institutions of the Sudan belt peoples shows us how this was accomplished among the Berbers, and in Egypt too among the *fallāḥīn*, though the given situation in Egypt when Islam made its appearance was quite different.

Four main Islamic culture spheres may be distinguished in the African continent: Egyptian and Maghribi bordering on the Mediterranean, and Negro and Hamitic south of the desert zone, each differentiated by the degree to which they have absorbed and been moulded by Islam and by the underlying cultural differences. The distinctions between the zones south of the desert (west, central and Nilotic Sudan, north-east and east Africa) are due more to differences in the African cultural basis than to Islam, but they are also distinct historical zones impinging very little upon each other.

We have said that although all the resources of Islamic culture were theoretically open to Africans, they were adopted only in part. Africans did not accept Islamic culture *in toto*. Islam made its impact as a legal culture; its theological, philosophical, literary and artistic values did not penetrate. These elements were not rejected by Africans, they were never presented to them. Islam came to West Africa from the Maghrib and into East Africa from Hadramawt, both among the less developed parts of the Arab world, and the legalistic aspect of Islam was so strong that students who went to the Azhar remained isolated against other currents from the seething Cairene world around them. At least they do not appear to have introduced new aspects of Arab civilization, so probably the gulf was too wide to be amenable to the adoption of new traits. Islamic culture was based on urban civilization and Africa had relatively few towns and cities; and where no towns existed, as among Bantu and Nilotic tribes, it could not penetrate at all. All the same, Islam in Africa flourished where there was some basis of urban culture, together with trading relations which ultimately stemmed from the city.

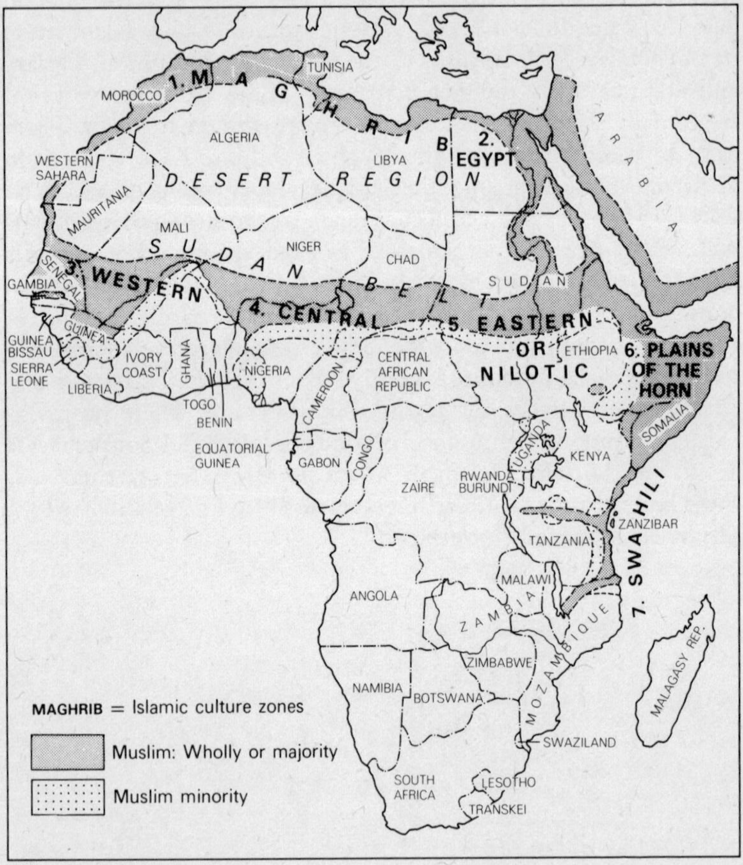

Map 1. Islamic culture zones

Chapter 1

Islamic culture zones: their history and characteristics

Islam in Africa may be divided into seven culture zones, so defined by reason of the pre-existing geographical, ethnological and cultural background of the inhabitants and the historical aspects of the penetration and impact of Islam. These zones will be treated as historical unities in themselves, though it will be understood that this is treating history from a special point of view, to provide the historical data on the processes and consequences of Islamization in the various regions.

1. Mediterranean Africa

The first two cultural regions, Egypt and the Maghrib, are those into which Islam first penetrated in the persons of the early Arab conquerors and became so deeply implanted as to influence all subsequent history and every aspect of life. The two regions are, however, clearly differentiated. This derives from the fact that their basic pre-Islamic cultures were quite different and each followed distinctive trends of historical development.

A. EGYPT

Egypt cannot be conceived of without the Nile which gave it a unity lacking to the Maghrib. Egypt formed a world in itself, and, though brought out of cultural isolation and subject to profound cultural change through its Mediterranean links and adherence to monotheistic religions, it has always displayed distinctive regional characteristics. Yet Egypt became, from the point of view of its Islamic orientation, relatively undifferentiated, belonging wholly to Arab Islam, though its regional uniqueness showed itself in a distinctive folk (*fellāḥ*) culture.

Egypt, though it falls into our overall view, will not come into our survey of the nature of African Islam. It belongs to Africa, yet has had little cultural influence upon Africa. What distinguishes Egypt is its geographical separateness and exclusiveness, as well as its relative degree of political unity, for political regionalism could never survive along the Nile valley up to the first cataract. Egypt was not isolated, of course; it had links with Europe, Berber Africa and south-western Asia, yet its links with Africa were largely confined to Nubia. Predynastic Egyptian cultures were basically African, though the influences which gave rise to its unique culture 5000 years ago came from outside Africa. Subsequently its cultural influence upon Africa has been confined to the dispersion of fugitive elements. This is due primarily to reasons of physical geography. The Nile upon which its life was dependent runs through formidable deserts; only to the south was the way open for communications with Hamitic and Negro peoples. For a long time Egypt controlled Hamitic Nubia and during the Meroitic period a derived Egyptian civilization flourished there. Attempts have been made, many of them fantastic, to show that Egyptian civilization had a profound influence upon Africa. Undoubtedly some cultural ideas and forms penetrated, but they were fragmentary traits transmitted through the untraceable process of culture diffusion which became indigenized and transformed. Many so-called borrowings simply derive from an African common source. Trading relations with the East African coast did not lead to cultural change. There is no evidence that any diffusion from Egyptian culture into Africa led to any radical new point of departure such as that accomplished later by Islam. Another consequence was that Egypt has had no political effect upon Negro Africa. Its contacts have been primarily with Hamitic regions, from the Nile valley or Red Sea coast.

Yet Egypt, because of its origins, was a part of Africa. African religious beliefs and social customs were the foundation of its unique culture, even if the initial impulse which led to its formation came from the East, whilst many elements survived subsequent cultural changes with extreme tenacity, even to the present day, within its folk culture.

The Egyptian has been distinguished by his strong attachment to cultural forms derived from life and work on a narrow strip of irrigated land, and at the same time has been a centre of urban civilization. With the decline of its own civilization Greek culture had its centre in Alexandria, yet this left the Egyptians, that is the peasant serfs, relatively untouched. More profound was the influence of the late Graeco-Semitic religious culture, Christianity. But the Egyptians did not simply take Greek Christianity. They expressed their own uniqueness within it. They adopted Monophysitism as a symbol of resistance to Byzantine imperialism and transformed the Greek alphabet as a medium for writing their own language, which remains the liturgical language of the Coptic Church to this day. After the Council of Chalcedon Egyptian Christianity became increasingly restricted within regional limits with the significant exception of its outreach into Nubia, Nilotic Sudan and Axum.

The Roman Empire unified the Mediterranean, its decline heralded its disintegration, and the Arab conquest finally breached the last remnants. The Egyptians welcomed the Arabs in A.D. 639 as signifying a change of masters from the yoke of Byzantium. Naturally they did not connect an Arab invasion with a cultural transformation since Islamic culture had not yet been formed and the Arabs showed a tolerant policy towards People of the Book. But the conquest meant that Egypt entered a new complex. Already separated from the mainstream of Christianity it entered the sphere of the naissant culture of Islam. For long it seemed to be a Christian enclave under Arab Muslim domination, but in fact it quickly became a country of dual religious cultures. Whilst Egyptian society and civilization continued unchanged and sociologically the lives of Christian and Muslim *fallāḥīn* could hardly be distinguished, the country became divided in religion.

Whilst Christianity declined in numbers of adherents, Islam rapidly expanded and brought new life to Egypt. Though the main centres of the evolving culture lay in Asia the Muslim world was a unified world and Egyptians participated in the process. But they became rigid conformists. Though the Fāṭimid dynasty, founded in the Maghrib, gained control of Egypt (969) and inaugurated there a cultural renaissance, Shī'ism never won over the Egyptians, presumably because it was an aristocratic rather than a people's religion, and it quickly disappeared once Saladin had dispossessed the last Fāṭimid caliph (1171) and set the country again along the path of conformity. After the Mongol conquests destroyed the Asiatic centres of Islam, Egypt became the main centre of learning, but the Ottoman conquest brought in a period of relative stagnation.

B. THE MAGHRIB

As the history of Egypt is unified, that of the Maghrib is disparate. Egypt has no history of conflict between desert and sown since its deserts are unsuitable for the nomadic life. It has rather been a dispersion centre for Arab nomads; those that migrated there hastened to get out, westward into the Maghrib and southwards into Nilotic Sudan. The political and social life of the Maghrib, on the contrary, was based on achieving equilibrium between nomads and sedentaries. That equilibrium was precarious because of the presence of great nomadic tribes. Consequently the Maghrib has a history of the rise and fall of states due directly or indirectly to the presence or invasion of nomads, and the greatest of all changes took place through the migration of nomad Arab tribes from Egypt in the eleventh century.

The Berbers had been little influenced by the Mediterranean civilizations which established outposts on or within their borders. In spite of successive alien dominations, mainly affecting coastal zones, the Berbers remained *imaziġən*, 'free men'. Of these alien conquests the only one to leave an indelible imprint upon the Berber soul was the Islamic. The result of contact was the Arabization of vast numbers of Berbers and a fusion of Berber and Arab custom. Politically, Arab domination was shorter-lived than any previous one. After the primary Arab conquest, Arabic became the language of the towns and administration, but the Arabization of the Berbers of the plains and mountains was a long process due primarily to the influx of the Bani Hilāl and other tribes from the eleventh century. The adoption of Islam preceded Arabization, but it did not truly begin to win the Berbers until it came to be seen, first, as something other than the tribal religion of the Arab conquerors, that is, when it dissociated itself from Arab racialism, hence the way Khārijism and Shī'ism flourished in the early centuries (with states like those of Tāhart and Fāṭimid) as Berber means of self-expression; but much more when Islam came to be seen as a cultural element which could be assumed as additional to Berber custom without displacing it. Consequently, when the Murābiṭ and Muwaḥḥid periods established the Mālikī code as the ruling Islamic factor, deviationist forms almost disappeared, and Berber reaction took other forms. Eventually in the fifteenth century the popularization of the religious orders and maraboutism gave Maghribi Islam its special imprint.

Coptic Egypt offered much less opposition to Arabism than the Berbers, but in time both Islam and Arabic deeply affected most aspects of Berber life, even changing custom, and forging a link between different social groups. But the fusion of Berber and Arab never became complete (as between Islamic and Berber custom), especially in western Maghrib (Morocco) where 40 per cent of the people still speak Berber dialects.[1] In western Sahara, south of Morocco, an influx of Arab Ma'qil tribes dominated the Berber nomads and all were arabized, but the Arabs did not penetrate into central Sahara where the Tuareg retain to the full their language and institutions. These central Saharan Berbers are very few, but those Tuareg who spread south to the borders with Negroland around the Niger loop have been more modified in their institutions through adaptation to their physical environment, and have been a factor in west and central Sudan history.

The next significant religious movement is the diffusion of Sufism which introduced into the rigid formalism of Mālikī Islam aspirations towards personal spiritual growth and union with God through mystical ecstasy. An early interpreter of Sufism was Aḥmad ibn al-'Irrīf, a Sanhaji Berber who lived in Spain (d. 1143). Esoteric Sufism reached its full flowering with Ibn al-'Arabī and the representative of this approach in North Africa was Abu Madyan (d. 1197). Masters of the Way increased in mountain regions, where many lived in their *zāwiyas*, surrounded by their family, disciples and servants.

From the fourteenth century Sufism tended to stagnate, and then suddenly it burst forth into a popular movement. Leaders like ash-Shādhilī (d. 1258) had taught their special ways which appealed mainly to a spiritual élite, but now their ways developed self-perpetuating organizations in the fraternities (*ṭawā'if*) which aimed, not merely at guiding members in mystical practice, but in binding them in allegiance to a master, and developed into a cult of saints as mediators with the spiritual world. This process began in the middle of the fifteenth century with al-Jazūlī (d. 1465/6). Neither the legalistic city religion, nor the mystical tradition of the early teaching Sufis, had penetrated and gained the hearts of the ordinary people, but the teaching, and especially the methods, of the new religious orders, suited and penetrated their ways of life, thought and emotions. Through these new impulses Islam gained an integral hold over the diverse classes of the Maghrib. The apprehension of Islam as a Maghribi heritage created a new historical departure-point, a new perspective, and, in a sense, a new system of society, Arabic names replacing Berber in tribal eponyms and each village, tribal section or family was related to a patron saint.

Whilst these tendencies were found in most Muslim countries, in the Maghrib they attained such a degree of diffusion that *maraboutisme*, to use the French term, became the dominant principle in Maghribi Islam. Mystical practices developed peculiar tendencies, whilst veneration for holy men often degenerated into hagiolatry. So Maghribi Islam gained the characteristic imprint it bears to this day. Berbers and Arabs, nomads and cultivators, mountain people and citizens lived in an atmosphere of the wondrous, of *baraka*, 'the sacred' power which emanates from saints, their tombs, descendants or anything associated with them. In their spread the orders penetrated Mauritania, Shinqīṭ being an important centre, and so into the Sudanese Sahil.

2. Western Sudan

Hamites and Negroes, the first nomadic pastoralists and the others settled agriculturalists, have always been closely intermingled and their different cultures and interrelationships are an essential aspect of the history of Islam in Africa. In the Sahara the two lived side by side. By the ninth century the Saharan Berbers had so increased in numbers, cohesion, mobility and power that they pressed upon the black cultivators of the oases and other cultivable parts within the Saharan wastes, and either pushed them towards the Senegal River or subjected them as tribute-paying serfs. Eventually the Berbers came into conflict with the Negro Soninke state of Gana[2] which had long dominated the southern Sahil bordering the Sahara.

The Sahara has never proved an insuperable obstacle to traffic and Mediterranean influences penetrated the Negro world. When Muslims gained control of the Maghrib the old traffic in gold and salt continued. Berber merchants not merely organized trans-Saharan caravans for trade with Negro states in the Sahil but established permanent residence in their towns and founded intermediate trading towns like Awdaghast. The evidence of Arabic writers show that Islam had penetrated peoples on the banks of the upper Senegal and in the Sahil region by the beginning of the eleventh century. Caravans crossed the Sahara to the Sahilian state of Gana to exchange salt and Mediterranean goods for gold and slaves. Gana allotted a special quarter with a mosque for Maghribi merchants. Special Muslim trading settlements like Kūgha, are also mentioned. In consequence, some Sudanese chiefs made a profession of Islam, in particular, Wār-Jābi (d. 1040), ruler of Takrur on the Senegal, a ruler of a Mande state (Malel) converted through experiencing the rain-making powers of a Muslim visitor, the ruler of Kawkaw on the Niger (before A.D. 985), and the ruler of Kuku in central Sudan.

The outburst of the Murābiṭūn in western Sahara ensured the definitive Islamization of Saharan Berbers such as the Goddāla and Lamtūna, but though it changed the political complexion of the Maghrib it did not greatly affect the southern Sahil except in one respect, that their conquest of the capital of Gana (1076), though ephemeral, broke its power and the state disintegrated into its constituent elements. All one can say of the Islamizing effect of this movement is that it brought about the conversion of the Soninke, and it now became the custom for chiefs on the upper Senegal (Tokolor) and Sahil (Soninke) and the trading class to profess Islam. The pattern which was to characterize Sudanese Islam now formed itself. It was a class religion of chiefs and traders, with a professional class of clerics, but it did not become the religion of the people. As al-Bakri observes of the chief of Malel, 'he is sincerely attached to Islam, as are his offspring and entourage, but the people of his kingdom remain polytheists (*mushrikūn*)'.[3] This compromise derives from the Sudan conception of society and the relationship of authority to the people who, of course, in their particularist societies did not feel the need for a universalist religion.

Islam now spread among the Soninke groups which had acknowledged Gana, such as Dyara (Nyoro region) and Galam (Bakel region), and into the trading settlements of Dya and Jenne in the Masina region. It is from these places that the Mande Dyula dispersion probably derives. Whereas the settled Negroid Fulfulde-speakers on upper Senegal known as Tokolor adopted Islam and in time became fervent adherents, the nomadic 'red' Fulbe speaking the same language resisted its encroachment because it limited their freedom, and only in recent times has their resistance given way. Berber movements, ending in that of the Murābiṭs, may have started the migrations which dispersed them throughout the vast Sudan belt.

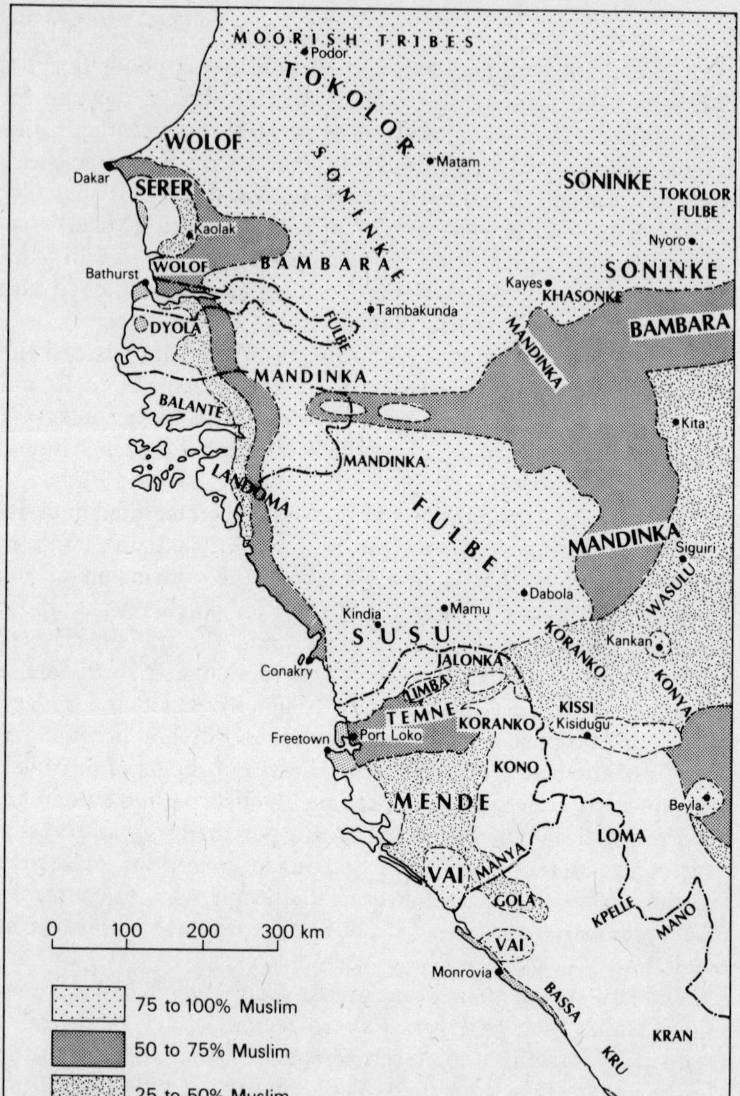

Map 2. Islam in West and Central Sudan

The key for this map covers the following three pages.

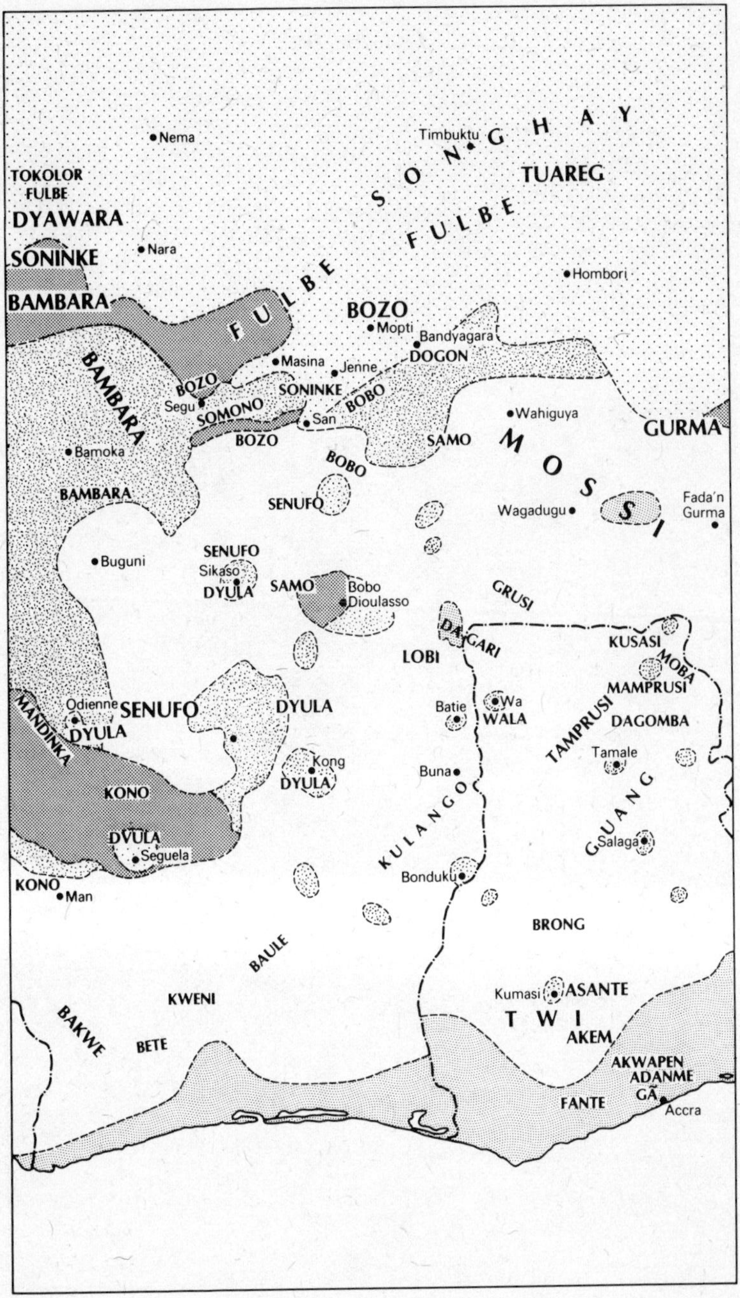

SONGHAY
Timbuktu
Nema
TOKOLOR
FULBE
DYAWARA
TUAREG
FULBE
Nara
SONINKE
BAMBARA
FULBE
Hombori
BOZO
Mopti
Bandyagara
DOGON
Masina
Jenne
BAMBARA
BOZO
Segu
SONINKE
BOBO
SOMONO
San
BOZO
Wahiguya
GURMA
SAMO
MOSSI
Bamoka
BOBO
BAMBARA
SENUFO
Wagadugu
Fada'n Gurma
Buguni
SENUFO
Sikaso
DYULA
SAMO
Bobo Dioulasso
GRUSI
DAGARI
LOBI
KUSASI
MOBA
MAMPRUSI
Odienne
SENUFO
DYULA
Batie
Wa
WALA
DAGOMBA
MANDINKA
DYULA
TAMPRUSI
Tamale
Kong
DYULA
Buna
KONO
KULANGO
GUANG
DYULA
Seguela
Salaga
KONO
Man
Bonduku
BRONG
BAULE
Kumasi
ASANTE
KWENI
TWI
BAKWE
BETE
AKEM
AKWAPEN
ADANME
GÃ
FANTE
Accra

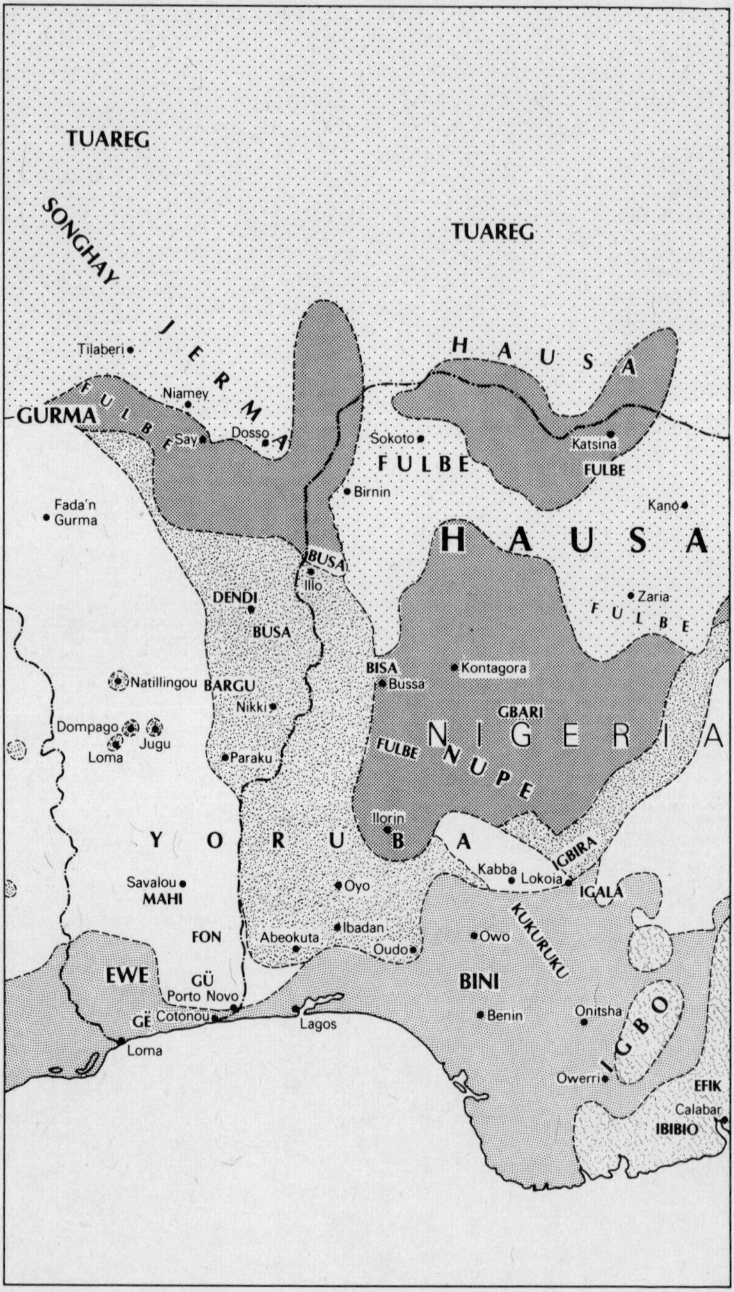

Map 2. Islam in West and Central Sudan (*continued*)

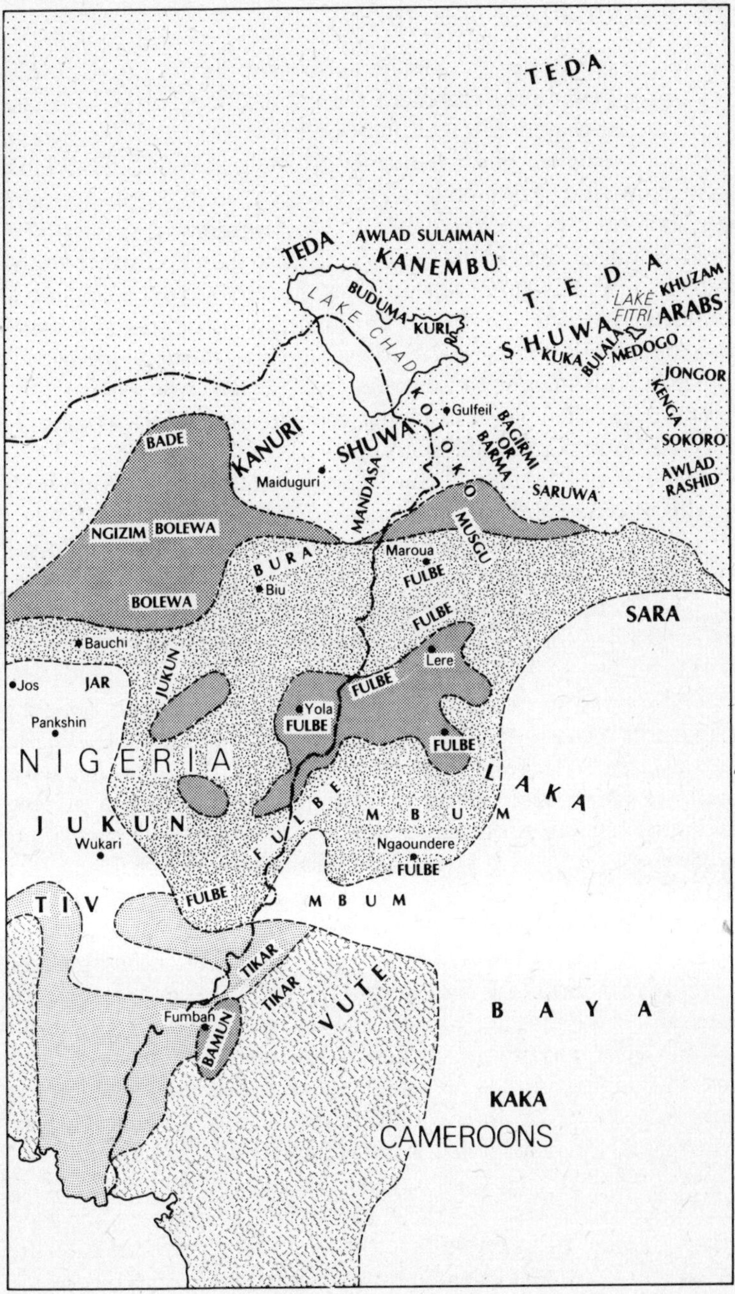
TEDA
TEDA
AWLAD SULAIMAN
KANEMBU
TEDA
BUDUMA
LAKE CHAD
KURI
LAKE FITRI
KHUZAM
ARABS
SHUWA
KUKA
BULALA
MEDOGO
JONGOR
KENGA
KOTOKO
Gulfeil
BAGIRMI OR BARMA
SOKORO
AWLAD RASHID
BADE
KANURI
SHUWA
Maiduguri
MANDASA
SARUWA
MUSGU
NGIZIM
BOLEWA
BURA
Maroua
FULBE
Biu
BOLEWA
FULBE
SARA
Bauchi
JUKUN
Lere
Jos
JAR
FULBE
Yola
FULBE
Pankshin
FULBE
NIGERIA
LAKA
MBUM
JUKUN
FULBE
Wukari
Ngaoundere
FULBE
FULBE
TIV
MBUM
TIKAR
TIKAR
VUTE
Fumban
BAMUN
BAYA
KAKA
CAMEROONS

Mali now became a great state under Sun Jata (*c.* 1250–55). His widespread conquests embraced the reduced state of Gana whose capital disappeared with the increased desiccation of the region. But the expansion and ascendancy of Mali, about which Arabic writers provide a fair amount of information, is not associated with any significant expansion of Islam. Mansas, the title of the rulers, went on pilgrimage, in one case so fantastic that Mali became well known in the Islamic world. They fostered trade, encouraged Arabs to visit their courts and introduced new features of civilization, but all this was so related to the State that it had no permanent effect upon Sudanese culture. As Ibn Baṭṭūṭa, who visited Mali (1352–53) at the apogee of its power, witnesses, Islam was hardly practised outside the ruling group.

Mali fell into decadence, the Mande decentralized into hundreds of village states, Voltaic Mossi states developed strong centralized structures, Tuareg became more menacing disrupting trade routes and causing insecurity in the Sahil, and Songhay with its centre at Gao (Kawkaw), having grown more powerful under the *si* dynasty, filled for a time under a new dynasty the vacuum caused by the decline of Mali.

The coming to power of *askiya* Muḥammad Turé in Songhay also marks a change of Islamic significance, though not leading to any decisive change in the relationship of Islam to Sudanese society. *Askiya* Muḥammad, having usurped the throne in 1493 and inherited a large empire created by the *sīs* and in particular his predecessor, *sī* 'Alī (d. 1492), based his authority on Islam rather than Sudanese symbols of power. Four years after his succession he set off on pilgrimage to Mecca where he was appointed *khalīfa* of Bilād at-Takrūr[4] by the Sharīf al-'Abbās. He encouraged the visits of Maghribi shaikhs, including the Saharan reformer al-Maghīlī, fostered the '*ulamā*', and even attempted to enforce Islamic legal provisions. Although the definitive conversion of certain Songhay groups may date from this period, his attempt to introduce Islam by force or otherwise among Bambara, Mossi (where his war was styled a *jihād*) and Fulbe of Termes and Nyoro failed. During this time Islam almost disappeared among the Mandinka of Mali and the pagan 'universal' cults like the *komo* attained wide diffusion and power. Sudanese rulers like Mansa Mūsā had been able to come to terms with these societies which formed a competing form of authority in a way that was not possible for a dynasty like the *askiya*. Only the Tokolor conquerors of the nineteenth century succeeded in breaking or curbing the power of these cults by ruthless suppression, but they sprang into new life after the colonial occupation.

Askiya Muḥammad's work and the power of his state were weakened and finally lost through the factional struggles of his successors and within a century of his coming to power an army of adventurers sent across the Sahara by al-Manṣūr, sultan of Morocco, captured Gao and destroyed Songhay (1591). No great power was now left in the Sudan. The rule of the pashas, confined to a limited stretch of the Niger loop, came to an end about 1660. The Islamic states were now ruined, pagan Bambara states of Segu and Karta became more powerful, and Islam as a determining factor in Sudanese civilization fell into complete eclipse. The only Muslims were the Tokolor of Futa Toro under a pagan ruling class, most of the Soninke, the Dyula colonies, families in the Masina region and along the Niger bend and, of course, all towns like Timbuktu, Gao and Jenne.

However, in the eighteenth century, a new outlook upon Islam which was to revolutionize the Sudanese scene, made its appearance. The movement began in Futas Jalon and Toro and stemmed from Pulo or Tokolor clerics who reacted against the Sudanese spirit of compromise and accommodation of Islam with African religion by manifesting a new Islamic spirit, exclusive, legalistic, intolerant and militant. No outside inspiration seems to be behind this change in Islamic outlook, rather it seems to derive from study of those normally neglected sections of their legal treatises which deal with the ideal Islamic state.

The new outlook appears first with a Pulo cleric in the mountainous region of Futa Jalon (Guinea) called Ibrāhīm Mūsā (d. 1751), who incited immigrant Fulbe to a *jihād* against the Susu-Jalonke inhabitants of the country. After prolonged struggles the movement was brought to a successful conclusion by a companion of Ibrāhīm Mūsā called Ibrāhīm Sori who became the Fulbe war-leader and *almāmi* (Ar. *al-imām*). In this way the *imām*, leader of the prayer community, evolved into the leader of the *jihād* and political chief. What the new state leaders sought to affirm was the primacy of Islam as the ruling factor in the community and the religious integrity of the secular political group. In Futa Toro (Senegal) the movement was inspired by Sulaimān Bal, whose death in 1776, when the *jihād* against the Denyanke rulers had just reached a successful conclusion, brought to power his lieutenant,

'Abd al-Qādir (d. 1806) who became the first *almāmi* of Futa Toro.

An interesting feature of the Muslim states formed in the two Futas was their method of government. The basis of authority was new to the Sudan state. The ruler derived his authority from God and ruled according to divine law. He was chosen according to custom which derived from the history of the *jihād* by an electoral body composed of the descendants of the Muslims who took part in the liberation movement and formed the new aristocracy. After the death of the first theocrat a council of hereditary electors made its appearance and a Muslim enturbaning, the principal rite in the investiture of chief *imāms*, consecrated the new ruler.

The next movement, which began in central Sudan in 1804 under the inspiration of 'Uthmān dan Fodio, will be treated in the next section. After that a Pulo shaikh, Ḥamad Bari, initiated (1810–1818) a revolution in Masina. Though initially inspired by the success of 'Uthmān dan Fodio in Hausaland, its development and fortunes took different lines for it led to the creation of an Islamic state as near the ideal nomocratic state as is likely to be achieved.

The state of Masina was destroyed in 1862 by a Muslim leader who initiated a new phase of conquest. This was al-ḥājj 'Umar ibn Sa'īd. Born in one of the first theocratic states, Senegalese Futa Toro, he spent many years in Mecca and Medina where he was appointed a *khalīfa* of the Tijāniyya *ṭarīqa* by Muḥammad Ghālī, Tijānī leader in the Hijaz.[5] His travels across Africa brought him into touch with all the theocratic states then existing, with new ideas and movements and with the menace of European expansion. His propaganda in his homeland having failed through the opposition of the established Muslim leaders, he formed a centre in Dingeray where he began his warlike career. He launched from 1853 a series of expeditions against pagans, Bambara in particular. Profoundly instructed in Tijānī theory as his writings bear witness, he lapsed from spiritual leadership but used Tijānī allegiance to bind his Tokolor followers to himself as *khalīfa*. Spurred on by an insatiable lust for conquest, he brought vast regions between the Senegal and Niger untouched by former *jihād* movements under his control, but lost his life in 1864 before he had had time to consolidate his conquests and establish a stable administrative structure. Although his son, Amadu Seku of Segu, was recognized as titular head of the vast empire, the provincial governors ruled independently. The most able was probably his nephew, at-Tijānī

(d. 1887), who gained control of Masina which he ruled from his new capital of Banjagara. Often in mutually hostile relationships, these rulers had to suppress the continual revolts of their subjects and face the steady penetration into interior Sudan of the French who eventually destroyed the last remnants of 'Umar's empire.

Coincident with French penetration into interior Sudan which began in 1878 was the rise of the Mandinka adventurer, Samori ibn Lafiya. Samori attempted to form a Mandinka empire in the region watered by the upper basin of the Niger and its tributaries. His career was brought to an end by the French in 1898.

3. Central Sudan

Central Sudan is that section of the Sudan belt which stretches from the Songhay of middle Niger through Hausaland, Bornu, Kanem and Waday to Darfur. Its history of Islamic penetration and influence is quite different from that of Western Sudan. One reason for this derives from the organization of trade routes. North African traders were active on three trans-Saharan routes into central Sudan. Ya'qūbī reports[6] commerce in slaves by that which ran from Tripoli through Zawīla to Kawār, then a considerable market-centre to which Negro chiefs and traders sent their slaves. The difference from the west is that the main points of commercial interchange were situated on these routes in the Sahara rather than on the borderland and the people whom the Arab writers mention most frequently are the Zaghāwa, nomadizing over vast wastes, whose guarantees of safe passage was necessary. Trade slackened during the eleventh century owing to disturbed conditions. Al-Bakrī reports that in his time (A.D. 1067) traders did not go south of Zawīla into Kanem (to him the Zaghāwa area in general) 'a region of polytheists'.[7] Towards the end of the eleventh century a ruling clan of nomadic Zaghāwa in control of the regions of Kawār and Tibesti extended their control over Kanem in the narrower sense, an ill-defined region north-east of Lake Chad. Although a nomadic state it adopted the divine kingship system and in time changed to a Sudanic kingdom in the fullest sense. This state ensured the safety of central Saharan routes. At the end of the eleventh century Hume, regarded as the first Muslim king, and his son Dunama (*c.* 1100–40), had a wide range of authority. Naturally Islam was adopted by the ruling clan in consequence of trans-Saharan contacts and pilgrimages to

Mecca became a feature, this Dunama being drowned near Suez during his third.[8] The state maintained relationships with Tunis, Tripoli and Egypt, and for a time controlled Fezzan. In time it extended its control over the So tribes of Bornu, west of Lake Chad, and Ibn Khaldūn records the gift of a giraffe to the Ḥafṣid, al-Mustanṣir, from the 'king of Kanem and Lord of Bornu'.[9] At the end of the fourteenth century internal troubles with an allied clan, the Bulala, caused the dynasty to transfer its seat of authority into Bornu west of Lake Chad which became the dominant state until the *jihād* of 1804 changed the political complexion of the region by consolidating the Hausa states.

The history of the region between Songhay and Bornu is confused. By the fifteenth century a number of town states possessing unique forms of government and institutions had differentiated themselves. The peoples of the region, collectively known as So or Saw, had developed a town-state organization, but the dynasties governing these states derive from immigrants from the north, from Kanem in the east, and in one case, Wangara, probably from the west. These dynasties progressively expanded and gained control of other small town states, and their home town, becoming dominant, gives the name to the state. The term 'Hausa' by which these states are known is a linguistic term rather than the name of an ethnic grouping (the word is actually the term for the left bank of the Niger), though at that time linguistic uniformity was far from having been achieved. The chief states were Katsina, Kano, Daura, Zanfara, Gobir, Wangara and Zazzau (Zegzeg or Zaria), the most southern, an amorphous state founded among uncoordinated tribes. West of Zazzau on the Niger was the Nupe state with an organization of considerable antiquity.

An unusual aspect of Islamic infiltration into the area is that Islam was not spread noticeably by traders, except perhaps in Katsina, although the walled towns had wide trade connexions, well-stocked markets and craft industries. Unlike Kanem these states do not seem to have maintained direct trading relations across the Sahara, but regions like Air, then part of the same 'Hausa' complex and not yet dominated by Tuareg, formed intermediary exchange places. The Hausa genius for assimilation quickly claimed any foreign Muslims who settled. Islam was introduced as a legal cult by clerics from Kanem and from west Sudan. These last are mentioned in the Kano Chronicle during the reign of Yaji (*c.* 1349–85) as Wangara and may have been

Dyula traders, but certainly some were negroid Fulbe.[10] They introduced an element of conflict into Kano state and the Chronicle shows something of the struggle between magico-religious powers, one native, the other intrusive. The conflict was resolved in the Sudanese fashion by absorbing Islamic elements into the state structure and town systems and thus neutralizing their power to change. A religious hierarchy was incorporated into the traditional structure to give the state Islamic support. These officials were appointed by the king and formed part of his entourage on ceremonial parades and accompanied his military expeditions. Muḥammad Belo wrote in justification of the *jihād*:

Islam was brought to this country [Bornu] by traders and travellers. Whoever wished adopted the faith; some practising it as sincerely as they were able, others mingling it with elements that nullified it. Such was the case with the majority of the kings of the country; they adopted Islam, confessed to the unity of God, observed ritual prayer and fast, yet never got rid of their inherited practices, nor abandoned one whit of their customs.[11]

The only attempt to form a great state was made by the *kanta* of Kebbi (d. 1545), situated on the borderland between Songhay and Hausa. At first allied with the Songhay ruler, Askiya Muḥammad, whom he helped deliver Agadez from Tuareg domination, he then broke with the *askiya* and, as symbol of Hausa resistance to Songhay aggression, dominated a wide range of Hausa states. But the power of Kebbi declined under his successors, Bornu dominated the eastern Hausa states, and by the end of the eighteenth century Gobir situated in the Sahil had become the most powerful state.

Diffusion of the new millennialist concept of Islam from western Sudan now completely changed the outlook and position of Islam in central Sudan. The preaching of a 'forerunner', Jibrīl ibn 'Umar, among semi-Hausaized Tokolor *torodbe* settled in the pagan state of Gobir, inspired the revolt of 'Uthmān dan Fodio in 1804 against its ruler. The impetus of the movement, which even drew in nomadic Fulbe, was so great that it spread Fulbe domination over vast reaches beyond the regions of highly developed states like Hausa, Nupe and Yoruba, to lands of uncoordinated small pagan groups in the plateau regions of Bauchi and Adamawa. Islam, which had been merely a class cult in the Hausa town states, only began to gain the cultivators after this *jihād* imposed on them a new ruling class, though it was not long before the Hausa genius for absorption led to the assimilation of their conquerors whose clerical leaders in fact were already Hausaized. They became distinguishable only through pride of origin, both religio-historical and racial fictional, over the Habe, their uncomplementary term for autochthones.[12] The creation of large numbers of slave villages, for whose members Islam constituted the only common denominator and binding factor, greatly helped the process. The Hausa proper changed only slowly in spirit and outlook.

The evolution of Islamic authority in central Sudan states after the *jihād* followed different lines from that in the two Futas and Masina. The various flag-bearers whom 'Uthmān had consecrated for the *jihād* ruled the conquered regions nominally as his representatives, in fact, as their personal states, and, though not the rule at first, their leadership also became hereditary. Many were pagan states (Yoruba Ilorin, Nupe, Bauchi, Katagum and Zaria) and though Islam was the basis for the conquerors' authority there was no Islamic unity between conqueror and subjected.[13] It is remarkable enough that such a conglomeration of loosely integrated states was able to maintain some measure of unity and was due to the two factors already mentioned, pride of race and Islam.

Bornu did not escape becoming involved in the new Islamic forces that had been let loose. It was first attacked in 1808, but survived a number of defeats owing to the crisis bringing to the forefront Bornu's own clerical leader in Shaikh Muḥammad al-Amīn, who, with the help of Shuwa Arabs, was able to preserve the integrity of the state at the expense of the loss of a few western provinces. Muḥammad al-Amīn became *de facto* ruler, but retained the *mai* as nominal king. His son, 'Umar, destroyed the old dynastic link, and during his long reign (1835–80) was able to maintain the unity and cohesion of the state against numerous external and internal threats. Under his successors, however, the decline was rapid and in 1893 Hāshim was attacked and killed by the adventurer Rābiḥ who was himself killed by the French in 1900. The nephew of Hāshim was recognized by the British as *mai* of Bornu when they established a protectorate.

South of Bornu was the state of Bagirmi, founded in the sixteenth century and Islamized in the seventeenth. It maintained a precarious existence, torn and ravaged in struggles with and between Bornu and Waday. The introduction of Islam into Waday, a region of many Negro tribes (basically Maba) with a large influx

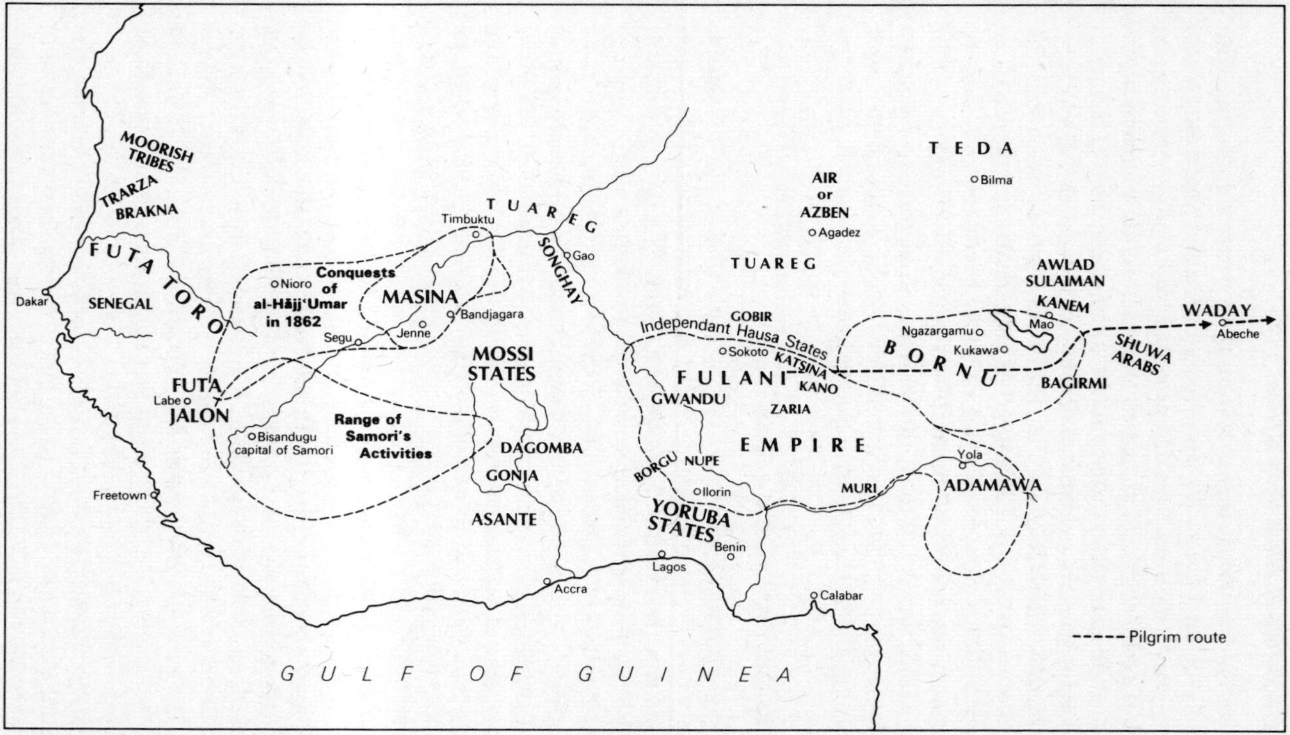

Map 3. Muslim theocratic states

of nomadic Arab tribes, dates from the seventeenth century with the formation of the Ṣāliḥ dynasty by ʻAbd al-Karīm (d. 1655?), an immigrant from the Nile. It developed into a large state with an elaborate hierarchized structure and an absolute monarch at the head, but at the same time subject to constant internal struggles and wars with its neighbours Darfur and Bagirmi. Like Waday, Darfur (the country of the Fūr, the dominant tribe) was under the Tunjur, pagan or semi-Islamized immigrants from Nilotic Sudan, about whom little is known but who may have been an important factor in the spread of the state system in these regions. Their hegemony was overthrown in the sixteenth century by Sulaimān Solong whose dynasty first introduced Islamic institutions. Darfur was annexed to the Egyptian Sudan in 1874.

4. Eastern or Nilotic Sudan

The geographical position of Nilotic Sudan has made it a zone of interaction between Hamitic, Negro and Arab Africa. The human foundation was eastern Hamitic or Kushitic. There were riverain Nubians, primarily Hamitic though formed through an early blending with Negroes, one of whose waves imposed their language; rainland cultivators also modified by a Negro admixture; and nomadic Beja, then much more widespread than today for they covered a vast area between the Nile, the Red Sea and the Abyssinian plateaux. South of the Hamitic zone lived many groups of Negroes and Nilotes.

At the time of the Arab conquest of Egypt there were two Christian Nilotic states south of Aswan; Maqurra with its capital at Dongola stretched from just south of the first cataract to about the junction of the Atbara with the Nile; whilst the other, ʻAlwa, stretched from thence up both White and Blue Niles, with its capital at Soba near modern Khartoum. Islam made its first appearance in the presence of the early Arab conquerors of Egypt, but its progress southwards was blocked by Maqurra. ʻAbdallāh ibn Saʻd, governor of Egypt, in fact led an expedition south from Aswan into Nubia and besieged Dongola in A.D. 651/2. The outcome of this expedition was a treaty of alliance and commercial interchange which lasted many centuries, peace being broken only by relatively minor differences until the rise of the Baḥrī Mamluk rulers of Egypt. Arabs settled among both Nubians and Beja in whose country they exploited the gold mines of ʻAllāqī district.

Such clans lost their Arabic and were absorbed into Nubians or Beja. One Nubianized Arab clan, the Banu Kanz, became a force in the borderland region and played an important role in the events which led to the downfall of Maqurra. Muslim traders were active even as far as the capital of ‘Alwa where they had a special quarter.

Although external influences were involved, Maqurra's collapse was due to internal weaknesses and disintegration. From the time of Rukn ad-dīn Baibars I (1260–77) a series of Egyptian interventions accelerated its disruption. At the same time, nomadic Arab tribes, encouraged to migrate southwards, found the lands beyond the inhospitable Nubian stretch exactly suited to their mode of life. From 1317, when an inscription records the rededication of the Dongola church as a mosque, Nubia can be regarded as an independent Muslim state. The old political structure disintegrated and Dongola decayed as the seat of authority and centre of commerce.

‘Alwa survived the decline of Maqurra and the history of its downfall is obscure.[14] It apparently broke up into its constituent chieftaincies through the weakness of central authority long before the founding of the Funj state on the Blue Nile (traditional date for the founding of Sennar town is 1504), which however inherited aspects of its state tradition. Before this an Arabized Beja family, the ‘Abdallāb, had become a force on the main Nile north of the confluence, having its centre at Qerri and possibly inheriting the hereditary title of *mānjil* from ‘Alwa. The conquest of Soba is attributed in late traditional sources to an alliance between ‘Abdallāh Jammā‘, the founder of this family, and ‘Amāra son of Dunqas, founder of Sennar, but this has been shown to be without foundation,[15] and ‘Alwa may well have disintegrated as a state long before 1504. The Sennar state expanded to embrace not only the Jezīra, the district between the White and Blue Niles, but also a considerable stretch of the main Nile. The ‘Abdallābī chief of Qerri, whose range of authority varied under successive *mānjils*, was tributary to the Funj.

The conversion of the Nubians of Marīs (northern Maqurra) in any numbers took place after A.D. 1300. Al-‘Umarī, writing about 1340, says[16] that the people were still Christians, though the king of the time was a Muslim.[17] The conversion and fusion of the population was not complete in 1596 when the Ethiopian monk, Taklā-Alfa, speaking of his journey through Dongola, distinguishes between Nobā and Muslims (*Taubalāt*), and also refers to ‘all the

Muslims (*Maslemān*) and the inhabitants of Dongola, Nobā and Jallāba Arabs'.[18] The Nubians became fervent Muslims and all trace of Christianity disappeared, but rejecting Arabic they remained strongly attached to their own language, customs and mode of life. South of this stretch Islamization proceeded along with Arabization. The wide dispersion of Arab nomads from upper Egypt was mainly responsible for an Arabization which embraced the Shā'iqiyya and Ja'liyyīn of the Nile and nomadic tribes like the Ḥalanqa and Kawāḥla. Arab nomads absorbed Hamitic clans as clients or serfs into their own tribal structure, whilst Hamitic tribes absorbed Arabs, frequently becoming at the same time Arab in language and structure.

The whole-hearted adoption of Islam came after the formation of indigenous clerical families who 'lit the fire of 'Abd al-Qādir' (that is, spread Qādirī allegiance) in one riverain community after another. The first teachers were immigrants such as Ghulām Allāh ibn 'Ā'id who settled in Dongola about 1360–80, taught the Qur'ān and *fiqh*, and founded a clerical family. After the fall of 'Alwa there was no comparable religious force to hinder the spread of Islam into the Buṭāna and south of the Nile junction. We do not know when the rulers of Sennar state became Muslim but it must have been about the time it was stabilized by 'Amāra Dunqas (traditionally in A.D. 1504) for it then gained wide inter-tribal relations. Relatively stable conditions under this state, whose organization and symbols of power were neither Arab nor Muslim, provided the conditions for the spread of Islam. But its rooting in the hearts and lives of the people was the work of definite missionaries, both immigrant and native. Of such was Maḥmūd al-'Arakī who lived during the first half of the sixteenth century. He studied Mālikī law in Egypt and on his return founded fifteen *khalwas* in his homeland along the White Nile.[19] The Funj state attracted scholars and holy men who found the soil prepared, by the vague diffusion of Christianity and the spiritual vacuum left by its disappearance, for the reception of Islam in a way which did not and could not happen elsewhere in Africa. Many early missionaries came from outside, generally the Hijaz and to a lesser degree from Egypt. The most effective were those who introduced Sufism in its popular form, such as Tāj ad-dīn al-Bahārī (*c.* 1550). From their Sudanese pupils many clerical lineages were formed. Nubians, Mahas in particular, migrated southwards in small groups, founded many colonies (for example, on Tuti Island and 'Ailafon), and adopted the Arabic language. These set a pattern of Nilotic Sudan Islam which contrasts with the religion of other peoples of the Sudan belt. The most important aspect was the harmonious blending of *fiqh* and *taṣawwuf*, the tempering of legalism with mysticism. The *fekis* were at one and the same time *fuqahā'* and *fuqarā'*. The prevalent *madhhab* was the Mālikī, pointing to the fact that early teachers came from upper Egypt and even the Maghrib.

The Funj dynasty exercised direct rule over the central core of the state in the Jezira between the two Niles and the rulers were recognized as overlords by a number of self-governing tribal states along the main Nile (the Arab-Baja 'Abdallāb, Ja'liyyīn, Majādhīb, Mirafāb, Shā'iqiyya, etc.) as well as by nomad tribes. As the power of the state declined these tribes repudiated their vassal status, the dynasty came to rely more and more upon a slave-recruited army, and lost the last remnants of its power in 1760 when Muḥammad Abu Likailik assumed control and founded a dynasty of regents.

When Muḥammad 'Alī undertook the conquest of the regions south of his viceroyalty of Egypt in 1819 there was no power on the Nile capable of putting up any strong resistance. The small tribal states on the main Nile and the remnant of the Sennar state succumbed easily, only the Shā'iqiyya putting up any resistance. The new administration, contrary to the pattern of authority throughout the Sudan belt, ruled directly through an impersonal bureaucracy which weakened indigenous political institutions. In consequence, the *fekis* became the main depositories of Sudan tradition, embodying Sudanese hopes and aspirations in a unique way.

The Turko-Egyptian conquest and subsequent changes in Sudan societies prepared the way for the only successful Mahdist rising of the period. Direct influences go back to the revival of the mystical orders inspired by Aḥmad ibn Idrīs, a Maghribi shaikh settled in Mecca, who early in the nineteenth century sent missionaries to Islamic Africa where they found a fruitful field for their message. These included the founder of the Sanūsiyya, but the most influential in Eastern Sudan was Muḥammad 'Uthmān al-Mirghanī (d. 1853) whose descendants in the Sudan became leaders of large sections of the population. The slave trade and army recruitment also prepared the way since they broke up communities and cults and the scattered units found a new hope and religious basis in attachment to Islam through such *ṭarīqa* leaders.

When in 1881 a Dongolawi *feki*, Muḥammad Aḥmad ibn 'Abdallāh, proclaimed himself the expected Mahdī, the right man and the right conditions combined to ensure a successful revolt. His *daʿwā* evoked at first only a limited response, and the established authorities, including the *ṭarīqa* leaders, supported the status quo. But the conditions of social change coinciding with the ineptitude of the administration allowed the naissant movement so to gather momentum that it won a series of initial victories. Having thus demonstrated the effectiveness of his divine mission the Mahdī quickly won over diverse elements of the population. When he died in 1885 at the summit of his success he was succeeded by his lieutenant, the Baqqārī, ʿAbdullāh aṭ-Ṭaʿaishī, who, though unable to carry out the Mahdī's programme of conquest, maintained the political unity of the vast state until his defeat by an Anglo-Egyptian force in 1898.

5. North-eastern Ethiopic zone

This region displays the greatest contrasts, not only geographically, but in human diversity, cultural stages, languages and religions. Its destinies have been tied indissolubly with the Red Sea more than with the Nile valley, and it was from Arabia that it received the imprint of Semitic languages and culture. Immigrant colonists from across the Red Sea formed the kingdom of Axum in the Tigrai region. In the fourth century A.D. Christianity became the royal cult and in time, in its Monophysite form, the religion of the people. The establishment of Islam in the Near East and Egypt broke its links with the wider Christian world. Yet Islam, the religion of the nomads of the plains, is not significant in itself in this region, but only in relation to this isolated Christian outpost, the focus of historical continuity, the state of Ethiopia.

It was natural that the heterogeneous peoples of the Red Sea towns and off-lying islands should come into contact with and adopt Islam at an early date (the Dahlak islands came under Umayyad control in A.D. 715). From these towns it spread among the nomads of the lowlands neighbouring the coast, like Beja and ʿAfar-Danākil. Well-frequented routes passed through Beja country to the Red Sea, ʿAidhāb in particular being a port of embarkation for pilgrims who had followed the desert route. From Zailaʿ trade routes ran inland by way of Harar up into the highlands. Islamic expansion was connected with trade, and traders from the coast were active throughout the region. The need for the Christian state to obtain its single bishop from Egypt meant intermittent contact with its rulers, but the isolation caused by Islamic control of the Red Sea and Egypt directed the energies of the Ethiopian state towards Hamitic Africa, a gradual expansion and a cultural revolution ensued, and the Negus became a nomad. During this period when Axum was consolidating and expanding over the high plateaux of Amhara, Gojam and Shoa, a number of Muslim states came into existence in eastern and southern Shoa through which trade routes passed—Ifāt, Adal, Mora, Hobat and Jidaya. South of the river Hawash, among settled Sidama and nomadic tribes, the rulers of other Kushitic states adopted Islam, the more important being Fatajar, Dawaro, Hadya and Bali. In the south-east, within Dawaro, the town of Harar developed as the only permanent and still surviving Muslim town with a unique Semitic language. Islam became the force of resistance against the expanding power of the Ethiopian state towards the south and south-east. From the time of 'Amda Syon (1329) it engaged in a long struggle for dominance over pagan Agao and Muslim states. Eventually the Negus was recognized as overlord and though warfare was continuous this had little to do with religion until the rise of the Imām Aḥmad Grāñ. In the sixteenth century under his leadership the Islamized nomads inhabiting the plains launched an assault (beginning in 1527) upon the Christian state and conquered it. The conquest, however, was ephemeral, for the force of the invasion quickly petered out after Aḥmad Grāñ was killed in 1542, and had little permanent effect upon the religious complexion of the highlands rooted in the national religious tradition. The danger came from another quarter with the invasion of the pagan Galla whose migratory waves, beginning early in the sixteenth century (*c.* 1537), so overwhelmed vast areas of the southern Sidama region that Islam practically disappeared there. It was kept alive in the city state of Harar, in coastal settlements, and by the nomads 'Afar and Somali for whom it formed an integral part of tribal tradition.

But the Galla invasion waves carried them on to the permanent occupation of the vast regions of the plateaux, still further contributing to their complexity and the isolation of provinces. Those who settled in the highlands proper became either Christian or Muslim. The eighteenth and nineteenth centuries, when the Christian state was weak through these invasions and internal troubles, formed a period when Islam made considerable new gains, particularly among Galla. Those in the central highlands of Wallo, Raya and Yeju found in its profession a means to enable

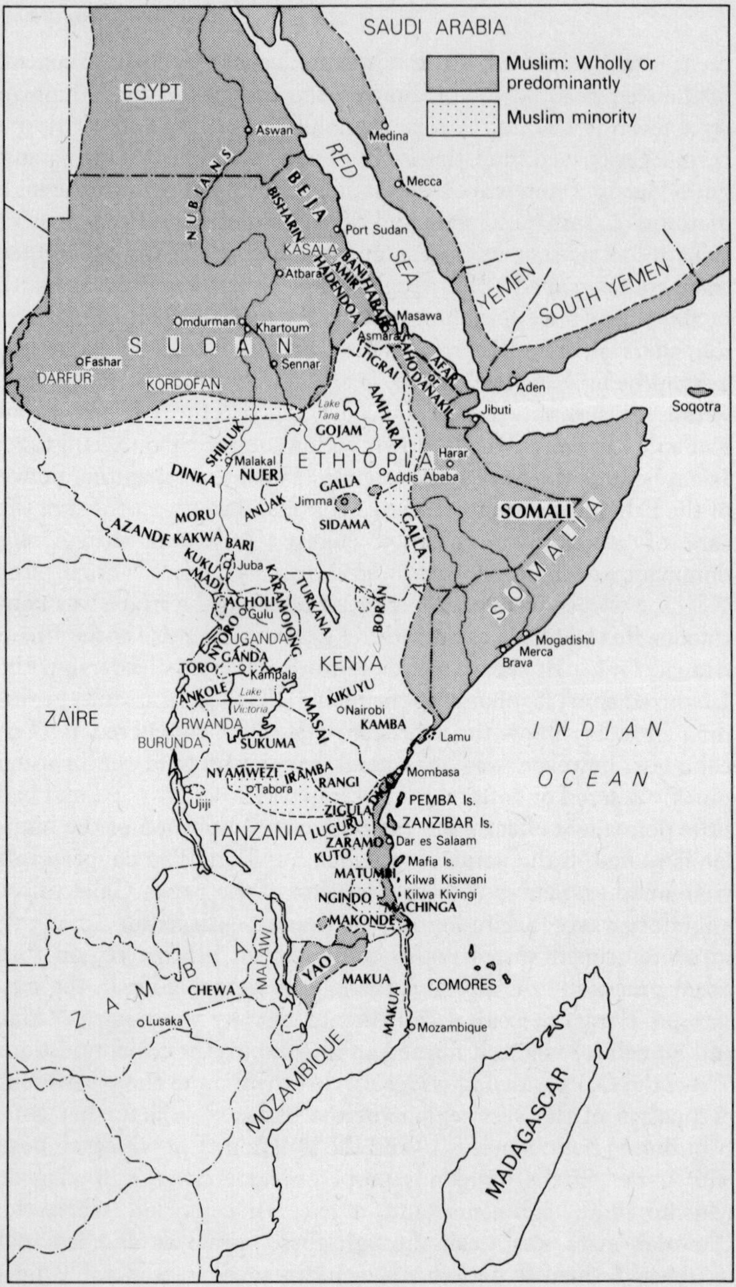

Map 4. Islam in North-East and East Africa

them to remain distinct from the Amhara. It was also an element in attempts made by Galla clans to dominate the Negus or highland regions.

In the south, in the territories of former Muslim Sidama states, Islam regained a considerable part of the regions it had lost to paganism by converting the Galla invaders through the agency of traders and settlements along the routes. In Galla *naggādi* means both 'merchant' and 'Muslim'. Throughout the whole Ethiopic region the religious orders also played a considerable role in the diffusion and consolidation of Islam.

Trading relations also carried Islam among the Galla conquerors of Sidama states in the region of the river Gibé (Gomma, Gera, Limmu, Guma and Jimma Abba Jifar) during the period from 1820 to 1870. Apart from town states like those on the coast (many however tributary to Ottoman or Egyptian powers), this is the only region where Islam became the state (as contrasted with tribal) religion.

In the north, in the region now known as Eritrea, where the Beja tribes of the plains had over a long period become Muslims, many Christian tribes adopted Islam in the nineteenth century. These included Tigrē-speaking tribes, the three Bait Asgede and the Marya, and the agriculturalist Belen (Bogos), Mansa and Bait Juk. These conversions came about not only through the normal processes, but also, at least among nomads, in consequence of their absorption of Arab and other immigrants who formed holy (*ṭarīqa*) families, performing ritual, clerical and magical duties on behalf of the whole tribe.

The progress of Islam was halted by the triumph of the monarchy and unification of the Ethiopian state during the second half of the nineteenth century. The energies and policies of the great emperors Theodore, John, and especially Menelik (1889–1913), not only brought about the unification of Abyssinia, but extended its boundaries to embrace the many Muslim and pagan peoples found in the present-day state of Ethiopia.

From the point of view of Islamic influence we may distinguish four spheres. (*a*) Coastal. Along the Red Sea coast a mixed population formed, primarily Hamitic (e.g. Zaila'wī) with a hybrid Islamic culture persistently reinforced from Arabia. The Banādir towns south of the Horn also belonged to it after their Somalization, though before they had probably had a proto-Swahili (i.e. Bantu) culture. (*b*) The northern and central plateau regions, dominated by the Christian Ethiopian state with deep-rooted non-African traditions, which maintained its unique identity in spite of being surrounded by Muslims. Here groups of Jabarti (Ethiopian Muslims proper) and the northern Galla (Yeju, Raya and Wallo) are Muslim. (*c*) The eastern and south-eastern plains and the Harar plateau region where live nomadic tribes of ʻAfar (or Danākil) and Somali, and where parts have been occupied by Galla. This area is now wholly Muslim. Islam's spread among the Hamitic nomads (Beja, ʻAfar, Saho, Somali and Galla) was not accompanied by Arabization as in Nilotic Sudan and this meant that they preserved their social institutions as basic features of tribal life, modified but not greatly changed by Islamic institutions. (*d*) The fourth significant Islamic region is south-western Ethiopia (Gibé region), where Islam superimposed itself upon the paganism of a group of Sidama and Mecha Galla tribes.[20]

6. East Africa

East Africa was apparently among the regions most accessible to the penetration of Islam. Muslim traders were present on the coast from the beginning, simply continuing the practice of their predecessors. Arabs divided the coast into four regions: (*a*) that of the *Barābara*, clearly Kushites, which embraced both angles of the Horn. South of Maqdishu came a zone of Kushite-Zanj interpenetration; (*b*) *Bilād az-Zanj* who possessed organized town states and were definitely pagan, with their king at Mombasa; (*c*) *Sofāla*, the land of gold, with a king at Ṣayūna, and (*d*) *Arḍ al-Wāqwāq*, the unknown and mysterious south. We must distinguish between the organizers of these coastal town states who were presumably Kushites[21] and the people inhabiting the coastal regions. Bantu, organized only as family groups, had been moving northwards, arriving in the south-Barābara coast A.D. 500–800. After Masʻūdī (writing A.D. 943) there is a hiatus in Arabic material for 200 years and when the curtain opens again the picture is different. From Idrīsī's account (A.D. 1154) it is clear that Islam had gained the Barābara coastal places, but not the Zanj south of them except the people of an island, probably Zanzibar;[21] in fact, he refers specifically to their pagan practices. Not until after Ibn Saʻīd (writing A.D. 1254) did Islam become the ruling class cult.

These small settlement states included Maqdishu, Brava, Merka, Lamu, Pate, Malindi, Mombasa, Mafia and Kilwa, which maintained commercial relations with Arabia, the Arabian Gulf, India and beyond. As on the Red Sea coast many were situated on islands. In the north Islam had penetrated among coastal Kushitic nomads and gained the ruling class of Sidama states, but south of the Horn there were no states, nor do there appear to have been nomads near the coast, for there were far more favourable regions inland for the pastoral nomadic life. These pastoral tribes rendered any penetration inland hazardous. Bantu peoples lived in family groups whose religio-social structure was unfavourable to the reception of a monotheistic legalistic religion. At the same time, the Muslim *Sawāḥila*, 'coastalists', as they were called, were preoccupied with commerce and interport quarrels and rivalries. Their outlook was towards the ocean and they do not appear to have contemplated the spread of Islam among Africans; rather, they themselves formed a new coastal community in which Islamic and Bantu elements blended, though with the non-African elements predominating. A type of civilization known to us as 'Shirazi' developed (1150–1500) which had unique features but whose source and inspiration are untraceable. This civilization, revealed mainly through its material remains, disappeared during the Portuguese period, after which developed the regional culture we call 'Swahili', which was overwhelmingly influenced by the Islamic culture of Hadramawt.

The equilibrium of coastal settlement life and commerce was abruptly broken at the end of the fifteenth century with the arrival of the Portuguese. Though they occupied only a few points along the coast, for they were concerned with Indian Ocean commerce, trade declined and so did the settlements since they had no other function. Tribal movements, Galla and Nyika in the north and Negro raiding bands in the south, also aided the process, some towns being completely abandoned. Portuguese domination of the coast lasted some 200 years. Their power steadily declined and they were driven away by the Arabs of 'Uman. The 'Umani rulers maintained loose links with the coast and some 'Umanis settled on Zanzibar Island. These Arabs were Ibāḍis but they made no attempt to spread Ibāḍism. On the contrary, this period saw the arrival of a steady stream of immigrants from Hadramawt, including many clerical leaders, who reinforced or introduced their own local customs (shown for example in *rites de passage*), but especially the Hadrami tradition of Islamic learning based on the Shāfi'ī *madhhab*. They also began to write Swahili in Arabic script with

Hadrami poetic and theme traditions. The fusion of the various Islamic elements, remnants of Shirazi, and new Bantu with the Hadramis, led to the Swahili culture synthesis as it exists today, Arab inspired and orientated as contrasted with Sudan Islam stemming from Berber Maghrib.

Although the coastal towns and islands acknowledged the suzerainty of the rulers of 'Uman their actual influence was vague and still diminishing when Sa'īd ibn Sultan (d. 1856), after establishing his position in Muscat, turned his attention to the African coast, making Zanzibar his seat of government. His reign marks a turning-point in East African history. Arab-Swahili penetration into the interior, beginning early in the nineteenth century, to exchange merchandise for ivory, with which was associated commerce in slaves as the carrying medium, began the process of turning the outlook of the coastalists inland upon Africa. But although the traders penetrated deeply into central Africa, beyond Tanganyika into Congo and Nyasa, setting up independent trading stations, they were not propagators of Islam. Only individuals closely associated with their activities like Yao traders and chiefs adopted an Islamic veneer, and even with the Yao Islam's real spread accompanied and followed the dominance of colonial powers.

During this long period of coastal settlement no Bantu communities had adopted Islam, in fact only those who were absorbed into or were closely associated with Swahili. Its effective spread into East Africa, mainly Tanganyika, really dates only from 1880 after the Germans took control of that territory. An aspect of European penetration is the way it facilitated Islamic expansion. However, its spread in East Africa is quite different from its spread in the Sudan belt in that it did not gradually penetrate existing communities, but, in the first phase, formed coastal Muslim communities which grew only through the absorption of Bantu individuals; and, in the next phase, its spread from about 1880 took place largely by individual conversion, though with considerable rapidity. The only people who may be compared with the Sudan pattern are the Yao who, becoming traders in the region between the coastal stretch from Kilwa to Mozambique and the interior, found it a valuable means of maintaining their distinctiveness, whilst at the same time ensuring that it changed their social institutions as little as possible. Swahili culture has influenced coastal tribes (Zaramo, Matumbi of Rufiji delta, and many others) whose distinctions are so slight that Islam may well aid tribal as well as cultural unification. But Islam in the interior, even when embraced by a significant proportion of the population, has not yet been truly integrated into the social structure of the Bantu peoples, whilst Nilotic and Nilo-Hamitic tribes have been completely unaffected.

Chapter 2

The process of religious and culture change

1. The spread and assimilation of Islam

The preceding sketch of Islamic culture zones, taking the regional or vertical view of the impact of Islam upon Africa, shows that the nature of its impact falls into four historical phases. We will outline these briefly since they correspond to four different degrees or types of Islam found in contemporary Africa.[1]

A. THE MAIN PHASES IN AFRICA

The first phase followed the conquest by the early Muslim Arabs of all the Mediterranean littoral from Egypt to the Atlantic coast of Morocco. Islam slowly won over the Egyptian Copts and the Berbers, but the Arabization of the latter derived mainly from a new break-in and dispersion of Arab tribes from the eleventh century.

The second phase began with the spread of Islam across the Sahara and up the Nile into the Sudan belt through the work of traders and clerics. Only the white nomads of the desert and Negroes of the Sahil belt and some other peoples on the river valleys of Senegal, Niger and Nile were Islamized. The feature of this period was the adoption of Islam as a class religion—the imperial cult of states like Mali and Kanem and as the cult of trading and clerical classes. Its penetration in numbers and quality was not extensive or deep. Religious life was characterized by forms of accommodation, by a dualism or parallelism of the old and the new—the African idea of the harmony of society maintaining itself over against any idea of Islamic exclusiveness.

The third phase from 1750 was marked by the appearance of clerics imbued with a new conception of Islam, intolerant, militant and exclusive of compromise with African religion, who waged the *jihād*, and whose impulse led to the formation of a number of

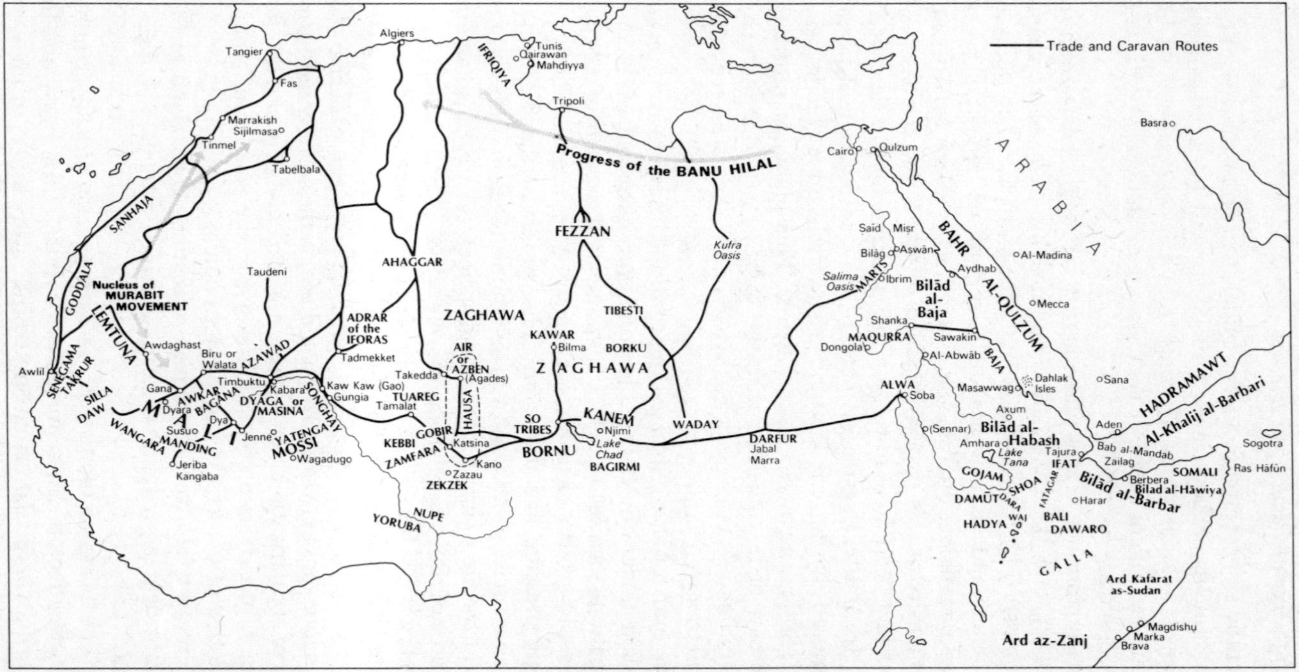

Map 5. States and trade routes in the northern half of Africa in the Middle Ages

theocratic states throughout the Sudan belt from the Atlantic to the mountains of Abyssinia—Futas Toro and Jalon, Masina, the successor Tokolor states deriving from the conquests of Al-ḥājj 'Umar, the Fulani states of central Sudan, and the Mahdiyya of Nilotic Sudan.

The importance of this phase is that it brought Islam from the periphery into the centre of communal life. The great change accomplished by the reformers lay in the stress they laid upon the uniqueness and exclusiveness of Islam and its opposition to the prevailing religious dualism and all-embracing tolerance. Although the intensity of this emphasis waned during the next phase, sufficient had been done to forge a new relationship between Islam and African life. Surviving aspects of the incorporation of Islamic law more fully into life is found wherever Islam is recognized as state religion, as in Northern Nigeria. This phase, or rather the latter part of it, coincided with the fourth phase, the increasing penetration of Western powers, by whom the states set up by these conquerors were suppressed.

The fourth phase witnessed the continued numerical expansion of Islam under the favourable conditions provided by colonial occupation—new facilities for communication, security of the trade routes and growth of towns, accompanied by a renewed surge of Islamic pressure and diffusion.[2] The impact of the West set in motion a social revolution in many animist societies, the foundations of the old unity of religion and society was weakened and the way opened for the adoption of a universal religion which could provide a stable framework of exterior observance and organization for life in a changing world. But the entirely new factor we shall seek to bring out in respect of religious change, since it is changing the relationship between religion and life, is the steadily increasing effect of secularization: the secular diffusion of Islam and the formation of neo-Islamic communities where the position of religion is like that of Christianity in Western lands.

To recapitulate: these four historical stages correspond to four different degrees or types of Islam existing contemporaneously in Africa:

1. The Islam of the first phase of expansion among Hamites. Preexisting factors differentiated two culture zones, Egypt and the Maghrib, where Islam is integrated into every aspect of life.

2. Traditional Sudan Islam, where Islam is accommodated into the indigenous system and embraces many grades of allegiance.

Religious dualism and tolerance is characteristic, with authority recognizing all religious usages.

3. Basic Sudan pattern, the result of the theocratic phase, where Islamic law is incorporated into the pattern of social life. Intolerance and at the same time parallelism.

4. The secularized religion of neo-Islamic communities and of the new men, the result of the simultaneous penetration of Islam and of Western secular attitudes.

B. THE PENETRATION OF ISLAM

The position as regards Islamic penetration is that the people of the first belt of Africa, that is, those bordering on the Mediterranean, are Muslim, though there remains a large and strong Coptic Christian minority in Egypt. The next belt, the Saharan, is wholly Muslim, but its few inhabitants, except for the Teda, belong to the Maghribi culture cycle. With the third belt, the northern Sudan, stretching roughly between 10° and 15° lat. N. across the continent, we reach Negro Africa. It includes the northern parts of Senegal, Mali, Nigeria, Niger, Chad and the Republic of the Sudan. In this belt of pre-desert steppes and dry savannas African Muslims reach their maximum density and Islam has made its deepest impact upon life. The Sudan belt divides into three areas: west, central and eastern or Nilotic, the latter differing considerably from the others owing partly to the wholehearted adoption of Arabic culture by the strong Hamitic element in the north. In the next belt, the southern Sudan, and that which follows in the Guinean or West African coastal tropical zone, Muslims are in a minority though there are important penetrations, notably among the Yoruba of Western Nigeria and in Sierra Leone (30 per cent Muslim) and Guinea (60 per cent Muslim). In north-east Africa most of the peoples, nomads and settled, ringing the Ethiopian highlands are Muslims. South of Muslim Somalia along the east coast there is a Muslim fringe where Islam is implanted in characteristic fashion, whilst the religion has penetrated deeply, if superficially, into interior Tanzania.[3] In central and south Africa Muslims are few, less than one per cent.

Islam penetrated easily into the northern Sudan belt where there were organized societies and states, though even in this belt there are few exclusively Muslim zones and some large groups (centralized Mossi states and Bambara village state organizations) remained uninfluenced until changes during the period of European occupation weakened barriers. Islam did not penetrate among the paleonigritic peoples of the southern Sudan belt, nor among chieftainless societies like that of the Ibo of south-east Nigeria, nor the highly evolved societies of the West African Guinean belt like Ashanti and Dahomey, except for the Yoruba and that mainly during this century. Although it spread among Hamitic nomads from North African Berbers to East African Somali, it did not penetrate at all among the Nilo-Hamites or Nilotic tribes living in what are now the Republics of Sudan, Uganda and Kenya. The chieftainless agricultural Bantu inhabiting vast regions in eastern and central Africa remained impervious.

C. FACTORS AFFECTING THE SPREAD OF ISLAM

Factors fostering or hindering the spread of Islam derived from both the historical conditions of penetration and the nature of the societies affected. Both objective and subjective factors have to be taken into account.

Historical factors include trading relations, immigration and tribal movements, political conquest and subjugation, and cultural assimilation. The role of nomads is important, yet they exercised little direct influence. Their role was largely unconscious, through their dispersion affecting settled regions, through cultural assimilation and the absorption of pagans into their tribal structure by assimilation and clientage. Camel-owning nomads provided a vital link with the wider Muslim world through the caravan trade they monopolized: Berbers on the Saharan routes and Kushite nomads in Nilotic Sudan and north-east Africa, especially Beja and Somali. Pilgrim traffic is another aspect as, for example, from the Nile to Red Sea Ports. Nomads influenced the spread of Islam less through religious zeal as through their alliance with a reformer and his small nucleus of devoted followers.[4]

The role of traders was more important than that of nomads. We can think of trading as a form of nomadism, but it is largely a movement of individuals and small groups. Islam has always followed the trade routes. Initially Berber merchants carried Islam across the Sahara into Sahilian states before the Murābiṭ movement got moving. All nomads in north-east Africa where trade routes link the Red Sea with the Nile quickly became Muslim, though south of Maqdishu where such routes did not exist Islam did not spread. It follows from this that its presence is most evident along such routes, though this cannot be taken as evidence of the Islamization of the people of the country through which the routes pass.

African trading communities like Soninke and Dyula in west Sudan, Hausa in the centre, and Nubian *jallāba* in eastern Sudan, formed trading colonies and these always included clerics. The clerical profession and trade were closely allied and in many regions the terms for 'trader' and 'cleric' (or 'Muslim') were synonymous. So commercial movement included or more generally combined with clerical nomadism. We find clerical Wangara (Mande) and Tokolor visiting and settling in central Sudan walled towns. The role of the holy man has been very effective in Hamitic Africa, but much less marked in its traditional form (the thaumaturgic leader) in Negro Africa.[5] Pular-speakers (*Hāl-pulār'en*, Tokolor type) as culture-bearers have been perhaps the most important factor in Islamic culture diffusion, whilst nomadic Fulbe (*heferbe wodebe*, the 'red pagans') have been the most refactory. No missionary agency in western Sudan could compare with the role of the miracle-working *fuqarā*' of Nilotic Sudan. The spread of Islam through trading colonies varied. The Dyula, for example, were not active propagandists within the pagan communities among whom they lived, but their settlements, islands of Islam in a sea of paganism, were potential centres of diffusion, and when other conditions were favourable, especially after the coming of colonial rule, they proved of great significance.

The adoption of Islam by ruling families came through trading relations, but the cause of its adoption comes also into the sphere of subjective factors—the prestige of attachment to a religion linking with a new order but without involving any real change. The nineteenth-century phase of militant Islam resulted in widespread nominal allegiance to Islam which, through breaking up local cults, their centres and practitioners, caused a spiritual vacuum and paved the way for deeper penetration.

The passive factor must also be taken into account. Any integrated society resists pressures towards cultural change and assimilation. The type of social structure of the society upon which Islam made its impact was important both for the primary adoption of Islam and the subsequent depth of change, especially the adoption of elements of Islamic social law.

In general, societies with organized states were most likely to absorb Islam into their system. Such states fostered and protected trade, both internal and long range. The security of the trade routes in Mali and across southern Sahara is stressed by Ibn Baṭṭūṭa. But the superficiality of Islamic penetration among the cultivators was revealed when Mali disintegrated, for it disappeared almost completely except for the threadlike dispersion of the ubiquitous Mande traders.

On the other hand, among stateless societies, Hamitic nomads adopted Islam easily and became fervent adherents, whilst uncentralized Negro peoples were completely unaffected. Similarly with such nomads as Nilotes and Nilo-Hamites like the Masai and Nandi with a system of generation-sets.[6] The zone of Hamitic nomads extended from the Berbers of North Africa and Mauritania to the Beja, Somali and others in north-east Africa. Arab bedouin, of course, form a similar type of stateless society. Although little is known about the process by which these Hamitic nomads adopted Islam they seem to have absorbed it easily, if guardedly as regards social change, and with apparent lack of conflict, which must mean that clerics were not deeply involved. Somali tradition links tribal beginnings with the absorption of an undemanding Arab immigrant. Peoples with this type of society, mutually hostile nomadic groups subject to all the vicissitudes and crises of nomadic life—drought, animal blights, and intertribal conflicts—found in Islam a means towards tribal cohesion and solidarity. But whilst accepting the religious aspects they did not accept its legal provisions freely. Among these peoples, however, extramural aspects of Islam, such as saint veneration, cultic aspects of the religious orders, and manifestations of *baraka*, all of which made little impact upon Negro societies, provided means for Islam to gain a real hold and penetrate more deeply. In such societies the conditions and nature of assimilation differ from those which prevailed among townsmen and cultivators.

Vast areas of Africa verging on the Sudan belt zone are occupied by uncentralized Negro communities; for example, the hundreds of communities in the southern Sudan belt. Into these Islam could not penetrate in any natural fashion. Where Islam has spread among stateless societies during the changing conditions of the twentieth century, as among the Bantu of East Africa, the nature of its penetration (by individual conversion) and degree of acceptance (maintenance of ancestor-conciliation) differ from that of north Sudan belt Negroes.

In regard to the spread and penetration of Islam the subjective aspects are equally important with the historical factors. These include:

1. The factor of religio-social reintegration, though this was limited to certain types of people. In the past when communal life was broken up through conquest, forcible removal and slave-raiding, or at the present day is imperilled or distintegrating through modern changes, families, or even ethnic groups, cast adrift from their traditional moorings, may welcome an allegiance which will give spiritual stability in a new ritual, help to reintegrate the social structure and foster wider relationships. Similarly with new groupings in towns, mines or agricultural schemes. The Manyema of Tanzania are such a dispersed group who found a new identity through adherence to Islam. But we may point to the fact that the adoption of Islam by the whole community did not upset society, which remained unified, and only through a long period was the actual social structure modified.

2. An important factor, in the past at any rate, derived from Islam's system of intellectual and material culture and the feeling of superiority this gave to its adherents. Whilst desire for superior knowledge and pride in the acquisition of Arab letters was formerly important, this desire is today being directed into other channels. Yet, allowing for this, many conditions still awaken the need for a religion of status.

3. There is also the factor of accommodation. Islam has been present in the Sudan belt for centuries and accommodated itself in such a way that it became a natural aspect of its environment. The difference between Islam as an impersonal and abstract system with a body of doctrine and a rigid legal code embracing, not merely ritual, but every aspect of life, and the diversified and complex African systems of life appears so profound that few points of contact seem apparent and the psychological shock of religious change to be as great as for an African converted to Western Christianity. This is not so in practice. The reason is that Islam in contact with Africans is characterized by a series of gradations which act as insulators passing on Islamic radiation gradually to animist societies. Aspects of Islam as cult and ethic are characterized by their individualistic form. All the forces of African conservatism would be arrayed against this, but in fact such individualistic elements as might undermine social structure are not stressed. Elements alien to the local genius were rejected and those adopted were moulded into conformity. Islam thus does no violent uprooting but offers immediate values without displacement of the old. It is not a question of either–or but of both–and. Further, the agents of Islamic radiation are people who, whilst possessing a supratribal outlook and more sophisticated cultural background, are Africans who can live happily in village life and take to themselves local wives. The children of many Muslim traders living in an alien community grow up associated with the culture of their mother, and it is from such beginnings that the Islamization of many villages can be traced.

4. But the attraction of Islam was not merely based on its social and cultural advantages; the religious factor was more important, however obscure it may sometimes have seemed, since it was the inner impulse of such movement of change. Religion is the vital cohesive factor in the Islamic system which gives meaning to the whole structure. What strikes people first when brought into contact with another religion is less difference in belief as difference in ritual and customary observances. Islam's most obvious signs are the prayer ritual, especially communal prayer, its death ceremonial, and its taboos. The question of power is also a consideration, and strong aspects attracting the animists are Islam's divining, magical and animistic practices; yet Islamic animism is not confined to the family and its land like the old, it is universal animism which enables the animistic Muslim to take his place in a universal society.

The religious conceptions of Islam, its expression of the ultimate meaning of man's existence, were not a primary element leading to its adoption, but once the religion has been accepted, new conceptions penetrate unconsciously through religious action. No acute tension seems to be set up except under special conditions such as their coming within the sphere of theocratic rule, and then only within the rulers' immediate political orbit.

D. STAGES IN CONVERSION TO ISLAM

The rapid conversion of pagans during the last century and the beginning of the present one is not difficult to understand. The agents of Islamic diffusion were people who were at a higher cultural stage than the pagan and possessed a supratribal outlook, but who were Africans. Thus Islam was mediated through kindred people. The times were ripe, for in other ages Islam made little appeal except to limited classes. Further, Islam came in a way that was apprehensible, in that the point at which it first met Africans was such that it seemed little alien to, or at least its adoption appears to offer little disturbance to, the old order and the inner man.

Three stages mark the process of conversion: *germination*, *crisis*, and gradual *reorientation*. Germinating in the deeper levels of individuals-in-society and in the collective consciousness, the seed eventually forces the shock of crisis. This results in a new attitude which in time profoundly modifies individual and social behaviour. These stages also help us to understand the different levels of participation which one finds in the Islam of Africa.

First stage. Preparatory. Contact of some sort, visits and settlement of traders and clerics, leads to the breaking down of barriers and the adoption of certain aspects, chiefly material, of Islamic culture—the wearing of Islamic amulets and dress. The religious system is not upset.

Second stage. Involves the assimilation of real elements of Islamic religious culture—ritual prayer and recognition of certain categories of permitted and prohibited. They are at this stage religious dualists, but these changes are accompanied by a weakening of the indigenous culture, until eventually the community reaches a point of crisis. This marks the beginning of the

Third stage. The dividing point when the old religious authority is consciously rejected, the village ritual pattern is disrupted, priests of communal cults lose their power, and the clergy take their place as the guides for the religio-social life.. Ancestor-worship must go[7] because it is the core of the old religion, but a great deal of the old is retained. Offerings continue to be made to nature spirits, and medicinemen since they are individual practitioners still flourish, but the dualism has changed to parallelism. Islam is now really influencing society.

The three stages are often paralleled by change over three generations. In religious change the family rather than the individual is the natural and significant unit. The process takes more than one generation and is a reciprocal interaction between three generations. We may express it in this way. A pagan family (generation 1) is subject to Islamic radiation. This affects their children (generation 2) who become Muslims in name, without discarding much of the old, but their children (generation 3), under the influence of clerics, learn to despise the old inheritance, and generation 1, in order to preserve its authority and maintain the unity of the family, now become Muslims. So the cycle is complete.

2. The results of the adoption of Islam

The process by which African culture was transformed and reconstituted as an African–Islamic culture may be shown thus:

ISLAM → AFRICAN CULTURE = interaction = ultimate synthesis

During the years when African Islamic culture was being formed Islam was in dynamic relationship with the religion of Kin and Nature in a dialectal process in which it could only triumph through either incorporating an Islamic institution like the *mahr* into the corresponding African institution, in this case the bride-price; or, where assimilation was impossible, as with spirit cults, tolerating them alongside Islamic institutions. At the same time, the ultimate effect of a universal religious culture like Islam is the gradual disintegration and reintegration, in fact, transformation, of the African culture. The process is such that the disintegration and reintegration seem natural since they are but the reverse and obverse of one process. The ensuing religious change is potentially, and in time actually, radical. Life becomes based on a new spiritual foundation and this must change the basis of society.

We have to take account of various aspects of this process: (*a*) the reciprocity of culture contact, leading to the weaving of a new religio-social pattern; (*b*) the actual process of assimilation; and (*c*) dualism, changing in the course of time into parallelism.

In this process of cultural interaction, whether the gradual change of one village group or the ultimate formation of an African-Islamic subculture, African culture was the passive factor and Islam brought the vital cohesive element. Islam dominated the life of the few towns such as Timbuktu, Gao and Jenne in western Sudan and trading settlements on the east coast, but the African influence was at least as strong, and generally stronger, in the life of the agricultural populations.

But though the African factor has been described as passive, this passivity does not mean that it was not a vital element. When assimilation took place between African and Islamic institutions, the basic institution into which the other was assimilated might be either, but was generally the African. For example, in marriage as a social institution, the bride-price system remained the basis and the Islamic system of payment to the bride (*ṣadāq* or *mahr*) was incorporated into it. With marriage as a *rite de passage* also, the indigenous element remained dominant and the Islamic aspect was negligible.

Other aspects might be remoulded to harmonize with the basic assumptions of Islam, but there were vast spheres of life, such as the ritual cycle of seedtime and harvest, which could not be remoulded or absorbed but which were vital for the wellbeing of the community. The association of two attitudes towards the holy took the form of dualism during the first stage, but this changed in time into parallelism. Whereas the traditional religious practitioners, especially priests acting as intermediaries with the spirits, tend to be displaced, the practitioners of magic-divination are not, but rather continue their techniques in spite of the fact that the cleric himself serves as a medicineman and seer. It is a question of their role in society.

Islam met the resistance of an integrated system of life informed throughout by religion. It could survive in the Sudan belt only by indigenizing itself. This was not accomplished by any reformulation which was impossible since it came as an inflexible legal system, but by inserting elements into the pattern of African life and society.

In the first stages of historical penetration it is found functioning as a class religion. Islam transcends the circle of the local community, hence intertribal representatives such as traders are Muslim. The clerical class as supplementary medicinemen and the royal clan also had intertribal functions and could adopt Islam without upsetting society. But as Islam becomes more widespread, and this holds particularly for the nineteenth century, the old religion (family, nature and mystery cults) is undermined and fragmentated. Many survivals remain but they become disparate episodes, since the old unity of life maintained by religion has disintegrated. So we get the early dualism changing into parallelism.

Religious dualism tends to be characteristic of the early stages after conversion to Islam. It continues to be true of the general run of imperfectly Islamized Bantu in mainland East Africa. Historically in West Africa it was found in all those, other than clerics and traders, who adopted Islam before the nineteenth-century era of clerical states. This was the coexistence and parallel functioning of two religions in the community. Ancestral rites, for example, might continue because they were vital for the welfare of the family and the maintenance of kinship structure. Similarly the rites of the mystery cults[8] or rites assuring the authority of the ruler[9] are not likely to be discarded until some other guarantee is assured.

Such dualism is to be distinguished from the parallelism into which it changes, which is a normal aspect of an integrated Islamic community. This is the parallel existence of elements from two religious cultures alongside each other. Thus, in introducing the newborn into human society the Muslim *'aqīqa* is adopted alongside the native ceremony and a Muslim name (Fulfulde *innde Muhammadiyya*) added to the pagan names (*yettode*) which bind the child to the family and clan. The difference from dualism is that the whole tendency is directed towards the formation of a unified Islamic outlook on life.

It is incorrect to talk about the adaptation of Islam to Africans. The process was one of accommodation associated with parallelism and this came about through African Muslims themselves. They did not so much adapt Islam, a legalistic religion, as secure the acceptance of certain Islamic customs in such a way that the customary framework of society remained intact, though there was gradual change in psychological attitudes towards social institutions. The clergy could not strictly adapt the law; their task was to get certain minimum Islamic requirements accepted into the body of custom. These elements, being unadaptable, changed custom as it were from within, gradually remoulding life in an Islamic direction.

The result is a fusion in life but not a true synthesis, the unyielding nature of the Islamic institutions precluding this. The parallel elements bear the mark of their indigenous origin. Everywhere the traditional world remains real and its emotional hold vivid. There is, therefore, an ultimate dualism in life, since this rests upon a double foundation. The degree to which the life of the different social groups rests upon each primary culture varies, the most evident contrast being between town and countryside. Yet at the same time, it must be emphasized, the ultimate result is balanced and coherent.

Connected with this making the best of two cultural spheres is the sex division of religion, men being Muslims and women pagans. This is found everywhere, not merely among the newly converted. More correctly, one should say, men are more deeply involved in Islam whereas women's participation is marginal, for Islam provided women little scope for ritual participation. Few women are able to perform ritual *ṣalāt*. Even in Arab-Hamite communities they rarely do so except after the cessation of menstruation when 'they are no more women'.[10] This ritual separation of sexes is found in practice throughout the Muslim world. In Egypt, for instance, on Friday whilst the men are participating in *ṣalāt al-jum'a* at the mosque, the women are at the cemetery or the *qarāfa* (city of the dead) making offerings for the repose of the souls of the family departed. *Ziyāra* to saints' tombs, so strong a feature in Hamitic Africa, is not found in Negro Africa. Consequently, to turn to wider social aspects, we find men involved in the Islamic aspects of marriage, such as the contract ceremony, whilst women order the transitional rites like the *jirtiq* ceremony in Nilotic Sudan. Similarly with other rites. It is women too who maintain the non-Islamic cults, such as sacrifices to nature spirits and the ordering of possession-cults like the *zār*, *bori* and *pepo*, as well as in quasi-Islamic cults, such as saint-tomb rituals and medicinemen practices in which men also participate in varying degrees.

THE DEEPER RESULTS

In spite of all that we have said there is a radical change. This must be emphasized because so often one hears people say that because the people of such a village sacrifice to spirits they cannot be good Muslims. It is sufficient that they claim and want to be accepted as Muslims. In time Islam revolutionizes the inner man. Its adoption means acknowledging a new nucleus to life and there follows a gradual reorientation of life around this nucleus. It also revolutionizes society. The acceptance of Islamic legal elements gradually affects the structure of society; for example, in communities where divorce was formerly unknown, its introduction affects the institution of marriage and therefore the social structure.

The possibility of change is accounted for by the fact that there ensues a gradual change in psychological attitudes towards social institutions. The point is that the old sanctity of custom has been undermined. The source of authority gradually changes. Islam might almost be said to have worked towards the greater secularization of society in that its adoption destroyed the overall influence of religion on life, by a dualism changing to parallelism, and was able to extend its own influence only over sections of life and even then incompletely. This meant that the non-Islamic aspect of life was sanctioned by custom, which no longer had its basis in religion, but instead the will and ethic of the community.

The regional culture of Egypt was, until the modern age effected such great changes, an integrated culture embracing all aspects of life and thoroughly Islamic. This is true to some extent of the culture of the Sudan belt, though the integration is much less complete since this belt is not homogeneous like Egypt, but embraces many peoples speaking different languages and following varied types of life. In Egypt one is simply confronted with a peasant and urban culture, the relatively few nomads living on the periphery of Nilotic life. On the other hand, not merely are the peoples of the Sudan belt not solidly Muslim, but their Islamic culture is not homogeneously Islamic. Yet equilibrium is attained between the Islamic and African elements in a relatively harmonious pattern of life. Eventually, the process of mutual interaction reaches its term and an African Islamic culture is formed.

The fact is that Islam is stronger when confronted with a diffused world view like that of Africans and, however gradually and however many compromises are made during the process, it does change the direction of institutions towards its own special outlook. Although African-Islamic culture was retarded and marginal it was successfully maintained around the unmodified core of Islam without being changed into something else by syncretism. From Islam stemmed a view of life and society which created a new community. All this holds for the past when the process could be carried to its full term, but today the impact of a third new world, the secular outlook, institutions and society, is changing the whole process and movement of change, and this process catches the Afro-Muslim communities when they are at diverse stages of Islamic integration.

3. Effect of Islam upon African religion and society

Islam does not explain the religion of any Muslim any more than Christianity does that of any Christian. A person's or community's religious consciousness is both less and more than the religion professed. The whole question of the actual faith of anyone or any community is very complex. The religion professed is a guide, generally the dominant factor before the modern secularization movement began, since it permeated the whole culture complex, but still it is only a partial guide. This wider aspect derives from the fact that we are born and brought up within a particular culture, and that culture, though in the case of Islam the dominant factor moulding it and giving it its particular ethos and outlook, yet embraces elements from other sources.

The religion of African Muslims for analytical purposes embraces three spheres of belief, ritual and communal relationship:

1. Islam in the strict sense. Islam based on the *shārī'a*, without those animistic and magical elements which are associated with the Islamic system because believed in and practised by Muslims.

2. Animism. Man in ritualistic communion with spirits. Three main spheres: (*a*) Kinship ritual. Man in communion with the spirits of his ancestors. These are generally vestigial among communities in the Sudan belt who have been Muslim for any length of time, though more recently converted, especially Muslim Bantu in East Africa, may keep up the ritual. Ritual involved in the *rites de passage* may also include quasikinship relationships. (*b*) Paganism or local religion: man in communion with the spirits of the locality he inhabits. The beliefs and ritual system connected therewith. This sphere may also include Islamic animistic elements such as beliefs about *jinn*. (*c*) A third sphere, the mystery cults, do not survive definitive Islamization, but there is a development of possessive-spirit cults.

3. Divination and magic, having two spheres, indigenous and Islamic, the latter embracing the lore of written as well as spoken charms and divinatory practices.

The spheres of life likely to be influenced through the adoption of Islam which will be referred to subsequently may be outlined.

A. RELIGIOUS BELIEF, RITUAL AND INSTITUTIONS

1. *The supernatural and man*

Disintegration of organized cults of ancestor and community spirits governing social life, and the redirection of worship to the one God. The coalescence of the high-God with the God of Islam: change from high-God or universal spirit to monolatry, then to monotheism. Disappearance of the cult of ancestor propitiation and change in status of mystery cults. The resistance of aspects of old cults and survival as vestigial institutions.

Introduction of the Islamic antithesis between good and evil spirits, with the possibility of the degeneration of old powers into evil spirits.

Change in ideas of morality. Sanctions of behaviour find a new source in a written law. Adoption of a legalistic morality in place of, or parallel to, aspects of traditional communalistic morality. Persistence of old ideas of the sacred. Adoption of Islamic taboos.

Islamic magical elements and methods of divination introduced parallel to indigenous methods. The cleric in his function as medicineman.

2. *Islamic institutions*

The communal aspect of Islam directed towards serving the Islamic way of life through its institutions.

Training, organization and functions of the clergy. Their role in communal rituals of family and community life, on conduct, in education and on the state.

Role of the Qur'ān school and legal training, and of the *ṭarīqas*.

Ritual action differentiating believer from unbeliever: the cult, ritual prayer, fast, almsgiving and pilgrimage.

Calendar. Adoption of a liturgical calendar of twelve lunations, with displacement of rites based on seasons.

Desacralization of the idea of sacrifice and adoption of Islamic idea of *ṣadaqa*. Influence of Arabic and enlargement of the means of expression.

B. SOCIAL, POLITICAL AND ECONOMIC LIFE

These spheres are interpenetrated and moulded under the influence of religion. In each a reciprocal process of interaction takes place whereby customary usages are reformulated under the influence of Islamic law, and, conversely, the application of Islamic law is modified or restricted by custom. The following is a selection of the changes which may take place.

1. *Social structure*

Influence of Islam's ideal of religio-social unity in inculcating a wider outlook. Its law changing social institutions.

The family. Disintegration of extended family into households. Change from patriarchal succession to succession in the direct line. Change in matrilineal system. Effect of adoption of Islam's system of inheritance. Reciprocal duties of husband and wife—modifications.

Kinship and marriage relationships. Clan taboo degenerating into a vestigial system with consequent breakdown of marriage prohibitions. Addition of Islamic marriage ceremony implying idea of contract between individuals, but little change in system of alliance between two families. *Ṣadāq* incorporated into bride-price guarantee. Effect upon exogamous rules of Islamic encouragement of first-cousin marriage. Increase of divorces accompanying adoption of Islam. Changes in status of women, segregation both ritual and physical, according to class, town life or prestige.
Effect of Islam upon social differentiation.

2. *The state and the legal system*

Islam as imperial cult, state religion or theocracy. Introduction of religious hierarchy (central Sudan).
The *Sharī'a* and its administration. System of *qāḍī*'s courts. Custom retaining its character of fundamental law, modified by limited adoption of Islamic regulations.
Separation of judicial and executive systems.
Adoption of elements of Islamic system of taxation.
Influence of the clergy as experts on revealed law in limiting powers of chiefs.

3. *Effect of Islam upon transitional rites*

Birth. Adoption of the *'Aqīqa*—naming, shaving, offerings and sacrifice.
Circumcision. Desacralizing of the rite. Effect upon initiation cults and age-grade societies. *Jando* compromise in East Africa.
Marriage. Insertion of contract ceremony into the African ceremonial. Lack of effect upon marriage as a transitional rite.
Funeral rites and customs. A sphere where Islamization is pronounced.

4. *Economic life*

Special consideration accorded to traders and trading. Creation of trading class. Effect of Islamic contractual law and prohibition of usury. Rejection of Islamic land law. Changes deriving from Islamic regulations relating to ownership of property, marriage and inheritance rules.

5. Material culture

Islamic sensitivity to nakedness leading to adoption of clothing as an element of surface uniformity.

Effect of ritual regulations upon personal cleanliness. Refinement in manners and material life through introduction to a more developed civilization.

Effect of Islamic taboos on certain types of food and drink, actions and representational art.

Chapter 3

The religious life of African Muslims

1. The unity of belief, ritual and institutions

Myth, cult and fellowship: this is the triple chord found in all religion whose interrelatedness it is necessary to keep in mind, for they are only unravelled by us, hence distorted, in analysing the religious life of a community. In a revealed religion like Islam these are shown in *Belief*, actualized in *Ritual*, as a *Way of Life* (moral conduct), based on the principles explicitly revealed (*waḥī ẓāhir* in the Qur'ān) or inspired (*ilhām* in *ḥadīth*), or implicitly expressed (in *sunna*) through the action of the Messenger. All this is manifested in the form of the religious institution, the *sharī'a*.

Islam for the ordinary adherent is not an intellectual exercise. It is absorbed and maintains its hold because it is a system of life. It teaches and binds by ritual, and issues forth in the relatedness and conduct of the community, and is organized and perpetuated in the institution. In practical life theology is not an important factor. The important thing is the performance of the rites and the adoption of such customs as differentiate the believer from others, for this means that the beliefs are accepted even though they are totally unknown. When beliefs are important they are based on experience. For instance, belief in angels is not very strong in the Maghribi Islamic world, whereas belief in saints is vivid because it is based on collective experience; saints do manifest their presence and power and intercession to them does have results. The affirmation of the unity of God, carrying out His commandments and offering Him homage in the form of *ṣalāt*, are more important than knowledge about Him.

Theology, therefore, is not taught because it is an unnecessary abstraction. Intellectual heresy, and curiosity too, is virtually unknown. Heresy can only be practical, in other words, nonconformity with accepted forms of behaviour. In traditional society, as contrasted with secular society, most people believe and conform because they are born into a religious community and accept what they are taught or absorb. This whole communal reference is changing in the Western world but in Africa it still holds wherever traditional life has not undergone disturbance.

Ritual, cultus or system of worship, is the key to belief. It is the means by which the individual is related to the universal. Practical religion consists of ritual and institutions, observances and rules. Rite is the connecting link (*religio*) between daily life and eternity. In the Islam of Africa as in African religion, whilst ritual and practice are fixed, the content and meaning of the ritual remains vague. Ritual shared with one's fellows, not merely contributes towards the integration of the individual's personality, but also the integration of the fellowship of believers. It is socially significant in that it brings the community together for regular customary and seasonal observances, thus confirming to its members and affirming before the world its significance as a religious unit. The fact that the Islamic yearly cycle of ritual observance does not synchronize with the agricultural year, affects the relationship of the cultivator and Islam.

The third element, the ethics of the community, is the minimum conformity of social behaviour required. Here Islam is specifically achieved. The life of a Muslim community is observably different from that of a pagan community. Each has its codes of behaviour and after a community becomes Muslim the basis of communal life changes. Here Islam makes itself felt throughout the aspects discussed later under 'the unifying features of Islam'.

The unique social institution in which all this is embodied is the *sharīʻa*, the most fundamental in Islam. It has important values and a unique function in the conservation and fulfilment of Islamic religious and moral values. The whole may be summed up in this form:

ISLAM

THEOLOGICAL EXPRESSION	RITUAL EXPRESSION	EXPRESSION as a WAY OF LIFE (Moral conduct)
The unity of God (*tawḥīd*)	The unity through acts of worship (*ṣalāt, manāsik*)	The unity of the believers (*Umma*)

SHARĪʻA

Many aspects of belief will be referred to subsequently in association with ritual action or communal religious functions where they find their natural setting. Here we will refer briefly to certain questions of change in beliefs and methods of transmission.

Among the means of communication of the underlying beliefs behind ritual and codes of behaviour must be mentioned poems, *mawlids*, and legendary stories, which not only convey to the illiterate the rudiments of religion such as the laws regulating ablution and prayer, but also give some idea of the attributes of God, the names of the angels and prophets and conceptions of the afterlife, about which more is known than perhaps any other aspect. Therefore, although little theology is actually taught, a certain amount of doctrinal lore is absorbed in so far as it is fused in everyday thought and language.

Although the majority of believers are illiterate yet behind is a body of fixed immutable knowledge and this filters down in some form through the Qur'ānic school where, besides Qur'ān memorization, pupils are taught the occasions and order of ablutions and prayer, legal aspects relating to society and traditional beliefs and legends.

Belief in God everywhere coalesces with the creator-god of African cosmogonies.[1] Belief in God does not acquire clarity as to His nature but as to His uniqueness and power. As elsewhere, *shirk* or association is regarded as the greatest sin without practical realization of what it really is. What is taught are the duties the believer should render, his obligation to offer God homage in the form of *ṣalāt* and to obey His will by observing His law. The old term for God is frequently retained alongside the newly acquired term Allāh. Thus among the Swahili the terms Allāh and Mungu are used as synonyms, the Arabic term in stock Arabic phrases and exclamations, whilst Mungu is always invoked in informal subjective prayer (*du'ā*).

Characteristic of African religion is its one-worldliness. African religion is eminently practical. Religion, whether the cult of spirits of ancestors or of nature or those of the mystery cults, sustains a moral order of society, and all ritual is designed to foster the well-being of the community. Those who conform prosper, those who rebel pay the penalty, and all this not in some future life but in the here-and-now. And society and nature, indissolubly one, embrace not only those members visible on earth, but also the unborn and those who have passed on, as well as the various nonhuman spirit realms with which communication is possible. There is only one world, having within it realms of existence, but all in dynamic interaction.

Islam changes all this, and here its ultimately revolutionary character upon the thought and life of the spirit as well as of social life is seen. Islam changes the very basis of society. It introduces a dualism of life and society utterly unknown in the old realm of the spirit. It introduces an ideological antithesis, formerly unknown, between God and the Devil, good and evil spirits, God and Man (subject and object), this world and the next, heaven and hell, permitted and prohibited categories of actions (based on a fixed law), believers and unbelievers (with the concept of belief and unbelief in the background), and even between the ideal and the actual, the ideal Law and the practice of the law.

The position of the Prophet as introducer to this dualism and bearer of the Law is not prominent in African, more especially Negro, Islam. Through recital of al-Jazūlī's *Dalā'il al-khairāt* veneration became strong in the Maghrib, but generally in Negro Islam it is recited as an incantation without invoking any image of the Prophet. The *ṭarīqa* revival in the early nineteenth century stressed his mediatorship,[2] hence those influenced (Nilotic Sudan, north-east region and east coast) observe a cult of the Prophet. Recital of *mawlid an-nabī* plays a role. Devotion is strong along the east coast, both in the form of honouring him and seeking his intercession, and is stimulated by recital of al-Barzanjī's *mawlid.* Such recitals take place on every occasion for rejoicing, festivals of birth, circumcision and marriage, on all communal religious occasions and particularly during Rabīʿ al-awwal, the month in which occurred the Prophet's birth. The *mawlid* of al-Barzanjī is also taught in Qur'ānic schools, a practice which seems to be peculiar to East Africa.

2. The unifying features of Islam

The unifying features found in the Islamic community are:

a. The law and its practitioners. The recognition of the law in theory is shown in practice through the acceptance of the clergy as guides of conduct. With them is associated the Qur'ānic school as an essential feature of traditional village life.

b. Recognition of the pillars as evidence of following the Islamic way: the testimony to the faith (*shahāda*)—the emphasis being on the 'testimony', that is, action—ritual prayer, fasting, almsgiving, with pilgrimage as an ideal goal.

c. The adoption of common calendar (lunar) rites and observances. This is an important feature in breaking the link with animist cults and in the consolidation of Islam.

d. Observance of Islamic categories of the permitted and the tabooed (*ḥalāl* and *ḥarām*): intoxicants, eating pig and carrion; contact with dogs; whistling. Prohibitions of mutilations, incising and tattooing. Method of killing which is *ḥalāl*. The disappearance of deformation customs and ritual killing are indexes to the depth of Islamization in the earlier stages of change.

e. Incorporation of a minimum Islamic element into the transitional rites (*rites de passage*) at naming, circumcision, marriage and death.

f. Islamic magic and divination. Acknowledgement of the efficacy of Islamic supernatural powers; the ability of the cleric to bring power into activity through ritual words and actions. The adoption of such Islamic elements as ritual prayer for rain, the formalized magic of medieval Arabic treatises, the use of amulets and divinatory lore.

g. Whilst Islamic magic is important, belief in saints is not to be included among the universal elements for it has not taken root in the Negro Islamic world, but it needs to be included here for it is strong in regions which have a Hamitic background—the Maghrib, Nilotic Sudan, and north-east Africa. Similarly with the *dhikr* practices of the religious orders.

A. THE LAW AND EDUCATION

In absorbing and sustaining belief the institution—the binding forces of the religious community—counts most. The institution is bound together by the *sharī'a*, sacred law, which theoretically governs the whole of life. The law in Islam may be equated with the Church in Christianity as the expression of God in the world. The *sharī'a* embraces all aspects of life, and though for practical purposes it is divided into sections and subjects there is no essential difference between *'ibādāt*, ritual, forms of worship, and *mu'āmalāt*, practical religious life-usages. Many spheres of Islamic culture had little or no influence upon Negro Africa—the penetration of Sufism in the *ṭarīqas* and saint cult was retarded or incomplete, whilst Arabic literary culture, theology and philosophy, sciences and arts such as architecture, painting and calligraphy and the practical arts, were either completely absent or very marginal. But the *sharī'a*, because it is universal and stable, is the factor which, above all, as new populations have been embraced within the sphere of Islam, has provided the Islamic norm, contributing more than anything else to create in time an Islamic community.

Reverence for the law assumes an importance which is quite disproportionate to observance. People do not accept Islamic law *in toto* when they become Muslims. Gradually it influences aspects of society, but in an unequal fashion. In the established Muslim community it rules wholly and indisputably in all forms of cultic expression and within the realm of family life; that is, all the regulations regarding marriage, divorce, inheritance, custody of children and the like are normally accepted, and even though in many other spheres it is ignored it is still the force which gives an Islamic expression to life.

Madhāhib

African Islam, both Hamite and Negro, is predominantly Mālikī for this code is prevalent in the Maghrib, Upper Egypt (Ṣa'īd), Nubia and throughout the whole Sudan belt. The Shāfi'ī code is that of most of Egypt[3] and East Africa, including Ethiopia and Somalia, since this was the rite of most of Arabia until Wahhābī rule brought the Ḥanbalī code to the fore. Nilotic Sudan is also Mālikī which points to the fact that the establishers of the law after the decline of Maqurra (from 1300) came from Upper Egypt and a few even from the Maghrib, for there was no link at that time with west Sudan. Through Egyptian and Hijazi links, the principal external contacts, some teachers adopted the Shāfi'ī code.[4] The Ibāḍī *madhhab* is found only among small groups in Algeria and Zanzibar, the first dating from the early days of Islam and the other introduced through 'Umani immigration but not spread among Africans.

The Ethiopian region is unusual in that historical circumstances associated with the introduction of Islam have resulted in a number of *madhhabs* being recognized in different parts of the region: the Ḥanafī at Massawa and elsewhere in Eritrea, in parts of interior Abyssinia and in a quarter of Harar city (Ottoman-Egyptian influence); the Mālikī in the interior of Eritrea (from Nilotic Sudan); and the Shāfi'ī in parts of Eritrea, in Harar and among Somali and Galla (from Arabia, especially Hadramawt).

The clergy and their training

Although Islam does not have a sacerdotal body it has its clerks or clergy. As an institution they are the specific conduits of Islamic tradition, whilst family and village institutions such as initiation schools are the conduits of the African aspects of culture. The cleric stands apart from the rest of the laity only as a lettered man. He performs specific religious functions. He leads in prayer, teaches the young to recite the sacred text, performs the first sacrifice at the great feasts, names the newborn, conducts the marriage ceremony, washes the dead and leads the funeral prayers. No function of village life is complete unless he is present.

The ranks of the clergy can be entered with a minimum of training since the merest smattering of Qur'ān recitation, together with some knowledge of the ritual and social regulations of Islam and the technique of amulet-making, enables one to join their ranks, though the acquisition of the knowledge to enable one to attain the higher ranks is a very arduous discipline. Thus throughout the whole of Islamic Africa except in the east every Muslim village has not merely one but frequently several clergy living the ordinary village life as cultivators or traders, yet at the same time representatives of the heritage of Islam. They are also found in hundreds of pagan villages where they are welcomed as a natural element in village life since they provide an additional link with the spiritual world.

Exceptional in this respect is the East African interior. Here we have mentioned the lack of true villages such as are found in the Sudan belt. People live in communities, it is true, but they are dispersed. Since East African Muslims think that they can only pray with a roof over their heads, they generally meet only for the Friday prayer. Among them too the clerical life is thought of as a profession; many are trained on the coast and become 'Swahilized' and though they may return to their own tribal area they tend to set up in towns or large centres and not in their local community. Thus we have the surprising phenomenon for Africa of Muslim communities without effective clergy on the spot for carrying out clerical functions.

Clerics are both settled and itinerant. In certain parts (among Soninke, Fulbe of Futa Jalon and in Northern Nigeria) the permanent clergy are loosely organized in a socially accepted hierarchy. The *imām* of the Friday mosque is responsible for such functions as marriages and funerals and other clergy have to consult him and obtain his permission before being allowed to conduct them. The *imām* controls the distribution of *zakāt* and receives fees, customary gifts and thankofferings on all special occasions. He is also responsible for the welfare of the local clergy. The *imām* of the district Friday mosque is appointed by the political chief in Muslim areas and by the Muslim community in pagan areas. In the latter case he has wider functions since he acts as 'secular' chief and liaison with the authorities.

In western Sahara and Sahil, among Moors, Tuareg and Sahilian Soninke are clerical clans whom the French refer to as *tribus maraboutiques* whose role within the tribal community is that of an hereditary order of clergy. The Kel es Souq are such a widely dispersed clerical tribe, influential among Tuareg and Negroes of the Niger buckle, acting as their chaplains, amulet-makers, secretaries and *qāḍīs*. This development is due to special social and political conditions deriving from desert life and politics. In western Sahara it was partly a Berber reaction against the domination of Arab ruling clans.

A characteristic of Islam in Africa is its physical freedom and mobility. The typical mosque is a marked-out square on the ground,[5] whilst many clergy are itinerant. Especially in central Sudan one comes across wandering friars with, slung around them, a goatskin or mat *sijjāda*, ablution jug, bookbag and pencase.[6]

The education of the cleric begins in the Qur'ānic schools which are found in every Islamic settlement and village. Anyone who thinks himself competent may open a Qur'ānic school on the veranda or in a room in his house or in its compound. He begins with the children of his family and then neighbours will send theirs. Schools are generally small, rarely having more than twenty pupils. Teaching is a pious duty and is not regarded as a profession exclusive of other occupations and teachers generally have some cultivation on which their pupils are expected to work, whilst others are traders. The teacher receives customary presents when the pupil reaches certain stages in Qur'ān recitation, on the festivals and other occasions. He is frequently the local *imām* or section cleric, and adds to his income by making amulets. Schools in villages may well be difficult to find during the daylight hours when the pupils are working in the fields, and lessons are given early in the morning and in the late afternoon or evening when they will be found chanting their passages by the light of fires. In towns, where the pupils do not go out to work, there are generally three sessions a day. On the East African coast every Swahili village and town has its schools, but in the interior among the dispersed communities they are rare, and the reason for this has been discussed. Girls are found in schools in many communities—in Senegal, among the Moors of Mauritania and the Sudan Sahil, frequently in Bornu, and among Swahili. Certain regions, central Sudan in particular, also have travelling schools. In Darfur[7] and Hausaland[8] a master will often take his pupils during the dry season on begging tours lasting from three to four months.

The training of clergy beyond the Qur'ān stage is based to a large extent on the system of seeking masters. In west Sudan centres of Islamic studies have tended to be situated in the Sahil among Moors.[9] Here it was chiefly a question of individual teachers and clerical families whose reputation attracted pupils and whose influence often extended far beyond the sphere of education. Towns like Timbuktu, Islamically more Moorish than Sudanese, and Jenne which was authentically Sudanese, had many recognized teachers of *fiqh*. Soninke, Tokolor and Dyula chiefly supplied teachers for Negro communities. In central Sudan the Hausa city states seem to have had relatively few local teachers. West Sudanese, many of them Pulo, migrated there, but though they left behind them a reputation they trained few pupils to maintain an enduring tradition. After the 1804 revolution, however, Islamic learning received considerable stress and has ever since continued to colour the outlook of Northern Nigerian life. The Kanuri of Bornu possessed a much stronger tradition of learning than the Hausa and the indignation of Muḥammad al-Amīn at the accusations of 'Uthmān dan Fodio is understandable. In Nilotic Sudan a tradition of legal learning developed early and along unique lines in that it was blended with Sufi tradition. There the Qur'ānic school was known as a *khalwa* or 'retreat', the term used for the centre of a Sufi director, since all spiritual direction was concentrated in the hands of *fekis* who were at one and the same time *fuqahā*', 'jurisconsults', and *fuqarā*', Sufi 'mendicants'.[10]

Teaching has been a strong feature in Swahili culture since the revival of Islam through Hadrami influence during the nineteenth century and even earlier. Of special interest are the lecture sessions called *darasas*, held in both mosques and teachers' houses, and intended, not for the training of '*ulamā*', but for teaching Arabic, *fiqh* and Qur'ānic exegesis to ordinary interested people.

Two only of the manuals studied and frequently learnt off by heart need be mentioned. These are the *Mukhtaṣar* of Khalīl ibn Isḥāq and the *Risāla* of Ibn Abī Zaid which are authoritative for the whole of the Mālikī Sudan belt. So reverenced is Khalīl's 'Summary' that if one mentions *al-Kitāb*, 'the Book', they think that it is this that is being referred to. The Qur'ān and Ḥadīth rarely form part of the training even of the higher clergy since, having the Law, they have no need for independent investigation of sources. The *Ṣaḥīḥ* of Bukhārī may be known but only as a pious recitation exercise during Ramaḍān. Theology is not studied since it has no practical significance; there were no sceptics or free-thinkers in traditional society. Many have acquired a sound knowledge of legal Arabic and compose devotional or legal books, but they are simply compilations, displaying no originality.

B. PRACTICAL RELIGIOUS INSTITUTIONS

1. *Ritual prayer*

Ritual action is the sign of allegiance to Islam. He who observes ritual prayer (*ṣalāt*) is a Muslim; so the Hausa asks, 'Do you pray?' (*Kana sala?*) for 'Are you a Muslim?' This is a sphere which in its public manifestations is exclusive to men.[11]

The first pillar of Islamic action is the *shahāda*, 'witness' to the faith, which emphasizes the contrast between believer and unbeliever, a distinction unknown in the world of ethnic religion. Islam brings a fixed system of belief and action, not variable according to family or locality.

Friday prayer is the most obvious sign of a Muslim community and is always a feature of the Muslim state.[12] After the 1804 *jihād*, if not before, each Hausa town had its *'īd* prayer ground and its Friday mosque. People from the surrounding villages and any nearby nomad Fulani came into town for Friday prayer.[13] In parts where Islam is well established, after the *khuṭba* exhortation in which the name of the ruler should be mentioned, a *wā'iẓ* or 'preacher' delivers a 'sermon' (*wā'ẓ*). In West Africa the *wā'ẓ* generally consists of Qur'ānic exposition in the local language and is often given daily during Ramaḍān. In East Africa, though Friday and festival rituals mobilize the whole community, they have nothing like the significance they have in the Sudan belt, with their spectacular aspects whereby the authority of the ruler is displayed, simply because there were no Islamic state systems.[14]

2. *Almsgiving*

Zakāt, like *ṣalāt*, is an important ritual provision, an involuntary social obligation[15] which is both a purification and a thanksgiving. In Africa it was levied by the Muslim community when living among pagans and used for the benefit of the poor and clergy. Not until the era of theocratic states and their successors did it become a state levy.[16] In these states, from Futa Jalon to Mahdist Sudan, where there was supposed to be religious uniformity, *zakāt* was paid to the head of the state or into the *Bait al-Māl*. At first it was allocated according to the legal provisions (fixed proportions for the state, *jihād*, poor, etc.), but later became a tax levied and allocated arbitrarily by the chiefs. Colonial governments suppressed this arbitrary form of *zakāt* and it has become a voluntary, but socially unavoidable, contribution claimed by the clergy on 'Ashūrā and at the end of Ramaḍān.[17] *Zakāt* is distinguished from *ṣadaqa* in that it remains a levy, even though left to the discretion of the individual, whilst *ṣadaqa*, purely voluntary, has acquired a special significance.

We shall be frequently stressing the importance of *ṣadaqa* in African Islam. The word has spread widely, among pagans as well as Muslims. The meaning and usage of the term cannot be taken for granted. It may mean no more than almsgiving, it may be an offering made in the name of God or the ancestors which is not consumed by the offerers but given to the clergy and poor. It has played a great role in desacralizing the idea of sacrifice. There are two forms of *ṣadaqa*: that which is offered at the great Islamic festivals and to sanctify family events at birth, marriage or death, or safe return from a journey and the like,[18] whilst the other is an offering which seeks to attract divine approval and protection for man's activities, such as *ṣadaqa* to ask for rain, or to seek the help of God's spirits at the stages of cultivation. The two ideas may merge. The common element in the two forms is that the *ṣadaqa* is offered in the name of God and not consumed by the offerers.

3. *Significance of the pilgrimage*

Pilgrimage to Mecca has played an important role in giving African Muslims a conception of Islam as a world religion and the consciousness of possessing a common religious inheritance. Travelling the whole way through Muslim lands gave the impression that Islam was the religion of Africa. In modern times many pilgrims have acquired some conception of pan-African and

Near Eastern political issues. It has significance too as a means of culture diffusion.

It is characteristic of converts to Islam to proceed on pilgrimage. This applies particularly to rulers, and there are many references in Arabic writings to the pilgrimage of rulers from Takrūr,[19] Māli, Songhay and Kanem; a Kanemi chief being the first recorded pilgrim.[20] The same practice holds today and new adherents, chiefs or the ruling élite in modern states, will set off soon after their conversion with a view to enhancing their status in the new religion. In these days of air travel this is easy, but in the past it was a long and difficult journey even for the rich and a perilous undertaking for the poor.

During the period of the great Sudan states pilgrims travelled by the northern route across the Sahara and then east to Egypt and down to the Hijaz. There is no record of any going eastwards (even the Fulbe clerics who went as far as Kanem-Bornu then crossed the Sahara), but after the fall of Nilotic Maqurra and 'Alwa and the formation of the state of Sennar, when Tunjur were apparently organizing intermediary states, central Sudan pilgrims began to use the eastern route to the Red Sea ports. Ever since there has been a stream of Fellāta (Fulbe) and Hausa pilgrims working their way along this route whose pilgrimage might take seven years or more.[21] The Muslims of Nilotic Sudan and eastern Africa in general, chiefly Kushite nomads, have not been so enthusiastic. Some Funj kings encouraged their *fekis* to go by paying their expenses,[22] but do not appear to have gone themselves. The Mahdī of Nilotic Sudan prohibited his followers from undertaking the *ḥajj*, and he and his successor recruited pilgrims in transit, generally willingly, into their armies.

4. The Jihād

The *Jihād*, 'striving' (in the way of God), is regarded by some as the sixth pillar of Islam for it is a *farḍ* duty. In the Sudan belt *jihād*, interpreted as war for the extension of Islam,[23] enjoyed a great vogue in the eighteenth and nineteenth centuries as an essential aspect of the theocratic movement which transformed Sudan Islam. The early theocrats endeavoured to follow the regulations, but again, especially in Northern Nigeria, their successors found means to avoid the rule of law or to interpret it in their own interests.

Although Muslim nomads have had practically no direct influence upon the spread of Islam in Africa, they have occasionally been enlisted in the cause of the *jihād* by an inspired leader. We think of 'Abdallāh ibn Yāsīn rallying Berbers in the 11th century (the movement of the Murābiṭūn); 'Afar of the Dankali plains carried forward to the conquest of the Abyssinian highlands by Imām Aḥmad Grāñ between 1529 and 1542; Fulbe roped into the *jihād* of 'Uthmān dan Fodio; and Somali enlisted by Muḥammad 'Abdallāh Ḥasan at the beginning of this century. Nomads were little involved in the movement of the Mahdī of Nilotic Sudan, though his successor made use of his own Baqqāra and 'Uthmān Diqna rallied a few Beja to the cause.

C. THE ISLAMIC CALENDAR

An important feature of the process of Islamization is the adoption of the calendar. This follows a year of twelve lunar months and thus is out of gear with the agricultural calendar based on the solar year followed by Africans. Consequently the Muslim agriculturalist follows two calendars, the Islamic for all that concerns its ritual cycle and the solar for the natural cycle of seedtime and harvest. After Islamization one is tempted to call them the religious and secular calendars, were it not that 'secular' is hardly a word that fits in with any traditional African context, since the natural cycle retains its own ritual observances in spite of the adoption of Islam.[24] The significant aspect is the role of the Islamic calendar in the attack on the old religion; it now becomes the official religious calendar and this undermines the old cycle of ritual observance[25] which loses the position it formerly held in the life of the community. Frequently the Muslim cleric replaces the pagan priest in performing agricultural ritual and propitiating the spirits.

The rhythm of life in traditional Islamic society, especially in towns, was informed by the liturgical calendar. The daily activities of everyone, shopkeepers and artisans, labourers and slaves, took their cue from the muezzin's call, the week's activity from the Friday prayer of assembly, and the succession of holidays, fastings and rejoicings from the yearly calendar. Observance of the liturgical year is also an important reinforcer of Muslim self-consciousness and solidarity, one of the things that in the modern world, when everyone uses the Julian calendar for secular life, emphasizes the fact that they are Muslims.

Most people have adopted the Arabic names for the months;

however when a month has special significance it invariably acquires a local descriptive name which is the one commonly used. Thus in Swahili, Shawwāl which follows Ramaḍān and opens with the Breakfast Festival (*'īd al-fiṭr*), is called *mfungo mosi*, 'the first releasing', the next month 'the second releasing', and so on up to the ninth. With Songhay Ramaḍān is *haume*, 'shut mouth' and Shawwāl *ferme*, 'open mouth'. Among Mande (Dyula, Mandinka and Soninke) the Islamic lunar months are given the names of the solar year months, taking as point of departure the *sun-kālo*, 'moon of deprivation', formerly 'the hungry period' before the harvest, now the fast month.

The year begins with Muḥarram, but the tenth night, the 'Ashūrā, is that to which African practices connected with the New Year cohered; though now, since it is continually moving around the year, they are disconnected from the agricultural season. These African rites are symbolic, intended to ensure prosperity during the new year—rites of purification, washing in the river, purification by fire and torchlight processions. Islamically, it is a day when special prayers are offered in the mosque, and sometimes predictions are made there for the coming year since on it God created the tablet of decree, the pen, fate, life and death; and exhortations are given regarding the duty of paying *zakāt*.

The next festival is the Prophet's birthday, *Mawlid an Nabī*, on twelve Rabī' al-awwal, known under a great variety of local names, that of Masina (centre Jenne) *mūlūd dõ-mba*, combines Moorish Arabic *mūlūd* and Mande *dõ-mba*, 'day of the great dance'. Celebration varies greatly, but on the whole one may say it is a characteristic of Hamites but not of great significance among Negro peoples.[26] Among the latter it is celebrated in some parts (for example, Bornu and Futa Jalon) with recitals of such poems as the '*Ishrīniyyāt* of al-Fazāzī in the Prophet's honour, but no *mawālid*.[27] However, wherever the collective *dhikr* of ecstasy is performed, that is, in Egypt, Maghrib, North Sudan and the east coast, there are special recitals of *mawālid* accompanied by *dhikrs*. In Nilotic Sudan the celebration was not observed until the period of Turko-Egyptian rule, but then attained great popularity, being celebrated even in small villages and with fervour and official recognition in towns.

The 26/27th Rajab, the night of the Prophet's ascension (*lailat al-mi'rāj*), is only observed by a few clerics in Negro Africa, but is a recognized school holiday. In Hamitic Islam the adherents of the orders hold recitations of the *mi'rāj* story which is similar in form to the *mawlid*, but describes the Prophet's nocturnal ascension through the seven heavens.[28]

Ramaḍān is preceded by one or two days of festival (like Shrove Tuesday), and in consequence the whole month of Sha'bān is often called as in Swahili 'the month of feasting' (*mwezi wa mlisho*). The fast is strictly observed for African life is so open that it is difficult to do anything else owing to fear of public censure. The month is of great significance even among Islamo-pagans. Among devotees of possessive spirit cults the month of deprivation includes the spirits whom God imprisons. This belief is found among devotees of Hausa *bōri*, Songhay *holē*, Nilotic Sudanese *zār*, and Swahili *pepo*, as well as among the similar type of Christian devotees in Latin America during Lent. On *Lailat al-Qadr*, taken to be 27th Ramaḍān, clergy spend the night in the mosque where the whole Qur'ān is recited in relays, and in some parts also the commentary of the two Jalāls.

Unlike the Prophet's birthday *'īd al-fiṭr*, 'Breakfast Festival', is a canonical feastday, hence it is universally observed, and does not call for special comment—the giving of *ṣadaqa*, the festival prayer on the *'īd* prayer-ground outside the town, followed by congratulatory visits, new clothes and feasting. In West Africa the *khuṭba* delivered in Arabic is frequently translated into the local language.

The approach of the 'Feast of Sacrifice' (*'īd al-aḍḥā*) is heralded by the appearance of flocks of sheep baaing through the streets of the towns. In East Africa the days which precede the *'īd* prayer on 10th Dhū'lḥijja are often the occasion for holding ceremonial feasts in commemoration of the dead, not to be confused with ancestor-worship. Although called 'the Great Feast' it is not an occasion of such rejoicing as on the lesser *'īd*, but is spent more quietly paying and receiving visits.

D. THE COMMUNAL MORALITY OF AFRICAN ISLAM

In practical Islam moral conduct is following what God allows and refraining from what He forbids. Theoretical and practical morality[29] for the Muslim means the study and practice of the way of life (*sunna*) of the Prophet, the exemplar who followed the right path; but since all this has been codified it is simply a matter of following the law. The social ethics of Islam are directed to maintain the harmony and solidarity of the community (manifested in the cult), the consensus (*ijmā'*) of the community being the criterion. A vast range of possibilities is open to Muslims through the *ḥadīth* system and consensus, the latter often taken to be whatever, on a support of *ḥadīth*, remains unchallenged. Apart from the law the Muslim has for his guidance books of conduct like part 3 of al-Ghazālī's *Iḥyā*, *ṭarīqa* manuals, and also the diversionary *adab* (*urbanitas*, etiquette) literature which quotes sayings and relates anecdotes from the lives of great Islamic figures. These sources do not have to be known directly, but all contribute towards the formation of the moral standard of the community.

All this vast literature, other than the legalistic, remained practically unknown to the clerical leaders of non-Arabic-speaking Africa. Therefore Negro Islamic mentality, that is, the clerical outlook, tends to be severely legalistic. When a community becomes Muslim a gradual change takes place in its ethical outlook. The theoretical sanction of behaviour is now a written law; this influences communal morality which becomes coloured by Islamic morality, the depth of colouring varying according to community, by length of Islamization and other factors, though remaining basically African. Sanctions of behaviour are, therefore, the harmonized ethic of the community, a blending of the indigenous and the Islamic. Practical ethics vary since, though Islamic legal morality is uniform, the basis differs according to the particular make-up of the people. The Islamic basis for the approved ethics of the community is more limited in Negro regions since it is based on a few Mālikī law books, but stronger in Arab regions like Nilotic Sudan where oral tradition is full of episodes, derived originally from *ḥadīth*, used to support practices and customs.

The duties incumbent upon the community are summarized in the maxim, 'to command right and forbid wrong', a feature of the theocrat's utterances; and right and wrong are defined by the law. In some states, as in the Masina of Shaikh Ḥamadu, the institution of censor of public morals (*muḥtasib*) was adopted. There is a list of things which are lawful and unlawful with a wide range of terms covering the various categories. Whilst some like *ḥalāl* (lawful) and *ḥarām* (prohibited) are everyday words in African Muslim languages the majority are known only to the clergy.

Although the communal aspect of moral conduct has been stressed, it should be mentioned that personal responsibility is a keynote of the Qur'ān[30] and its outreach in institutions; the five pillars, for example, are duties incumbent upon the individual. Similarly with duties which are *wājib*, such as obedience to parents, wife's obedience to husband, almsgiving (other than *zakāt*), and support of relatives. Social harmony involves the stressing of positive virtues such as benevolence, humility, truthfulness; and, negatively, condemnation of envy, hatred and the like. African clergy had no use for the abstract element in these terms, but for practical elements like stress on the care of orphans. They also stressed such aspects as the duty of *ṣalāt* as paramount over all these. Arabic abstract terms are concretized, thus *tawba*, 'repentance', through the influence of *jihād* movements, became 'submission'. Similarly taboos, such as prohibition of swine flesh and intoxicants, are readily comprehensible.

E. ISLAM AND THE TRANSITIONAL RITES

Religion plays a vital role during the rites which mark the major transitional phases in the individual's life which ensure protection during these dangerous stages.[31] They are organized as significant communal events. These turning-points of life quickly absorb an Islamic element because such absorptions do not modify the social structure. This is a sphere where the parallel existence of the two heritages is very evident, with only occasional blending as in the East African *jando* initiation rites. But the Islamic element is important in that it hallows the event, and in death rites it is dominant. Old ideas may cling to naming and death rites, yet they are transformed when given an Islamic character. The rites carried out in different parts of Africa vary considerably, even among the same people, through the amalgamation of distinctive African rites with the fixed Islamic rite. With circumcision the Islamic element is minimal since it is not an Islamic ritual occasion, and with marriage it is mainly legal.

The essential elements of the first of these rites, naming on the eighth day after birth, comprise the pronouncement of the name, a sacrifice (*'aqīqa*) and shaving. East African Swahili vary most from the norm,[32] and among Arabs and Hamites the naming and *'aqīqa* are frequently dissociated. In Nilotic Sudan the ritual sacrifice is now generally omitted and the ceremonial reduced to simple naming (*simāya*). Negro Muslims place much more stress on the naming. This derives from their belief that a person's name is especially related to him, partaking in some sense of his spirit. Some Songhay believe that at the naming the *biya* (soul or personality) of an ancestor enters and the baby becomes a person.[33]

West and central Sudanese maintain the three essentials of naming, sacrifice and shaving. Among Songhay of Gao the *bongo kyebu*, 'shaving of the skull', takes place in the morning with representatives of both families present but not the father. The cleric chooses the name with the aid of a *sibḥa* (rosary), proclaims it and prays. The animal is sacrificed and a woman shaves the child's head. If it is the first child the mother remains with her own mother for forty days until after her purification. Many variations are found among the Songhay owing to their different ethnic constituents and the influences brought to bear on them; some, for instance, have adopted Tuareg customs.

Among Soninke we find simultaneous naming, throat-cutting and shaving. In western Guinea they go further by including the pounding of rice simultaneously with the other elements. The rice is then made into ritual sacrificial *tyobbal* cakes. Thus custom was adopted first by the Fulbe of Futa Jalon which was the diffusion centre for Islam in the region. The cleric places the knife on the victim's throat, recites a ritual formula, and at the same moment that he utters the name and cuts, the pestles pound and the grandmother shaves. The *tyobbal* is the real *'aqīqa* for the sacrifice is frequently omitted.

Almost invariably the mother's purification ceremony takes place on the fortieth day after birth. In Nilotic Sudan she goes to the Nile accompanied by her female friends to rid herself of the contamination of childbirth.

Circumcision in Islam differs from other rites in that it is not associated with any ritual of initiation. It is an individual rite, a ceremony of purification, whereas initiation in African life is also a social rite.[34] Wherever the age set organization was an important feature of the traditional structure circumcision formed part of the collective rite. Where not previously practised it was incorporated into the initiation rites. The new, therefore, is linked with the old, but the old provides the basis and only traditional ritual experts are normally involved. Later, the Muslim cleric may be allowed a sphere, and later still, after Islam has triumphed over the mystery cults, the role of the local witch-doctor, for to this is the cult priest then reduced, fades away.

Change in this sphere is related to Islamic pressure against mystery cults. Among Mandinka, in general only recently Islamized, the initiation rites and the cults they exist to serve, are still prevalent. These initiation ceremonies, generally in three stages of circumcision, retreat and coming-out ceremony, are today being weakened, less by Islam, than through modern pressures; for example, the shortening of the retreat in the 'bush' to a token ceremony. The only example of a synthesis between the old and the new is found in the East African *jando*,[35] performed by detribalized in Tanganyika, which is an initiation into Islam.

Swahili delay the ceremony until a group is ready, a house is set aside and enclosed by a fence. The operation as a rite of purification is performed by the cleric (*mwalimu*) or village head (*shehu*), but the period of retreat is under the control of the traditional officiants, *makungwi*. After the confinement they are brought out by their grandfathers to the feasting place and given seats of honour. The only ritual aspect is the recital of *mawālid*. The Songhay have a collective circumcision but have eliminated the old ritual elements, though still allowing a role for individual non-Islamic practitioners. Clerics chant the Qur'ān into sand which is scattered on the floor of the circumcision hut to expel and protect against spirits during this critical period, and at the same time Gabibi pagans bury their charms in the four corners of the hut.[36] Although nowadays in more sophisticated parts of Africa boys are often sent to the hospital or dispensary for the operation, there is generally some element of initiation.

None of this elaboration is found among Arab-Hamites and Hamites. You will find collective circumcision, and those circumcised together may have a special relationship, but nothing more. In Nilotic Sudan as in Egypt it is an individual event. Among riverain tribes like Ja'liyyīn it resembles a bridal procession, hence the saying, 'the Arab is a king on the day of his wedding and the day of his circumcision'. The boy is kohled and hennaed, mounted on a horse, invested with the protective *jirtiq* and sword and garbed in women's robes and ornaments—all to protect against the 'eye'.[37]

With marriage again the Islamic factor remains constant since it is based on written law, but the indigenous elements, the actual transition rites, vary from people to people. The general form is marked by three stages: the proposal and engagement (*khiṭba*), the Islamic contract ceremony (*ijāb* and *qabūl* known as *katb al-Kitāb*) and the ceremonial surrounding the transference of the bride and her transition from one state to another. The adoption of Islam affects marriage more in legal and social aspects than as a transition rite.

Marriage remains a contract arranged between two families, not as in Islam between two fathers. Discussion of the marriage payments forms the essential part of the engagement ritual. The marriage settlement is known as *ṣadāq* throughout the Sudan belt and as *mahr* in parts of eastern Sudan and north-east and east Africa. This is legally the property of the wife and there would appear to be ground for conflict since its adoption would undermine the social purpose of marriage money. This is solved by inserting the legal *ṣadāq* (not a very high sum) due to the wife into the indigenous system of compensation to the bride's kin. Swahili, for example, recognize both *mahr* paid to the bride and a marriage settlement called *kilemba*, 'turban money', paid to the bride's father, as well as *mkaja*, 'travail money', paid to her mother. The indigenous system allows for the provision of a dowry but customs differ as to who provides it. In West Sudan it is generally remitted by the future husband to the bride, in central Sudan it is property brought by the wife to the marriage. It frequently balances the bride-compensation and consists of clothes, household utensils and food. Among Arab *abbāla* (camel nomads) in Nilotic Sudan, the husband's family pays *mahr* to the bride's family and '*adal al-bait*, consisting of money and goods, to the bride's mother for her trousseau and wedding expenses. This is a sphere where it is impossible to generalize since there are so many variations and exceptions.

The essential feature of the Islamic marriage is 'the declaration and acceptance', the same as in a commercial transaction. The general pattern does not differ greatly. The male relations on both sides (in West Africa generally without the groom and the fathers who are represented by *walīs*) meet before the cleric. The bride's *wali* announces the amount of the bride-price and the cleric proclaims the acceptance of the settlement, recites a formula which binds, and leads the recital of the Fātiḥa. This ceremony may be performed before the customary rites commence (even months before) or inserted in the middle.

The rites fall into two parts, the division being marked by the meeting, either the transference of the bride to the groom's house, or the leading of the groom to the bride's house as among Swahili. The Hausa have seven days festival, the first three take place at the bride's house, then, after the contract ceremony, the bride is conducted to the groom's house where the ceremonial is completed. Songhay of Gao region and Fulbe of Gundam and Duentza, influenced by Tuareg, set up a primitive house or tent in the compound of the bride's family where the marriage is celebrated.

The Islamic elements in the rites consist of the henna ceremony,[38] the bathing and veiling of the bride, and the *walīma*,[39] the statutory feast held after she has been transferred to the husband. Many associated elements are Islamic in the sense that they are traditional in the Islamic *'urs* in most lands, but their introduction need not necessarily be ascribed to Islam.

Islamization is more obvious in funerary rites than any other sphere, and there is general uniformity in the ritual pattern. The distinctive elements are: ritual washing and incensing with prayer, definite types of grave clothes, the use of the stretcher and expedition between death and burial; separation of the sexes; graves of specific type and orientation; mourners' assistance in carrying the stretcher; funeral prayers (*ṣalāt aljināza* and *talqīn*), with the casting of earth on the grave; widow's ritual mourning, with washing, seclusion period and purification; and after the burial ceremonial gatherings with prayer and recital (Qur'ān or *Dalā'il*), and *ṣadaqa* offerings and feasting on first, third, seventh and fortieth days after death.

The greatest difference is between the after-death rites of black and white Muslims for the former cease to be concerned with the deceased after the fortieth-day sacrifice. The ceremonial consists of various forms of *ṣadaqa* or sacrificial almsgiving. In the early transitional stages of Islamization there may be confusion. Hausa may regard offerings as being to a man's *kurwa* (personality soul), to the powers of the unseen world or to God for the repose of the soul, but once the fortieth-day ceremonies are over there are no subsequent offerings, certainly among deeply Islamized, such as would constitute a cult of ancestors. In addition to *ṣadaqa* another aspect stressed in some West African societies is the settlement of a man's obligations. Repose of the soul depends on ritual prayers at burial, offering of *ṣadaqa* and settlement of debts and obligations. Indifference to the dead is, therefore, the result of the adoption of Islam. Thoroughly Islamized societies have full confidence in the efficacy of the rites severing the link with the dead and have no fear of being harmed by them for neglect. This indifference cannot be regarded as a natural consequence of adopting Islam, since if we turn to white 'Hamitic' Africans (Maghrib, Egypt, northern Nilotic Sudan and north-east Africa) we find, on the contrary, that as in Asian Islam, they continue to venerate the dead, both those of the family[40] and holy men emanating *baraka*.

In Nilotic Sudan the near relatives spend from three to seven days squatting on mats (*furāsh:* hence the mourning period is called *ayyām al-furāsh*), to receive visits of condolence. On the last day the whole Qur'ān is covered by simultaneous recitation of different sections. On the fortieth day *karāma* is made with consumption by the poor only, and women are then allowed to visit the grave. This they continue to do on Friday evenings and special offerings called *raḥmatāt* are made on the last Friday in Ramaḍān.

The Sudan belt peoples traditionally had no burial places. Burials took place in the courtyard of the house in which a man died or outside the village. Islam did not lead to the introduction of cemeteries except in Sahilian towns. Graves were shallow, the process of disintegration rapid, and within a few months no traces were left. Today all towns have cemeteries whose emptiness on Fridays contrasts with the women's religion of the Arab-Hamites.

3. Influence of the saint cult and religious orders

Islam has its clerical order but no priesthood. This lack is compensated through the order of *baraka*-possessors who act as mediators bridging the gap which separates God and man. The saint cult and the orders in the form mediated by family *ṭarīqas*, though they are different spiritual forms in that one is based on the mediation of a saint and the other on techniques for attaining ecstasy and communion, are essentially linked together. Here again the distinction between black and white Muslims manifests itself. Their development is characteristic of what, for want of a better term, I have called Arabized Hamities as in Maghrib, Mauritania, Sahil and Nilotic Sudan, and as eastern Hamites or Kushites in north-east Africa. On the other hand, neither aspect deeply influenced the Negro Muslim world.

Public opinion canonizes certain men whom God gifts with *baraka* or 'holiness' so that they manifest *karāmāt*, miracles or charismatic gifts. Such men become the centre of a cult, but it is more especially after their death that the true saint cult is seen. Hamitic Africa is dotted with the *qubbas* of these men. Throughout nilotic Sudan can be seen whitewashed domes rising from square walls, which house the *turba* over the remains of the saint. At the foot of the grave is a small box for offerings (*zuwāra*), and in front a *ḥōd* of sand for taking as *baraka*. We have said that the true saint cult is not an integral feature of the Islamic scene in Negro Africa. This weakness may be due to the fact that belief in miracles on which it rests is linked with an historical and static view of the universe and does not accord with the Negro view of a dynamic universe. The cult of ancestors is not bound up with their graves. The lack of *qubbas* and *maqāms* in Negro Africa and consequently of visitation rites[41] needs bringing out as an aspect which emphasizes the deep difference between the Islamic consciousness of Negro and Hamite. The concept and feeling for *baraka*, such a feature of traditional religious consciousness which actually crossed the Sahara to impregnate Moorish Islam and up the Nile into Nilotic Sudan, did not penetrate beyond the Sahil. The word itself, it is true, passed into Negro languages, but the meaning behind the usage of the word is more like 'blessing' than the force peculiar to certain persons and objects. Consequently, the practice of drawing the power (*li 't-tabarruk*) is rare among Negroes except such as are connected with Arab-Hamites.

The position with regard to the religious orders is not quite analogous since they are found everywhere, but their function in the community and practices do not compare in Negro and Hamitic regions. They have a very reduced role in Negro Africa, where they are more in the nature of an Islamic grouping and rivalry. This seems to be connected with the fact that the saint cult did not accompany their diffusion, whereas in Nilotic Sudan it was integral. The technique of rhythmic breathing, with silent or audible ejaculations of the divine names and phrases, was not transmitted among Negroes, whereas this is essential to the *dhikr* among those with a Hamitic background. The *sibḥa* or rosary to enable one to perform individual *dhikr* tasks is used by all initiates into a *ṭarīqa*, but mainly as an adjunct to ritual prayer. There are no dervishes, even in Hamitic regions they are rare. Asceticism is alien to the deeper religious life of the Negro to whom it seems life-denying.

Negro Africa knows only two *ṭarīqas* of any significance, Qādiriyya and Tijāniyya, whereas Hamitic Africa has hundreds. Their profound role in the Maghrib has been mentioned.[42] The sixteenth-century maraboutic movement in Mauritania, which was in part a Berber reaction against Arab domination and marked tribal origins with an eponymous saint ancestor, introduced the Qādiriyya into the western Sahil where it influenced Negroes in the borderland. Its leaders played a role among travellers and traders, and acted as a conciliatory force in the endemic rivalries among nomads. In Nilotic Sudan we have mentioned[43] the function of the orders, the *dhikr* association and devotion to saint-mediators in spreading and adapting Islam to the needs of the people. The orders spread among Hamites in the north-east, and saint migrants from Arabia became eponymous ancestors of Somali and 'Afar lineages. But Negroes did not have the same customs as nomads, nor apparently the same spiritual needs as Hamites; their needs unprovided for by the Islamic legal cult finding other outlets. The spread of order allegiance in an attenuated form among Negroes began in the nineteenth century after the revival which stemmed from two Maghribīs, Aḥmad at-Tijānī (1737–1815) and Aḥmad ibn Idrīs (1760–1837). The Tijāniyya spread throughout Islamic Africa, not only southwards across the Sahara into west Sudan where the conquests of al-ḥājj 'Umar are responsible for its wide diffusion, but also into Nilotic Sudan, chiefly among westerners settled there, whence it penetrated into Ethiopian Galla states around the river Gibe. After the death of al-ḥājj 'Umar, Tijānī influence waned, but from 1920 it grew rapidly in West Africa, and since 1950 has enjoyed a special vogue in central Sudan, in Northern Nigeria its adherents coming into acute rivalry with the traditional Qādiriyya.

The Idrīsid revival, which stems from Arabia where Aḥmad ibn Idrīs did his teaching work, affected eastern Sahara, eastern Sudan and the north-east zone, particularly Somalia. This came about through the work of Aḥmad's disciples, in particular Muḥammad ibn 'Alī as-Sanūsī (1787–1859), Muḥammad 'Uthmān al-Mirghanī (1793–1853), and Ibrāhīm ar-Rashīdī (d. 1874), who each received a call to found derivative but distinct orders. The Sanūsiyya, a remarkable force in bringing religious unity to Libya, spread south into Chad region. From the Rashīdiyya in 1887 branched out another derivative, the Ṣāliḥiyya, which spread in Somalia. Besides Arabian 'Asīr the original Aḥmadiyya continued in Nilotic Sudan and Somalia.

The continuing influence and popularity of the old order, the Qādiriyya should not be underestimated. In the form of Moorish family *ṭarīqas* it became a force in the western Sahil. But its influence was always diffused as compared with the hereditary centralization of orders like the Mirghaniyya which became a political force in eastern Sudan. But the Qādiriyya was spread throughout the whole of Islamic Africa. In Senegal there was considerable rivalry between leaders, but its most outstanding manifestation was in the Murīdiyya. It has been a strong religious influence in Nilotic Sudan and Eritrea, mainly through the influence of family groups like the Ād Shaikh. In Ethiopia it predominates in coastal towns and in Harar territory, and is found among the Galla of the Gibe region and in southern Somalia.

The religious action of the orders has been effective both on the surface and in depth. They have been a factor in the interchange of men and ideas, and have opened the way for a few to enter into a dimension of Islam deeper than the legalism which tends to predominate in Negro territory by their stress on ethical aspects, whilst the mystical aspects have penetrated more among the Arab-Hamites. Although they have been the cause of rivalries and internal stesses their influence did not instigate the *jihād* movements as is sometimes stated. The early *jihād* leaders, though attached to a *ṭarīqa*, were inhibited from the deeper reaches of Sufism through their worship of the law. Later leaders, however, arose out of *ṭarīqas*, which were an important element in the pre-*jihād* careers of al-ḥājj 'Umar of west Sudan and Muḥammad Aḥmad, the *mahdī* of Nilotic Sudan.

Although we have claimed that in Negro Africa the orders were adopted without their characteristic elements and compared with their role elsewhere the *dhikr* recitals were a mild exercise, whilst their leaders were not real charismatic figures, yet, by linking the individual with a ritual leader (*muqaddam* or *khalīfa*), they created a fraternity which might be moulded as a potential or effective social force whose members could cooperate in social and economic activities.

4. Other Islamic movements and sects

A. MILLENARIAN MOVEMENTS

Messianic expectations require special conditions for their manifestation. They played no part in the history of the Sudanese states when Islam was the cult of certain lineages and occupational groups and the soil unfavourable to the propagation of universalist ideas. The first stage was the revolution in the Islamic atmosphere caused by the formation of theocratic states under the inspiration of a messianic leader who departs from the scene before victory is fully achieved. These movements constituted a social and political, as well as a religious, revolution. The theocrats attacked *mushriqūn* (polytheists) and *kāfirūn* (Muslim pagans) to establish the universal state, but these messianic states degenerated into anarchy or despotisms. At the same time came the gradual penetration of European powers. Many clergy affected by these conditions felt the call to proclaim themselves forerunners of the End. The real messianic figure in Islam is the Mahdī, and at this stage societies experiencing social dislocation and change were often receptive to this appeal.

Expectations were in the air at the beginning of the nineteenth century. Muḥammad Belo said that his father, 'Uthmān dan Fodio, was the *mujaddid* (renewer) and *Quṭb* or pivot of his age, though not the Mahdī.[44] This sort of thing helped to quicken expectations and Belo mentions the appearance of mahdīs during the early days of the *jihād* who had to be suppressed. Others appeared during the period when Nigeria was under Fulani rule. Then, after the British took control, reaction against 'Christian' overlords and measures they took such as the emancipation of slaves, sometimes took the form of the rise of mahdīs.[45]

These manifestations were largely confined to Northern Nigeria and Senegalese Futa. After the death of al-ḥājj 'Umar many individuals appeared who claimed to be his messianic successors, proclaimed the *jihād*, mustered a following and fought both Tokolor chiefs and French. Western mahdīs include Amadu Ba (1867–75), Mamadu Lamīn in the Bakel region influencing Soninke (1885–7), Samba Diadana (1888), Mamadu Bubu of Cognangol (1895), and the Tokolor, Amadu Alfa Musa (at Galoya 1895).

The point about these manifestations is that they were mainly local affairs, natural in a transitory period, born of the activities of clerics in an atmosphere of social disruption. The evanescent and limited range of their appeal derived partly from the nature of the agitation and the response of the people to whom it was addressed and partly from the watchfulness of both African and Western rulers who quickly suppressed them before they could spread. There was one exception.

The only successful Mahdist movement was that in Nilotic Sudan[46] and in consequence of the achievement of Muḥammad Aḥmad that country can never be the same again. It not only affected that region but also Adamawa and Bornu, and companies of 'westerners' are said to have served in the armies of the Khalīfa

'Abdullāh whose family was of Takrūrī origin. There was a recrudescence after the rise of 'Abd ar-Raḥmān, son of the Mahdi of Nilotic Sudan, whom many regarded as the unmanifested Nabī 'Īsā,[47] but with the growth of modern nationalism in the Sudan the influence of this neo-Mahdiyya moved into other channels.[48]

B. SECTARIANISM

In Western thought a 'sect' is regarded as a group which has broken away from the parent religious community because of differing views. On such criteria Shī'ism is not a sect in its origins, since it springs directly from the main stream of Islamic development, which branched into two streams, following different interpretations, hardening into doctrines, about the origins and ordering of Islamic society. The Shī'a movement, however, showed a tendency to keep on splitting, with the result that it now consists of a number of schisms, characterized by group solidarity and exclusiveness.

An aspect of East African Islam which immediately catches the attention of the visitor and consequently has been given undue prominence, is sectarianism. Shī'ī places of worship are ubiquitous and their communal and commercial activities are inescapable. This sectarian communalism seems to contrast with the rest of Africa which is solidly Sunnī, but in fact is confined to settlers from the Pak-Indian subcontinent. The important aspect is that this invasion of a different form of Islam has had no effect upon African Islam. Practically no Africans have become Shī'īs. The Asian Muslim diaspora remained distinctive, only slightly modified by their changed environment. Unlike Arab settlers they have not married Africans, nor adopted Swahili language and culture (they use Swahili simply as a code language). Between them and African Muslims there has been no real cultural and social dialogue such as would lead to significant change. As for the rest of Africa, the Shī'a are quite outside African Muslim comprehension; the vast majority, even of clergy, having no idea that they exist.

No account is necessary here but one may mention that the Shī'ites include Ithnā-'asharīs or Twelvers and two Isma'īlī sects, the Musta'līs, generally known as Bohoras, and the Nizārīs who acknowledge Karīm, the Aga Khan, as their forty-ninth Imām. The result is that East African towns present an appearance of Islamic racial and sectarian diversity manifested by the presence alongside each other of Arab and African mosques, Ismāʿīlī *jamāʿat-khānas* and Ithnā-ʿasharī *imām-bāras.*

At the opposite extreme to Shīʿism is Ibāḍism. Historically Ibāḍī movements were found in North Africa where Tāhart, an Ibāḍī state, had relations with Negro states across the Sahara, but there is no sound evidence that Ibāḍism spread south and its later reduced role to tribal Saharans precluded expansion. More important were the relations of the Ibāḍiyya of south-east Arabian ʿUmān with East Africa. These strengthened after the Portuguese were expelled from their coastal stations, and especially after Saʿīd ibn Sultan made Zanzibar the centre of his East African state. ʿUmani Arabs formed plantations on Zanzibar Island and parts of the coast but they did not spread the Ibāḍī *madhhab* among Africans, regarding it almost as a tribal religion. Now with the change of authority in Zanzibar its influence is fading.

Some of the new movements, like the Ḥamālist, which appeared in former French West Africa are regarded as sects since they have changed aspects of Islamic ritual regulations and therefore are condemned by the legalists as deviationists (*ahl al-bidʿa*). The Lāyen sect, founded by Limāmu Lāy (d. 1909) and restricted to the Lebu of Cap Vert (Dakar), is a real deviation since it repudiates the Ramaḍān fast and the restriction of the number of wives to four.

A real deviation which made its appearance in Africa under European occupation was the Aḥmadiyya of Qadiyān (now centred at Rabwah) which claims Mirza Ghulām Aḥmad (d. 1908) as its Messiah. Entering British West African dependencies from the sea (1921) emissaries found neo-Muslims susceptible to their propaganda. They succeeded in building up communities by individual conversions in coastal Ghana and Nigeria, but in Northern Nigeria they came up against the entrenched prejudice of legalistic Islam. In East Africa, on the contrary, the first missionary in 1934 found entrenched Islam on the coast and the neo-Muslims in the interior, among whom a few converts were made. But once East and West African Muslims realized that Aḥmadīs were regarded as deviationists by the rest of the Muslim world they had little chance of any wide success.

Aḥmadīs form new communities—that is what condemns them in African Muslim eyes—clearly distinguished from other Muslims by their whole attitude and outlook, by such non-conformism as refusal to pray behind a non-Aḥmadī *imām*, by deviations from

Islamic law or simply from African Islamic practice, such as their allowing women to enter mosques. Their influence has been greater than as reckoned in purely quantitative terms. They have shown enthusiasm for education, and through their aggressive propaganda and literature, especially their translations of the Qur'ān into African languages, they have provoked discussion and controversy.

5. African religious elements

Relationship with traditional culture remains vigorous among cultivators who comprise the majority of African Muslims. This is marked in the more narrowly religious sphere where beliefs and rituals concerning spirits remain a stronghold of traditional consciousness. Communities faced with inescapable change cushioned the impact by holding on to certain religious possessions as symbolic and practical guarantee of their identity. In this aspect communities vary considerably. Among the longer established there is normally no conflict between the faith professed and the practices observed. The two elements we have shown run parallel; both have become an integral part of culture. Cultivators clearly had to maintain their traditional relationship to the land, and Islam, introduced by way of trade routes, had no rural basis. Naturally ceremonies concerned with the cycle of seedtime and harvest continued with little change except that God is addressed as well as spirits. Although in the early stages old practitioners continue to function, the tendency towards the displacement of traditional religious authority leads to their substitution by the Muslim cleric in his role as medicineman. Islamic prayers are introduced, but prayers directed to God are supplemented by prayers directed to spirits; naturally so, since the latter are omnipresent and directly concerned with man. God's sovereignty is not regarded as being in any way compromised, that is, if such questions ever enter anyone's head for controversy of this nature is practically unknown.

God is supreme, that everyone accepts for it is the foundation of Islam, but at the same time the agents of Islamic diffusion showed by their practice that God allows to exist a realm of subsidiary powers both good and bad, vouched for by the Qur'ān itself under the terms *malā'ika*, *shayāṭīn*, *'afārīt*, and *jinn*. Islam, therefore, reinforces the belief in powers, but at the same time there are changes. A spirit dualism is introduced and some inherited spirits are relegated to the category of black spirits. In Hamitic societies nature spirits are incorporated into the realm of *jinn*.[49] Here occurs another distinction between Hamitic and Negro Islam in that *jinn* beliefs in their traditional form are found mainly among Arab-Hamites; the meaning behind the word in Negro Islam, if adopted at all, is often quite different.

The ancestor cult has found no niche in the sphere of African Islamic life. This is because it was too authoritative in the old life and Islam seeks to become the chief governor of life. In the early stages, however, offerings to ancestors, as intercessors and intermediaries in the chain of supplication reaching to God, may continue. But that in itself signifies change since prayer is proffered through or for instead of *to* the intermediary,[50] and such offerings take the form of *ṣadaqa* which implies a fundamental change in the idea of sacrifice.[51] The idea of almsgiving which can be offered by anyone substitutes itself for offerings to spirits for their own use which are offered by the family head or ritual sacrificer. In the Sudan belt this stage is quickly reached and even prayer and *ṣadaqa* of this nature go relatively quickly, but in East Africa it still survives and one finds a situation of practical dualism.[52] This seems to be due to both internal and external causes; the fact that Bantu society needs to maintain lineage authority by this means more than Sudan Negro societies, and that Muslim Bantu communities so rarely have a cleric who can take the place of the old ritual agents.

Another form of spirit cult that must go is the mystery cult, characteristic especially in West Africa, and the reason is, as with the ancestor cult, the role it plays in the government of society.[53] Another type attacked is that represented by 'idols', like Mande *nyana* or *dugu da siri* spirits which are related to *boli*, a tabernacle, a sacred object serving as the transient and temporary dwelling-place of a spirit which may be summoned there when certain rites are performed.[54]

But other spirits are a different matter and spirit propitiation continues in Islamic societies for God is felt to be remote and little concerned directly with the affairs of men. No one is really afraid of His wrath and punishment if He is not given His due of prayers, but the spirits are near, watchful, jealous, greedy for offerings and resentful of neglect. So the vitality of spirit cults derives from concern with this-worldly aspects of human life, not very evident in Islamic cult. The spirits are strictly neutral but easily aroused to side with or against one. So their help and protection are sought, and they are coaxed and propitiated by means of offerings. The change brought about by Islam is seen in ritual change. The clergy do not deny the reality of spirits since they themselves believe in them, but, seeking to maintain the sovereignty of God, they try to get people to cease making offerings at *boli* and similar objects, for this is idol worship, as well as to spirits as independent powers, guarantees of sanctions of conduct, that means especially those belonging to communal cults.

Possessive-spirit cults are found in Abyssinia and Nilotic Sudan (under the term *zār*), in central Sudan among Hausa (*bori*), Songhay and Zerma (*hole*), among Swahili (*pepo*) and among Negroes in the Maghrib (*dīwān*). All these terms mean 'possession', though fusion of the phenomenon and the spirit is normal. The spirit gains such a relationship with a person that it can take possession of the body whenever it wishes. This is disturbing and the purpose of the rites is not to exorcize but to gain control of the spirit so that it may be summoned at will, kept appeased, and used to cure psychological troubles. The rites which are elaborate involve especially drum rhythms and the ecstatic dance. These initiatory societies of ecstatics are found especially among women, that is, those excluded from full participation in the rituals of Islam, and also among socially penalized minorities such as Negroes in the Americas and in the Maghrib. Spirit possession is a symptom of religious change and was not normally found among pagans. They are not cults of the natural community, but embrace a limited circle of initiates. At the same time, their beliefs and practices may affect the whole community and are a factor in any assessment of its religious consciousness.

Other aspects of religious life which can only be mentioned briefly include divination and magic. Of these divination is perhaps the most important since its usage extends over so many spheres. Islam, it should be pointed out, is tolerant of these sciences; it recognizes that magic can be used to work evil and so provides remedies, but African witchcraft is totally outside its purview. The role of divination cannot be overestimated, but with such a vast subject we need only indicate the ease with which Islamic methods penetrate, the cleric in his role of diviner, and alongside this the persistence of old methods and their practitioners. Muslims do not have a special class of diviners like pagans, for divination is one of the functions of clergy, but specific diviners flourish even within long-established Islamic communities like Tokolor. Islam does not change the psychological attitude to the practice, but exploits it. The normal Islamic method is mechanical, by the manipulation of sand, book of magic or Qur'ān, numerals or rosary. Then there is the sphere of divination proper: by dreams, ordeal, spirit possession and necromancy. The *jihād* leaders of the last century all employed the dream method (*ṣalāt al-istikhāra*). Before making a decision they went into retreat to receive guidance, consequently their followers regarded their orders as the oracle of God.

Similarly magic is a vast sphere but does not call for any detailed reference here. The role it has played in Islamization has frequently been pointed out.[55] Magical procedure has nothing in itself to do with religion since it is based on mechanical manipulation of words and objects, yet it is one of the functions of the Islamic cleric whose most called-for activity is the writing of amulets. The efficacy lies in the belief that the power inherent in the words and phrases of the Qur'ān, the names of angels and *jinn*, and certain numbers and symbols, can be transferred to objects and protect their wearers. The power is also related to the person writing the amulet. With the written amulet is frequently associated a magical object, an aspect inherited from the old world. Although the practice of white and black magic are distinguished there is no essential difference and they are operated by the same person. The distinction is a moral one, not in method employed.

Witchcraft is distinguished from sorcery. The sorcerer, we have shown, is really the magician, using material means or spirit agencies, in his antisocial aspect, but the witch, 'eater of souls', is an involuntary worker of evil, either individually or as a member of a guild. His quality is inherent, not acquired. As has frequently been stated, witchcraft is a state whereas magic is a technique; you are born a witch but made a magician. Islam has no remedy against witchcraft and everyone seeks help from traditional practitioners for protection and remedy.

Chapter 4

Influence of Islam upon social life

1. Islamic universalism

Africa is a region of particularist societies and Islam, being a universal religion, introduces a new outlook. It introduces Africans to Time, to an historical view of man in relation to the universe. It broadens conceptions of communal relationships. This is achieved primarily through the sharing of common ritual and, to a much lesser degree, social institutions. Islamic ritual has significance, not only in its specifically religious context, but as a manifestation of an Islamic thread linking communities connected in no other way. Social life begins in the family where children receive their training in African ways, but in inculcating an Islamic spirit and outlook the Qur'ānic schools are important. The change from pagan to Islamic after-death practices contributes greatly to the process. The community was based primarily on kinship, on the one hand, and on occupation of territory in common or exploitation of a common stretch of Niger or Nile, on the other; both of which had a religious basis, family or territorial religion. When Islam is adopted the concept of community is extended to include all who observe Islamic ritual and custom. Ritual brings the community together for regular observances like Friday or *'īd* prayers. In this way Muslims affirm for themselves and before the world their significance as a people linked, if not united, by Islam. The life of integrated Islamic communities is a mosaic of Islamic and indigenous elements in complex combinations, but running through the web of life of different peoples the Islamic elements form a uniform, abstract, impersonal thread showing little significant variation. Thus a Muslim can participate in ritual prayer in whatever country he is in. The change brought about by Islam in this respect should not be exaggerated, the old bases of community remain paramount and the ideal of the unity of believers a superimposed linkage, yet our first fact must be to see Islam as a factor in community relationships.

2. The Islamic community

We have just emphasized the place of ritual in Islamic universalism, but what about the linking threads of Islamic social institutions? Here the communities have asserted their distinctiveness and show wide divergencies. Custom seems to have an autonomy of its own. Although Islam changes the religious basis upon which the social structure depended it does not thereby cause social disintegration or even radical change. In long Islamized societies present custom is the integrated result of a long process of change before pressure from Islamic law; in other societies the process has only just begun. Consequently, we are presented with extreme variations in the custom of different societies, and generalizations become impossible. Each people, each clan, each family frequently, varies. All one can do is to indicate tendencies and the range of possibilities for change.

A. FORMATION: THE PROCESS OF SOCIAL CHANGE

Social change in Negro society has been conditioned by the fact that Africans did not come into contact with integrated 'civilized' Muslim communities from whom they were divided by deserts. Thus change towards an Islamic pattern of life passed through a series of gradations by recognition of aspects of the Law. The spread of Islam came through the agency of African Muslims who had formed a pattern of Islamic life. The popular religious revolution which transformed the religious consciousness of the Maghrib in the sixteenth century did not penetrate in the same way the western and central areas of the Sudan belt. The difference is seen most clearly in the contrast with Nilotic Sudan where Arabization and Islamization were integrally associated, and its inhabitants deeply affected by the people's religion of Arabia and Egypt. Thus in western and central Sudan changes in social institutions were likely to come, less from direct contact for nomads did not accept Islamic social law, than from clerics perusing law books which they regarded as revelation itself.

Since African religion manifests itself throughout all spheres of life, the adoption of a religion characterized by rigid ritualistic and social institutions expressed in written law is bound to affect social as well as specifically religious aspects of life. The process of social change followed the same lines as in other spheres in that a reciprocal process of interaction took place whereby an African Muslim community was formed. In this process Islamic customary usages were adopted into indigenous custom which was then remoulded through reciprocal interaction. Conversely, and this is especially true with social institutions, custom restricted or blocked completely the application of many aspects of Islamic law.

Social institutions take longer to change than religious elements. We have shown that the influence of the *sharī'a* is more evident in the sphere of ritual, since this is at first additional to the old order, than in anything that might endanger structural institutions. Thus people will adopt food taboos, the ritual method of slaughtering animals and of performing ablutions and prayer, but regulations concerned with family relations and inheritance are adopted only through pressure or under special environmental conditions. We can illustrate this with the Tuareg. Those of central Sahara, who now number not more than 20,000, after a millennium of Islamic allegiance, have still not adopted these regulations, whereas those living about the Niger bend and Sahil who number about half a million have been more influenced. Whilst descent by the maternal line in succession to power is recognized among the Tuareg of Hoggar and Air, the Ullimmeden and Igellad of the Sahil follow the paternal line. Here the change of environment set in motion the trend towards modification of custom. Teda chiefs in the Sahara have tried to substitute the *diya*, 'indemnity', for the vendetta but any success they have achieved is as much due to their coming under French administration as from any pressure from Islamic representatives. The custom of widow inheritance is in vogue among Dyula trading communities in West Africa, yet Islam as represented by their own clergy, makes no attempt to change the custom.

With the adoption of Islam kinship loses its religious basis,[1] yet it is not weakened but maintains an autonomy of its own. Negro societies have a guaranteed structure of social stability so long as they remain agricultural and maintain customary institutions, and, if Islam is introduced in the natural way by Africans, the social structure is not upset. We have shown[2] how when Islam is adopted by whole communities, family or village, the group remains a unity, distinguished by its own pattern of culture and a social life ruled primarily by custom, often in contradiction to the abstract rules of Islam.

One primary consideration rules people's adoption of the

sociolegal elements of Islam—the maintenance of family or clan solidarity based on custom; anything that might menace or undermine the group is barred. Islamic law has definite individualistic elements and against the introduction of these all the forces of African conservatism are arrayed. In practice the socially disruptive forces inherent in Islamic individualism are reduced to the minimum since many provisions of the law are not insisted upon except under conditions of violent change or by a reformer or zealous *qāḍī* eager to put pressure upon colonial authority. For example, in a pagan community an individual's observance of Muslim prayer is not going to upset the family unless accompanied by non-participation in community ritual. At a further stage, when the whole group is Muslim, Islamic inheritance provisions, for example, are simply ignored. At a still later stage, a compromise may be reached, the Islamic provisions are applied to part of the deceased's estate, but the rest divided according to clan custom. Among many Dyula a family head's rosary, prayer-mat and other symbols of authority, as well as wives, will go to the brother who succeeds to his authority; the land he farmed remains communal property, but implements and other removable property are shared according to Islamic provisions. Islam, therefore, has affected only the division of personally acquired movable property.

Resistance to social change was weakened where Arabization accompanied Islamization as in the Maghrib and Nilotic Sudan. In these societies the degree of change depended upon the type of life, nomad or cultivator in rainland, riverbank or mountain, and upon the way and nature by which Arab-Islamic social elements were assimilated. In eastern Sudan immigrant nomad Arab tribes absorbed indigenous Beja-type nomads through forms of association like clientship (for Arab kinship has little to do with blood relationship of which it is an artificial extension), and those who were absorbed adopted, not only the Arab form of social structure, but also features of Arab customary life, so that they became indistinguishable from an Arab tribe of the same region, marks of distinction being blurred by the fact that immigrant Arab tribes reciprocally adopted Hamitic customs like the *jirtiq*. In Arabized Sudan, not merely nomads, but settled riverain *sāqiya* and Jezira rainland cultivators, all adopted as a feature of their Arabization the Arab tribal structure and customs. The nomadic Beja of the Red Sea Hills region and the Barābara or northern Nubians eking out a meagre living on a barren stretch of the Nile banks,[3] contrary to the southern Nubians, were not Arabized and kept their own forms of social structure and customs. Similarly with the Berbers of the Moroccan mountains at one extreme and the north-east Hamitic nomads like the 'Afar and Somali at the other.

B. THE ISLAMIC SOCIAL PATTERN

We have stated that ritual observances rather than observance of Islam's social laws designate that a community is Muslim, but we need to look at specific features making up the Islamic social pattern which, as they take hold, give the community a social as well as ritualistic characterization.

If given time Islam succeeds in implanting many of its social features. This is most evident in towns. Thus west and central Sudan towns like Timbuktu, Jenne, Sokoto and Maiduguri are as clearly Muslim towns as are towns in Arabized Africa like Omdurman at the junction of the two Niles, or Fez, Marrakish and Qairawan (to mention Maghribi towns where traditional life remains more marked than places like Casablanca). But the dualism in society becomes apparent once one moves out of the Sudan towns mentioned into the neighbouring villages of Songhay, Bozo, Hausa or Kanuri agriculturalists. On the other hand, the Arabized villages of Nilotic Sudan are as clearly Muslim as Omdurman.

The first institution which Islamic law stands to affect is the primary one of the family. Islam cannot help but change this through its regulations regarding marriage and divorce, custody of children, mutual relations and responsibilities of husband and wife, the system of slave-wives and its inheritance regulations. Islamic law recognizes the simple matrimonial family of man, wife or wives, and children, and the Mālikī system gives absolute authority to the husband as its head. But the African family is the extended family and family authority is quite different. The tendency of Islam would seem to be towards its disintegration. In general, the extended family with its traditional head remains the significant social unit and authority, but there are modifications. We see this among Hausa where pagan families may be composed of some thirty to eighty persons, whereas long-Islamized families are reduced to the household family unit. A common Hausa family consists of a man and his married sons. Of course, there is every gradation, since many Hausa are in the process of change, some being still pagan, so that actual societies are situated at varying points in the Pagan-Muslim continuum. All one can do is to point out the Islamic trend.

Islam tends to bring the actual father into great prominence than is customary in unmodified Sudan belt societies, and this helps to bring the elementary family out of complete obscurity. This often comes about through the stress placed on parental authority, the inculcation of a son's duties to his father and the father's to the son, and through the father being responsible for his children's marriages and their being allotted some share of his personal property, though at the same time the extended family remains the primary social cell and rights of succession to headship and communal property remain unchanged. Even in towns where the small family unit may be found the link with the countryside frequently remains strong and the family extended.

The Islamic facility for divorce has varying effects upon the family according to the nature of the African system. The wife-mother element is unstable and the pattern of matrimonial alliances may be changed, but does not necessarily result in the disintegration of the family. Polygamy is not common among Songhay of Gao region but divorce is prevalent, and the family is changed in this respect that children who live with both father and mother are rare.

Islamic influence tends towards making a person's tribal and social status dependent upon the paternal line and many African societies are matrilineal. Its effect varies greatly, depending upon the strength of underlying factors and external pressures, and generally a compromise is reached. Many East African Bantu among whom Islam has spread relatively recently are matrilineal and are at various stages of reaction to Islamic regulations. Whilst clan membership among the Zaramo is matrilineal, inheritance of property is patrilineal. The matrilineal Yao in Portuguese East Africa, southern Tanzania and Malawi, who adopted Islam as a distinguishing feature during a very short period, in this following the Sudan-belt pattern of group conversion, have maintained their social institutions relatively unmodified, whereas other East Africans who adopted Islam piecemeal have been involved in bitter conflicts between Islamic and customary law.

In Nilotic Sudan the adoption of the patrilineal system of descent accompanied the process of Arabization. Most riverain (Nubian-type) and nomadic (Beja-type) peoples followed the matrilineal system and through their use of this system Arabs are thought to have gained political power.[4] After the decline of Maqurra when Arab tribes poured southwards an extraordinary process of assimilation took place, by which Arab tribes assimilated weak Hamitic nomad groups, strong Hamitic nomads absorbed numerically weak Arab clans but were Arabized in the process, and settled Nile-bank or mainland cultivators (eastern Sudanic language-speakers) also underwent Arabization by some unknown process by which they kept their distinctive ways of life and customs intact but became Arabized linguistically and adopted an Arab *nisba* or lineage, that is to say, the Arab system of patrilineal descent. The strongly patrilineal traits of the Arabs account, at least in part, for the rapid introduction of Negroid traits among the southern nomads as well as those who settled. Mixed blood children (Arab father and Negro mother) belong to the father's group. This contrasts with the matrilineal Tuareg where the children of 'nobles' and their Negro slave women belong to the 'inferior' line of their mothers. Where the Arab spread in this way Hamitic peoples (including Nubian-speakers), both nomadic and settled, felt the need for such assimilation as would turn them into Arabs.[5] A similar process took place among Berber tribes in western Sahara though under quite different conditions of change.

A unilateral kinship group is frequently distinguished by a name and close relationship with an animal, plant or action, regarded as 'sacred' and taboo to that clan. Islamic pressure is not specifically exerted against such beliefs since they have no religious significance, but the tendency among the longer Islamized is to change their attitude to the taboo (for Islam has its own animal, drink and action taboos) and consequently to break down marriage prohibitions between members of the same clan. Islam has its own categories of allowed and prohibited in marriage and here there is ground for conflict with African custom in early stages. Islam encourages marriage between any class of cousins, and among the Saharan nomads, with the exception of the Teda, the tendency is towards endogamy, but many Africans regard marriages between parallel cousins as incestuous. It will be understood that change of this sort is no Islamic index. Marriage between cousins, whilst common amongst Arabized peoples, is prohibited among such self-conscious Muslims as the Somali and marriage can only be contracted between a man and a woman of different lineages. This question is closely bound up with inheritance regulations and changes tend to be synonymous. African custom normally prevails but the long-Islamized may be found observing Islamic categories and even *kafā'a* (compatibility) regulations.

Islamic marriage forms are always adopted. These include contract, slave and gift, whilst widow inheritance is prevalent in many communities. Contract and slave marriage are well known and Islamic regulations are followed, but there is controversy over the other two. Marriage by gift was in vogue among many peoples of the Sudan belt. A man who wishes to honour a cleric or seek an alliance with an influential person, orders his daughter to be prepared for marriage, announces before witnesses the prospective husband's name and sends her over to his house as a form of alms (*ṣadaqa*), without requiring *ṣadāq*.

Widow inheritance is a common traditional practice maintained by Muslims but modified by Islamic provisions. Few practise the true levirate like the 'Afar inhabiting a barren stretch of the Red Sea coast. Stricter Muslims avoid infringing the law as far as possible. If the elder brother already has four wives he may divorce one or waive his claim in favour of a younger brother or cousin. In many cases, however, it is believed that the contract ceremony cannot be performed again, since the taking of the widow is not regarded as a new marriage. But there are many variations in Muslim families. Sometimes there may be a new contract without the necessity of providing a new *ṣadāq*. By arrangement a widow may be allowed to marry outside the family, sometimes without and sometimes with the repayment of *ṣadāq*.

Slavery played a great part in the social system of Sudan belt states in particular, and even today has left traces which affect social relationships. Many West Africans had an elaborate system and a compromise was achieved with Islamic law. Under this system the lot of slaves ameliorated itself with each successive generation and the gradations from the captured- or bought-slave to serfdom and even clientship are clearly shown by the terminology employed. Slaves 'born in the household' became more like serfs in status, for according to customary law they could not be sold. Islamic law could theoretically affect this situation in that it decrees that descendants of slaves remained slaves and could be sold. However, Africans tempered the letter of the law, whilst Islam provides for change in the status of slaves by emancipation through purchase or gift. Among Hausa the occasion when such a serf paid over his redemption money and received his freedom paper was celebrated like a baby's eighth-day naming. The cleric shaved his head and sacrificed a ram at the same time as he gave the freed-man a Muslim name. Such a freed-man continued to regard himself as a client of his former master. Today this relationship is dignified by being regarded as one of patronage (*walā'*) rather than clientship, but still a social distinction remains between freemen and descendants of slaves which operates especially in marriage alliances.

3. Religion and types of life

A study of the relationship between religion and life would be incomplete without referring to the fact that different patterns of life mean different degrees of apprehension and involvement in Islamic culture—life in desert and steppe, rainland or riverain cultivation, in urban market-places and mosques. Similarly with women, slaves, smiths and the bard-genealogists. Saharan life seems at all times to have generated a 'molecular humanity'[6] which divided ethnic groups into castes or at least rigid classes: warrior nobles, Berber tributaries and clerics, *ḥarrāṭīn* or black oasis-cultivators, blacksmiths, serfs and slaves,[7] to such a point that the prime distinctions between men derive from ethnic-social criteria.

Participation in Islam varies according to class. Warrior classes of Moors and Tuareg do not concern themselves with it but expect the *zwāya* or *inislimen* class to perform religious duties vicariously on their behalf. Class distinctions may be transcended in the strictly religious sphere, though rigid in any question of marriage relationship; but practice varies, the Targi 'noble' prays alongside his black slave, but not the Nigerian Fulani chief. This 'molecular humanity' also distinguishes peoples of the Sahilian or Sudan belts, more particularly the Atlantic group, comprising Serer, Wolof and Tokolor, and settled Fulbe and Soninke. As with the native institution of *griots* or minstrels, the clerical class was outside the sphere of direct warfare, though like *griots* they accompanied the warriors to stimulate. This kind of distinction is found in West Africa with the *zwāya* of the Moors and the *mori-ke* of the Mandinka, and in East Africa among the Somali between the *waranleh*, 'warrior', and *wadād*, 'cleric'.

Although they could not marry outside their caste men were not tied to that profession; many were cultivators, and *griots* and *laube* (wood-workers) have often become traders. Men could escape their restrictions to some extent and such changes are becoming more marked today. All one can say of the effect of Islam upon traditional social differentiation is that it had no effect, except by adding new categories of clerics and traders, though these were less subjected to caste restrictions. There are even legalists who supported such a pattern of stratification on the grounds of *kafā'a* or marriage equality regulations.

The relationship between Islam and trading has frequently been stressed and need not be elaborated. Trade has an important place in Islamic tradition and there is a body of legislation governing contracts, exchange, loans, market conduct and the like. Urban and trading life involve abandoning, or at least independence from, family and local religion, and Islam provided a spiritual basis for life in a new dimension.

The role of the town is integral to Islam. It acts as a base where Islam's universal and impersonal aspects can be maintained. In the town *qāḍī*'s courts can function and the law can operate over a wider field of social relations. It is the site of the regional *jāmi'* and a centre of clerical training where teachers can draw pupils from different social groups. In fact, the Sudan belt town resembled a collection of villages in social structure, each section having its own council of elders, consequently individuality is not pronounced. But its primary function as a regional centre of trade, embracing a heterogeneous population, distinguished it from a village. Some were ports like Timbuktu on the Niger loop and Mombasa on the Indian Ocean, with links across desert and ocean; others were centres of internal trade like Jenne and Kano, with streets of artisans plying specialized trades. In central Sudan they were the seat of political authority, but elsewhere central authority was not normally based on the town. Towns which came into existence as the seat of a new theocracy like Sokoto or Hamdallahi, not developing commercial activities (like Omdurman), declined or disappeared with the theocracy.

The north-east and east coast towns had an entirely different character from those of the Sudan belt. Primarily trading centres, they were strongly influenced from Arabia whose coastal towns they closely resembled. Harar, heterogeneous in population but with its core of citizens speaking a city language, was almost unique. These towns were the stabilizing factor for the Islam of the region as well as diffusion centres. When the southern Ethiopian regions overwhelmed by the Galla invasions became more stabilized, trading connexions from Harar carried Islam among the immigrant groups. Today Sudan belt towns like Kano in Nigeria and Omdurman at the Nile junction retain much of their traditional character despite the appearance of modern-styled structures.

Islam has had little effect upon agriculture, with the notable exception of the agricultural settlements in Somalia and Senegal whereby labour was sanctified under the aegis of a *ṭarīqa*. It has had no effect upon customary land law, and this was one sphere which even the theocrats never sought to bring within the provisions of the *sharī'a*. It is also noteworthy that the *waqf* system was not transmitted to African Islam.

The trader is a Muslim and the cultivator is a pagan (*paganus*), so we get occupational religious parallelism. The Muslim trader in his cultivation is a pagan, just as the pagan trader is a Muslim. Although Islam may be introduced into agricultural rites (the cleric pouring a libation of washed-off Qur'ānic texts supplementary to, or in place of, traditional rites), this does not make the rite Islamic, though it shows the increasing influence of Islam. Islam has a ritual rain ceremony which is in vogue among cultivators. Craftsmen similarly fall into this practical dualism. Here the distinction between Hamitic and Negro Islam is found. Whereas craftsmen in the Maghrib have their patron saint, Hausa craftsmen have their patron spirit. As Professor M. G. Smith remarks; 'Despite the long centuries of Islamic proselytization in Hausaland, the market derives its mystical charter and its economic vitality from the traditional pre-Islamic spirits.'[8]

The relationship between Islam and other aspects of material life should not be completely overlooked. For example, the Islamic taboo on nakedness and the adoption of clothing is one of the evident signs of a desire for identification with Islam, and this has economic aspects such as the relationship of Mande Dyula and weaving. We have referred to the ritual segregation of women, but their physical segregation is based on class, town life or prestige—non-Islamic factors, though justified by clergy on Islamic grounds. The following statement by K. M. Barbour concerning Islamic influence on house architecture can apply not merely to the Eastern Sudan but to much of the Sudan belt

> The design of a house is strongly affected by the social customs of the Sudanese, and these in turn are to be explained in great measure by

their adherence to Islam, at least throughout the northern and central provinces. Except among some of the very poorest, the settled Muslims regard the seclusion of women, and their protection from the eyes of men other than their near relatives, as of the greatest importance. Almost more necessary, therefore, than shelter from the elements is the possession of a high enough wall around a man's property to protect its inmates from observation by strangers.[9]

In such regions women rarely go out except at night and then covered in some form of enveloping garb. Although this kind of architecture existed in this belt before the coming of Islam, it has become a sign, a significant symbol, of Islamization. The Omdurman woman behind her mud-brick walls on the Nile banks and the Hausa woman behind her high fence of millet stalks treasure this 'protection'.

4. Influence of Islam on the state and legal system

Three types of Islamic states were found through the Sudan belt: states where Islam was the imperial cult, the state religion or a theocracy. Because states like Mali or Kanem-Bornu are known as Muslim states, since the rulers professed Islam, we tend to ascribe to Islam an influence upon their civilization quite disproportionate to the facts. These states (and the 'state' was the ruling clan) showed themselves receptive to such Islamic features as would reinforce their authority. Rulers encouraged and utilized Islamic representatives, traders in the economic and medicinemen in the religious spheres. But the important factor is that the basic features of authority and organization remained indigenous. We have shown that though Islam gained a real hold over certain groups it was not until the nineteenth century that it spread widely in consequence of the formation of theocratic states whose main principles were the subjugation of the state to the written law of God and uniformity of religious allegiance.

Both regal and theocratic types tended to converge towards states in which Islam is recognized as the state religion. Theocratic states could not maintain their original principles; whilst in the other type, as Islamic allegiance broadened, Islam came to be manifested through the channels by which the state acts, especially the legal and taxation systems. In consequence of this dual upward or downward movement there were various grades related to the history of Islamization; in some states Islamic institutions had a strong function, in others both pagan and Islamic institutions were found.[10]

City states, like Zaila', Harar and Maqdishu in north-east Africa, belonged to the state religion category, developing Muslim patterns of government, administration and legal procedure. The Nilotic state of Sennar falls into the same category for, although Islam was adopted into an indigenous type of Sudan state which retained traditional ceremonies, functionaries and institutions, the religion was spreading simultaneously with great rapidity among the tribes of the Nile banks, the Buṭāna, and Jezīra, and acquiring a deep hold.

Although the Fulani states of Northern Nigeria appear in certain aspects to be a continuation of the Hausa states, retaining many Hausa institutions, they were new creations in that they were Muslim in spirit and outlook, which could not be said of the states they supplanted. There was an Islamic norm against which the actions of the rulers and officials could be measured and criticized, whether or not anyone would dare to do this.

We have indicated elsewhere that the theocratic state is the most interesting feature of Islamic development in Africa. Within these states a rigid application of Islamic law was sought, for the reformers had no experience of the compromise and balance between the ideal and the actual practised elsewhere in the Islamic world, since the previous states where Islam was merely a class religion were not of this nature. The formation of these states constituted a social revolution, set in motion by settled Fulbe, a reaction by their clerics (*torodbē*), conscious of the superiority of their Islamic (and also racial) inheritance, against their subjection under pagan regimes to various forms of inferior status. Consequently, the success of the revolutions resulted in a reversal of roles: Fulbe *torodbē* becoming rulers over pagan Susu-Jalonke in Futa Jalon, over pagan Fulbe rulers in Futa Toro on the Senegal, over pagan Bambara overlords in Masina on the Niger and over Hausa in central Sudan. In these states Islam became the core of a new aristocratic principle, the primary factor being the role played by an ancestor in the original *jihād*. The system of succession was based on the revolutionary one of service to the cause. In Senegalese Futa the leaders of the revolt against the Denyanke formed a fixed elective body which sought to follow early Islamic practice by nominating the *imām* from among their own members.

THE APPLICATION OF ISLAMIC LAW

Islamic law, we have pointed out, was accepted in theory without conscious movement towards its corresponding social pattern, except in urban centres. If adopted arbitrarily it would have been liable to cause social chaos, but in fact a system of compromise was adopted. The old pattern remained dominant. Consequently, though the theoretical legal position was the dominance of the *sharīʿa*, with recognition of custom where this was not in conflict with the *sharīʿa*, in fact, it was the other way round, and custom was the dominant and integrating factor. The foundation was customary law modified according to community by Islamic regulations. We are not implying that the influence of Islamic law was negligible. On the contrary, we have shown that it was the great moulding, as well as universalizing, factor. Apart from that, simply as ideal law, we have stressed its importance in creating in people's minds a Muslim outlook and attitude.

The African conception of the judicial function is not based on rigid interpretation of a fixed written law since this did not exist. The aim of the authority, family, clan, village or tribal court, is to restore social equilibrium. Reconciliation, not the letter of the law, was the guiding factor. After becoming Muslim the community, if left to itself, does not feel any conflict of laws—there is only the practice of the community. This harmonization of custom and *sharīʿa* was guaranteed by the fact that the depositories of the law were the elders of the community. They might consult the local cleric, but the clergy (provided that there was no enforcing external authority such as a nomocratic state or colonial power) were admirably adjusted to the situation. Disputes were settled within the family or local community. Trouble arose after the formation of nomocratic states which set up *qāḍī's* courts to which appeal might be made by an aggrieved individual or party. This was often regarded as treachery to family authority and cohesion. But in general the harmonious integration, or at least functioning, of custom and *sharīʿa* was achieved owing to the elders being the guardians and guarantors of custom.

With this system there were no *qāḍī's* courts except in towns,[11] and then chiefly in the successors of nomocratic states and where set up under colonial rule. But even *qāḍīs* proved adaptable to local conditions (in West Africa at least, though the Shāfiʿī *qāḍīs* in East Africa were more rigid) for they manifested elasticity in arriving at decisions since they were not required to show the process by which they arrived at them. The *qāḍī* might make use of assessors (*muftīs*), but the decision was his alone.

The *qāḍī's* jurisdiction was limited by both executive (*siyāsī*) and customary law. In regard to the authority of the latter among the Somali I. M. Lewis writes: 'Claims for the return of bride-wealth are outside the jurisdiction of the Kadis' Courts whose concern is solely with the specifically Islamic personal dower (*mahr*).'[12] A working equilibrium between these three spheres of law, Islamic, customary and administrative, is the normal pattern in the administration of justice, but the theocrats sought to enforce only the *sharī'a* and abolish the others. Their only official tribunals were those of the *qāḍīs* when administering justice. But in these states too the flexibility of African practice was apparent and *qāḍīs* were frequently guided by social necessity; even the theocrats never touched customary land law. The *sharī'a* was the theoretical system in force when the British took over the Fulani states of Northern Nigeria, a system they could understand and which they confirmed. Here the rulers found the *sharī'a* a means by which they could maintain a sphere of independence from the protecting power, enabling them to resist suggestions for change as contrary to divine law, whilst at the same time themselves making use of *siyāsa*.

5. The role of Arabs and Arabic in Africa

Arabs have manifested unique characteristics of assimilation and assimilability. They are easily assimilable into another environment and coalesce with the indigenous people,[13] and, at the same time, they impart their linguistic, religious and social characteristics. Thus in Nilotic Sudan they have mixed with both Hamites and Negroes, and though they became considerably modified in physical characteristics they transmitted their language, social patterns (tribal system) and ethos (pride in an Arab *nasab*). Even though Arabs have not been missionary-minded, transmission of their Arab heritage and Islam have been synonymous.

Although the process of migration has been continuous three main migratory periods may be distinguished:

a. In the first millennium B.C. South Arabians crossed the Red Sea, ascended the Ethiopian plateau and from their fusion with Hamites came the Abyssinian type, whilst their Semitic dialects, relatively isolated in the mountains, developed special forms and characteristics.

b. The dispersion of Arabs consequent upon their expansion under the impulse of Islam during the first Islamic century which established Arabic in Egyptian and Maghribi towns and throughout the administration.

c. Nomad Arab migrations between the eleventh and fifteenth centuries, one process leading to the Arabization of a large part of the Maghrib and the other to the Arabization of eastern and part of central Sudan belt.

Muḍarid tribes of Hilāl and Sulaim, followed by Maʿqil (Yemenite), who had moved into Upper Egypt proved an embarrassment to the Fāṭimids who encouraged them to proceed to the conquest of recalcitrant Maghrib. Leaving Egypt in the eleventh century they had reached Morocco by the end of the twelfth and in time they changed the whole linguistic and social complexion of North Africa and western Sahara. This migration did not have the effect in Morocco that it had elsewhere. Here Arabization, still only partial, rather spread from the towns into the surrounding countryside. The Maʿqil, meeting with formidable physical and social barriers in Morocco, moved south to the domination of the Berbers of Mauritania which brought about their eventual Arabization.

A synchronous expansion resulted in the Arabization of Nilotic Sudan. Rabīʿa tribes had been present in Nubia and Beja country from the tenth century, but had themselves been absorbed and had become Nubian or Beja in language and custom. After the fall of the state of Maqurra, Juhaina tribes passed beyond the inhospitable Nubian stretch into the steppes of Kordofan, Darfur and Waday reaching as far as Lake Chad by the sixteenth century. The Arab tribes which entered Nilotic Sudan have been considerably changed through assimilation with Hamites and, to a lesser degree, with Negroes; whilst those of central Sudan have, through intermarriage with Negroes, become dark or black in colour, and have changed their mode of life, cattle nomadism replacing camel nomadism with all that stems from such a change. But language, religion, mode of life and cultural features distinguish all these Arabs sharply from the people among whom they live.

Arabization is especially associated with the spread of nomads, as in the Maghrib, and with Arab political domination, as in Egypt. During the primary dispersion of Muslim Arabs, Arabic substituted itself easily for the language of those with a Syriac-Aramaic or Coptic background. But the immigration and settlement of individual traders, even in considerable numbers, does not lead to Arabization. Arabic did not become the lingua-franca of the East African coastal towns though Arab influence was strong on many aspects of life; instead, the immigrants were captured by a Bantu language. Where Islam's spread was accompanied by Arabization there was generally greater social change than among Hamitic nomads who retained their languages—Tuareg in central Sahara and Niger bend, and among Beja, Saho, 'Afar, Somali and Galla in north-east Africa.

The role of Arabs in the history of Africa is too vast a subject to be treated here, but we need to stress the effect of their language. The spread of a religion possessing a sacred scripture sets up an interrelationship between the sacred language and the languages of the people who adopt the religion. This is especially the case with Arabic. In Hamitic-speaking Africa Islamization was accompanied by Arabization, and the effect we have shown to be profound, but in Negro Africa Islam was spread almost entirely by Africans and Arabic was not envisaged as a living language. Thus the great divide between white (Hamitic) and black (Negro) Africa has been perpetuated by language, for whilst the spread of Islam has been accompanied by the absorption of words and expressions into African languages, in Negro Africa the mediating factor has been the law books in the memories of the clergy. Arabic in Negro Africa was wholly a sacred language with little or no secular usages. Few colloquial or daily-life words penetrated, but the language of the law books has enriched the languages of Muslims with hundreds of religious, political, commercial and abstract words and expressions. The difference this has made is evident when one compares the means of expression available, for instance, to Swahili in East Africa with those of animist Nyika inhabiting Kenyan coastal stretches who speak related Bantu languages.

Another effect was to stimulate Africans to write their own languages in Arabic characters, sometimes with the use of additional signs. Harari, a Semitic language, is unique, but Tokolor and Fulbe in Futas Toro and Jalon, Hausa and Songhay, and Swahili corresponded through the medium of their own language and even transcribed poems and other compositions.

The impact of secular culture has not missed even this sphere. Arabic had stimulated Africans to write their own languages, but the effect of the West has been to spread the usage of the Latin script and it has all but substituted itself in the writing of Hausa and Swahili, both languages where the usage was greater than elsewhere. One reason for this easy conquest is that the Latin is more suitable than the vowelless Arabic script for expressing African languages. Another cause derives from the ambivalent attitude of African Muslims towards Arabic as a sacred script. Clergy did not encourage its secular use. They wrote their compositions in stilted Arabic and vernacular writing in Arabic script tended to be mainly for secular usage such as commercial correspondence. Thus there was no stimulus to compose in one's own language. Hausa clergy employed the term *Ajami* (Ar. *'ajamī*, *'ajamiyya*, 'outlandish') for vernacular texts written in Arabic characters.

Chapter 5

The African Muslim in an era of change

1. The spread of Islam

Africa is passing through an era of dynamic change. This change was set in motion in consequence of the new relationships to life and the world brought about through almost the whole of Africa falling under the control of European powers during the last quarter of the nineteenth century. Paradoxical as it may seem, Islam enjoyed more favourable conditions for expansion under colonial rule than at any other period of history. During this period of stability Islam not merely consolidated the gains made during the period of theocratic conquerors and states, but also spread far beyond its former confines. European occupation aided this outburst both through the direct action of the administrations and the conditions deriving from that occupation.

The French and British administrations displayed an ambivalent attitude towards Muslims; on the one hand, they feared that they might prove intransigent to their rule, and, on the other, they tended to favour Islam as something known which could be recognized in a way difficult with pagan cults and their authorities. Because of their wider contacts and experience Muslims were employed as subordinates in administrative services, whereby they acted as intermediaries between the administration and pagan populations. Whilst the French reduced or eliminated the temporal power of Muslim chiefs, the British confirmed them over both pagan and mixed populations, thus enabling them to employ the principle of *cujus religio cujus regio*. Consequently chiefs could exert indirect or direct pressure, especially upon office-holders. The recognition of Islamic law, placing it upon what appeared to the uninitiated to be an equal footing with French or British law, signified to pagans that there were advantages in calling oneself Muhammad and wearing a gown.

More important aids to the spread of Islam came from the indirect impact of new changes. The most immediate derived from the suppression of warfare and the creation of firm stable administrations. This enabled movement over vast areas to become possible and the people who were quickest to take advantage of a wider field of operation were those who had already acquired a universal concept, the Muslim traders, though in other respects, as we shall see, they were walled-in within an Islamic view which insulated them against new conceptions. New means of communication enabled traders and other agents to gain access to regions formerly closed to them. Considerable movement and intermingling of peoples took place, and as people experienced wider ranges they felt the need for a more universalized outlook. This had a disintegrating effect upon pagan institutions.[1] Over vast areas, and not merely the Sudan belt, Islam was the only universal religion on the scene, and, as compared with Christianity, was indigenous, in the sense that it had become a natural aspect of African life. The field was left wide open for Muslims to proselytize.[2] A religious label acquired a significance formerly unknown and there was no alternative to that of Islam. Among modern changes which helped its spread and enhanced its attraction, especially for the disinherited, was the growth of towns. In towns Islam tended to become the religion of the majority, especially since Christianity with its emphasis on the new literacy, became the religion of an élite.[3] Christianity anyway was confined to the coastal belt and all towns in the interior took on a Muslim tinge, even in the midst of full pagan village culture like Bamako in Bambara country. Pagans who went to Bamako became Muslims as a matter of course as they put on a gown.[4] Even West African coastal towns gained a significant proportion of Muslims, not merely through immigration but by conversion of individuals.

During the twentieth century Islam began to spread into the southern Sudan belt. It had little effect upon the basic population of the hundreds of small chieftainless groups where the extended family or village is the largest political unit. But these are not the only inhabitants, there are neo-Sudanese currents which pass through and beyond this belt. Among these (such as Nupe and Bariba), though not all (Jukun or Kororofa), Islam has had more effect. Again, in western Guinea the Susu had become Muslim through impulses emanating from Futa Jalon and the tendency was maintained, and during the nineteenth century

Islam was spreading among the Temne and in the twentieth among Mende.

At the same time, peoples in areas of integrated animism, like Bambara and Mossi, and the inhabitants of the mid-Guinea forest belt in West Africa, remained bulwarks of resistance provided they remained at home. Some of these long-resistant peoples have been succumbing recently,[5] just at the time when, as we shall show, the values and attraction of Islam is weakening and change to the traditional type of African Muslim community is ceasing to be a possibility.

Nilotic Sudan provides a special situation. Contrary to the tendency elsewhere, the colonial period, which began with Muḥammad 'Alī's conquest in 1820, did not witness any great expansion of Islam among pagan societies. Formidable barriers separate the north, related culturally to the Arab world, from the south, which ethnically and culturally forms part of black Africa. The ground had not been prepared in any way. On the contrary, instead of the peaceful penetration of traders and their settlement as was the normal pattern (regarding as out of tune the phase of militant Islam), the southern Nilotic Sudanese had been subject during the nineteenth century to organized slaving expeditions and ruthless exploitation. Consequently, no southern communities accepted Islam, only those uprooted by the slave trade who were Arabized and assimilated into northern society, and in borderland regions where pressure was stronger and the breaking down of barriers more effective.[6] During the Condominium period (1898–1956) the British, recognizing this acute cleavage, pursued a policy of discrimination and religious protection in both north and south, leaving the south to stagnate (until 1946) under the plea of allowing it to develop 'along its own lines'. One effect was to limit any possible, but unlikely,[7] spread of Islam among southern pagans.

Islamic expansion within the sphere of the state of Ethiopia was contained after its unification in the second half of the nineteenth century. There was an expansion of the state religion and this century it has been spreading among many pagan communities in the south. At the same time, a movement into Islam is evident, largely by a slow process of individual conversion. This is most evident in towns, and in Addis Ababa the Muslim population is increasing through both immigration and conversion.

We have previously shown how, although Islam dominated the eastern coast where the Swahili subculture was formed, it had not spread inland. Towards the end of the nineteenth century multiple causes led to the simultaneous spread of both Islam and Christianity into the interior of Tanganyika. Islam's main spread was between 1880 and 1930. The Germans, though favouring Christianity, were involuntary agents of Islam. They made Swahili the official language and employed coastal Swahili extensively in the administration. These Swahili reversed coastal history by working actively to convert to Islam. The interregnum bridging the transition from German to British rule (1917–23) witnessed an intensification in its adoption by communities inland from the coast and along trade routes. Its spread, however, was tempered or modified by the simultaneous diffusion of aspects of Western culture, including Christianity, and this resulted in many neo-Muslims taking an attitude towards religion as something adopted, not inherited like coastal Islam or ancestor ritual.

We have to mark a divide about 1950 when African societies were nearing self-government. After the great surge in expansion and influence during the colonial period, Islam's expansion has slowed down. This process is linked with the growth of nationalism since it began during the closing stages of colonial rule. There came a feverish desire to grasp the new instruments of power. These are all secular and do not include Islam. Islam is losing its former values, its prestige as a civilization, and seems to lead nowhere. Islam to the new men, including the Muslims among them, becomes associated with things that limit and retard. Among such are traditional education, Arabic and its script in non-Arabic-speaking Africa. At the same time as its spread is slowing down, its influence is waning. These changes are linked with the whole changing atmosphere in Africa.

Islam is still spreading in certain areas: Guinea, Sierra Leone, Mali, parts of Nigeria, Northern Cameroons, and in East Africa. It is spreading in two ways: mainly by the traditional way of family conversion in areas more remote from strong Western influence, but also by individual conversion which in the past was the case only with such people as detribalized slaves. Islam is offering itself to the new men and urban proletariat as a personal religion, with positive and negative appeals for its adoption. If under changing conditions it is felt to offer social and individual harmony it is likely to be adopted. In other cases, where it is stressed as 'the religion of the African', its appeal may derive from more negative aspects. A consequence of this mode of expansion of both Islam and Christianity is that a mixture of religious allegiance is found within the same family in certain areas in both East and West Africa.

2. The Muslim in a changing Africa

A. REACTION TO THE CHALLENGE OF THE WEST

We have shown how Islam progressed numerically under the conditions provided by the European occupation. But how has it fared in other ways and what has been the reaction of Muslims to Western civilization?

The reaction, response and adaptation of peoples to colonial rule and secular civilization has varied according to their particular make-up, social systems and physical environment, on the one hand, and the nature and force of the impact, on the other. The attitude of Muslims towards Western culture was fundamentally negative. Islam protected them from the impact of secular civilization (which they classified as 'Christian', for how was it possible to think otherwise?), by the fact that it had come to Negro Africa as a culture complex. It was a universal religion whereby they had transcended tribal or local religion, with a ritual, rules of conduct and social institutions common to diverse groups. Muslims, feeling culturally and spiritually superior to pagans, were resistant to another civilization, even though conquered by its representatives. This resistance shows us the reality of the change Islam had accomplished in the lives of those who had assimilated its culture. Other insulating factors derived from the fact that the established Muslim communities of the west and central Sudan belt lived deep in the interior, removed from the main impact, and not of great importance from the point of view of economic exploitation. Further, it was the policy of the colonial governments to keep Muslims isolated. Their reaction, therefore, was a self-protective withdrawal.

Another consequence of the rapid spread during the colonial period has often been the superficiality of its impression. J. A. K. Leslie writes of Dar es Salaam:

> The vast majority of the population are Muslims, but many of these are really pagans in Muslim clothes (for only a very small minority are prepared to admit being pagan in town); in any case the observances of Islam are strikingly absent here; this is not confined to town, but is true, to a large extent, of the whole coast, though in the town the rules

of religion, like all rules, are more than usually evaded. Most take only to the social aspects of Islam, cleaving still to the ancestral religion of their tribal areas. Many can observe the ancestral religious rites at home, making journeys or sending remittances from town: such rites, for example sickness, are a significant item of expenditure. Some have adopted Zaramo spirits for medicinal purposes. There is a lot of tolerated 'Islamic' magic, in the form of divinations, charms and talismans. Muslim and pagan are inextricably mixed in town, but some at least of the Christians like to keep apart: particularly those who have retained touch with their Missions (a supervision which Muslims do not have—and this is another of the attractions of Islam) . . .

The attraction of Islam in Dar es Salaam is that it is the religion of the majority, and the donning of a *kanzu* is a simple but effective membership card enabling the country bumpkin to be accepted as a civilized man; it is also in sympathy with Bantu conservatism and reliance on elders, tradition and continuity, its accent on the community rather than on the individual; it has enabled its adherents to laugh off the material success of the 'new man' and to retain their own self-respect though lacking in wealth, education and hustle . . .

These attractions must be weakening now, since new currents of thought are directly opposed to the spirit of Islam; the new leaders are almost exclusively Christian, and many are educated; they attack the power of the elders and advocate the equality of young and old.[8]

A practical syncretism is common. Thus L. V. Thomas writes of Dyola in Lower Casamance:

In certain villages only the marabouts can 'perceive' the traditional water spirits (*anmāhl*) and ghosts; only they can create protective gris-gris. . . . In short, one finds the juxtaposition and interpenetration of beliefs rather than genuine substitution. One may well find oneself confronted by a new functional specialization, the God of Islam intervening in affairs of a more general order, whilst the traditional spirits preserve their importance in the private domain, in the resolution of conflicts concerning custom, and on the occasion of the dramatic moments of life. . . . In the same sphere of ideas we may mention the successive participation (we have known a *chef de canton* in turn animist, Christian, Muslim, then atheist!), or simultaneous participation in two religious systems: such a one, for example, has his son baptized according to Christian, Muslim and animist rites, the blessing of three Gods being far better than that of one only.[9]

This sort of thing illustrates what I have had to say about the special situation of Islam in Africa as compared with countries where it is fully integrated into life. In modern Africa a religious label has become a useful sociological symbol, but its acquisition does not entail deep personal and social change. In the past its adoption by a community would have been the beginning of a slow movement towards the prevailing pattern of African Islam. But today the whole outlook has changed and is changing even for traditional Muslims. This is due to the encroachment of a third new world. The Western secular outlook on life and the material forces accompanying modern evolution modify the data and direction of change. This is stronger than Islam's power to change. For cultivators the effect is still slight, but for all brought into more direct contact with new ways of life, work and political and economic institutions, it is considerable.

The power of resistance inherent in Islamic societies has ensured that the process of change has been gradual and restricted in operation, allowed to influence only limited spheres of life. In the political sphere, having once adjusted themselves to the colonial rulers who accorded them a favoured status, Muslims clung to the status quo, fearing the loss of privileges, and reacted against the brash nationalism of the new men.

In their response to Western influences the peoples of north-eastern Sudan have been more responsive than those of western Sudan. This is due to the fact that Western influences penetrated eastern Sudan from Egypt up the Nile and affected Muslims first, whilst the southern pagans were left isolated and neglected. In West Africa, on the contrary, Western influence came from the sea and made its first and deepest impact upon pagans. At the same time, in eastern Sudan religious leadership remained strong and permeated and regulated the activities of the new men, so that you may find modern politicians with the religious outlook of a medieval Muslim and religious leaders with that of a political opportunist.

Gradually the resistance of consolidated Muslim communities has been breaking down. They found it impossible to insulate and immunize themselves completely against the new forces; they found themselves lagging behind the more responsive pagan societies in economic, technological, educational and political development; and finally with independence they found themselves within multireligionist states. But their traditional social systems and cultural forms are not being transformed in the way they are in other communities, showing how effective Islam has been in changing their community life. Still the trend of change is persistent, and any society which resists becomes a backwater, like

Zanzibar where the traditional Islamic outlook held up the pace of change until the dam burst in 1964.

From what has been said about the spread of Islam in the preceding section it will be realized that people are at different levels of participation in Islamic culture. This is an aspect which makes the study of modern change in African Islam differ from that in long-established Muslim lands where the whole population has been Muslim for centuries. On the broadest level, we need an awareness of three spheres of participation:

1. Regions of established Islam; that is, in Hamitic regions, the Sudan belt, and a thin line along the east coast. Here we have what is basically a medieval legalistic type of Islam. Islam dominates the outlook, though within this sphere are many degrees of participation due to factors such as occupation, as, for example, between nomads, cultivators and townspeople.

2. Regions into which Islam has penetrated within the last hundred years at a time when Western influences were simultaneously penetrating. Consequently the neo-Muslims are influenced by varying degrees of secularization and Islam is a 'religion', not permeating every aspect of life.

3. Regions basically pagan, with strong Christian and secularist influence, where Islam is weak, represented by recent converts and by immigrant Muslims from other regions. The reactions of a Muslim minority differs from those of the other two categories.

B. THE IMPACT OF SECULAR CULTURE

The formation of Islamic regional culture zones which was outlined in the first chapter presents the historical aspect of the impact of Islam upon Africa and provides the foundation upon which any study of contemporary change must be made. There is now a third factor in this scheme of culture contact: Western secular culture, whose impact challenges all previous norms and standards. Although contact with Europe goes back to the period of Portuguese expansion the impact of secular culture is relatively recent. The changes that began during the period of colonialist rule have since been accelerated by the political changes that have taken place during the past fifteen years.

Like all other Africans Muslims are undergoing intellectual, moral and social change, and are confronted by acute problems of readjustment. In estimating the influence of Islam and the way

Muslims are being changed we will take as given the historical pattern and characteristics of traditional African Islamic life, with its medieval outlook and its parallelism of African and Islamic ideas and institutions, which has monopolized our attention in earlier chapters, as an indispensable background to discussion of contemporary change.

In the contemporary scene of contact, reaction and adaptation we are confronted by three cultural fields: local African culture, that is, regional cultures, the inherited traditions and customs of the local folk culture; then there is African Islamic culture which has been the main theme of this book; and thirdly, comes Western secular culture.

In the Arab world only two cultural spheres are in interaction, for though it is possible to separate pre-Islamic elements such analysis tends to be artificial since in an integrated Islamic society the elements of the pre-Islamic past have no separate autonomy. However, when it is a question of Islamic and secular culture in the Arab world there is no real integration and each is autonomous. But with African societies, who are at different stages of integration into an Afro-Islamic amalgam, the pre-Islamic elements frequently remain fully autonomous. At the same time, it must be realized that whereas the African and Islamic elements were closely integrated in traditional Afro-Islamic culture, the new elements from Western culture are kept rigidly apart.

Modern changes have set a new series of largely secular parallel phenomena alongside the Afro-Islamic. New elements whose adoption could not be avoided were either segregated or adopted parallel to the old without ousting it. Here are a few examples of the triple parallelism now found in Islamic life:

Regional culture	*Islamic culture*	*Secular culture*
Customary law	Islamic law as civil code	Secular law as penal code
Elders' court	*Sharī'a* court	Civil court
Family instruction	Islamic education	Modern education
Initiation school	Qur'ān school	Secular school
Folk medicine	Medicine based on medieval authors	Modern methods of medical treatment

The Western impact has been very unequal in its effect upon different societies and in different regions, upon different classes, and upon pagan and Muslim societies. I have generalized as to the contemporary results in West Africa in this way.[10]

In the sphere of Sudan village culture the local culture field remains dominant, modified in varying degrees, according to region, people and class, by Islamic culture, and to an even lesser degree by the infiltration of Western influences.

In the sphere of Sudan urban life the three patterns operate with quite different emphases from those within village culture. The Islamic is the dominant culture pattern, Western influence is affecting economic and material life, and the old culture, originally the village civilization, is weakest for it consists of disparate elements of old social patterns, together with remnants of cults and practitioners, which, divorced from their natural setting, become perverse and non-functional in the life of society.

If we turn to West African coastal urban centres once more the emphases are different. The new world, secularized and materialistic, is the dominant element, the local culture comes second, and the Islamic is a semi-integrated intrusion, not only in a place like Cotonou (Dahomey) where Muslims number only 6 per cent as contrasted with 70 per cent Christians, but even in a place like Lagos where the population is 50 per cent Muslim. The influence of numerous Christian churches is prevalent, along with neo-African culture in its changed urban form. Within these towns there are also two kinds of Muslims divided by a great gulf: (*a*) immigrants like Hausa from the interior who remain relatively unchanged in their new environment and belong to the first category; and (*b*) secularized Muslims, converts who belong to the region. Another aspect of these coastal centres is their Islamic diversity and disunity, different groups following different *imāms*, with their own *jāmi'ṣ*, a diversity increased by the intrusion of the Aḥmadiyya. In village communities of the same region the village civilization remains dominant, but is affected by the strong secularizing influence radiating out from the towns, and with very little or no Islamic influence.

In East Africa we have the exact opposite since Islam is fully integrated in the island and coastal centres, though diversified through the immigration of Asiatic Muslims belonging mainly to Shī'ī sects. Western influence as well as Islam came from the sea and at the same time Islam spread among coastal and inland

Bantu. There is a great contrast between the old backward coastal centres like Lamu and modern Dar es Salaam.

Whereas the interaction of African and Islamic cultures goes back over many centuries and has created an Afro-Islamic culture amalgam, Africa has only experienced the full impact of the West during the present century. We have to take account of the fact that the centre of gravity varies in each of the different areas, and that it can change, and is now changing. The predominance of the new secular world is increasing even more rapidly now that Africans have gained more control over their own affairs in the political sphere at least, yet wherever Islam is firmly established as a culture it will remain the centre of gravity.

Yet today traditional Islamic culture is being influenced, but by regressing rather than changing to face the challenge of a new world. During the past twenty-five years, as more and more aspects of the secular and materialistic civilization became open to Africans, primarily through education (from which Muslims voluntarily cut themselves off), Islam lost much of its appeal as a civilization. Whilst colonial rule lasted Islam could still command some prestige, but today the values attached to a divine law and an Arabic education are being undermined by the values attached to secular education, freedom from religious restrictions, and the material benefits derived therefrom. The real undermining of Islam, advanced in the Maghrib but only beginning in sub-saharan Africa, is due to the fact that secular civilization challenges the very principles upon which Islamic civilization is based.

3. Islam and secular nationalism

A. ISLAM AND THE STATE

Political changes have been taking place at breathtaking speed throughout Africa. Between 1956 and 1962 the greater part of Africa became independent. In this fast-changing scene there are limits to the comments it is wise to make in this kind of survey, but we may give some indication of the part Islam has played within the new states.

Most of these countries have only a territorial unity for they embrace peoples of astonishing diversity in language, type of life, customs and stage of modern evolution. They are also distinguished by religious diversity. Only Somalia (100 per cent), Mauritania (96 per cent), Gambia (90 per cent), Niger (85 per cent),[11] and Senegal (85 per cent) are almost wholly Muslim.[12] Guinea (60 per cent), Mali (60 per cent), Chad (50 per cent) and the Sudan (60 per cent) have significant Muslim majorities. Nigeria is a Muslim stronghold since its Northern Region is two-thirds Muslim and Islam is widely professed in the Western Region, though insignificant in the Eastern. Others have a Muslim minority: Portuguese Guinea (36 per cent), Sierra Leone (30 per cent), Liberia (10 per cent), Upper Volta (22 per cent), Ivory Coast (20 per cent), Ghana (5 per cent), Togo (2·3 per cent), Dahomey (6 per cent), Cameroon (30 per cent), Ethiopia (33 per cent), Uganda (5·5 per cent), Kenya (4 per cent) and Tanzania (25 per cent).

After the formation of these states the universalism of Islam, the way it can transcend tribal particularisms, might have been expected to appeal to nationalists. In fact, the new leaders have little use for it, even if Muslims. The main reason, as we have already indicated, is that the new men associate Islam with conservative and backward elements, whilst the conservatives, the privileged and clerical classes, were frequently satisfied with the status quo, distrusted the new tendencies, and were lukewarm or opposed to the new order.[13]

Apart from the Mediterranean lands which fall into a special category since their affinities are closer to the Near East than to Africa, the influence of Islam in politics is most evident where Muslims form the majority, that is, along the Sudan belt, especially in Mauritania, Senegal, Northern Nigeria, Niger, the Sudan and, on the east coast, Somalia, but elsewhere its influence in political life is negligible.[14] The impartial attitude of the Western administrators towards the religions practised by the peoples they governed has been inherited by African politicians. As these regions moved towards independence Muslim minorities were concerned to gain recognition as communities possessing special legal, educational and social interests, but not to proclaim their Muslim solidarity against Christian or secularized pagan Africans.

Further, the state seeks to be all-powerful and distrusts other 'powers' like Islam or the Christian Church. Therefore these must be watched, controlled and, if necessary, curbed. The new rulers do not show the deference towards Islamic leaders and institutions shown by colonial officials. The new élite do not owe their status to birth but to modern education and their own efforts. They seek to break the power of the genealogical élite, to evolve new ideologies (like *Négritude*), and foster institutions suitable to the age. Their driving power derives from secular nationalism, hence they are cautious in their attitude to religion as a power belonging to a repudiated past and aim to keep it out of politics.

The important point is that Islam does not form a rallying cry, it is not thought of as a basis for the unity of the state (except in three Hamitic Islamic states, Mauritania, Nilotic Sudan and Somalia). This is due to the fact that their subjects profess different religions. Faced with the need to transcend tribal boundaries they do not wish to have to deal also with religious divisions, but seek a *modus vivendi*.

The Sudan Republic, however, differed from this pattern and followed a unique religious policy. The Egyptian occupation and the Mahdiyya had eliminated local chieftaincies and the British did not attempt to restore them; they even destroyed that of Darfur which had resurrected itself after the Mahdiyya. This left the religious leaders as the natural leaders of the people, associated in contrasting ways with the unsophisticated population, on the one hand, and with the educated classes, on the other. It is the latter aspect which is interesting and contrasts with West Africa. So strong was the prestige and influence of the religious leaders that the nationalist movement had to plant itself on the two most powerful forces, the Mirghaniyya or Khatmiyya led by Sayyid 'Alī al-Mirghanī (d. 1968), and the Neo-Mahdiyya or Anṣār group led by Sayyid 'Abd ar-Raḥmān ibn al-Mahdī (d. 1959).

The ethno-religious cleavage between the Arab-Hamitic Muslim north and the Negroid Animist-Christian south presented the new republic with acute problems of national unity. The pace of political development had been set by northerners whose common profession of Islam provided a measure of unity; while Christianity had spread in the pagan southern region, tribally very diverse, disunited and backward. Since these contrasts made for political instability the new government sought, by plain overt as well as hidden pressure, to spread both Arabic and Islam in the south and to suppress Christian missions. This was a secular attempt to solve a problem, religious imperialism in the service of the state, a nationalist rather than an Islamic and anti-Christian policy as such, with the aim of national integration and unification. The consequence is that Islam has suffered a great setback. In the eyes of southerners its image is tarnished, and its natural, even if slow, progress halted.

Other African states, facing a similar problem of creating a secular state in countries whose inhabitants profess different religions, have recognized the changing position of religion in life and adopted a policy more adapted to the secular state. The example of the Sudan has acted as a deterrent to any attempt to impose religious uniformity. They guarantee freedom of religion, honour all the religions of their people, and at state ceremonies invite Muslims, Christians and pagans to offer prayers and libations.

In the neighbouring country of Chad we have the opposite situation from Nilotic Sudan. In Chad European influence came from the sea and affected the southern pagan Bantu who adopted Christianity and welcomed modern education and social changes, whilst the Muslim north remained much more backward. This disparity faced the newly independent government with acute internal problems of readjustment and unity, but it has followed a secular policy. Similarly, in the Cameroon Republic the same contrast occurs, though here the leaders of the predominantly Muslim north (the President is a Muslim) have had a moderating influence upon the more advanced Christian-Pagan south, divided by deep cleavages.

B. ISLAM AND POLITICAL PARTIES

Islam has not so far been a strong factor in internal political life. Once political parties were formed the nationalist programme secularized itself. Naturally Islamic influence has been more pronounced in states wholly or predominantly Muslim and we have just referred to the coincidence of religious and political leadership in the Sudan Republic, the Anṣār with the Umma Party and the Khatmiyya with the Ashiqqa Party. The Sudan though does not mirror the normal trend of Islam and politics in Africa. In strongly-Islamized Senegal the Christian, Leopold Senghor, was elected as president, and there can occur such shifts as that of the Murīdiyya *ṭarīqa* leadership's support from Lamin-Guèye's *Section Française de l'Internationale Ouvrière* to Senghor's *Bloc Démocratique Sénégalais*.

Few political parties have labelled themselves Muslim for the whole concept is secular, though Islam was involved in some parties. The *Union Socialiste des Musulmans Mauritaniens* is in a wholly Muslim country. In Ghana Kwame Nkruma reacted strongly against the Muslim Association Party as introducing religion into politics, and when he came to power in 1957 he banned parties representing religious or ethnic interests. Islam has been a factor in regional politics in Nigeria, but has been modified in the federal sphere as dangerous since the southern politicians, whatever their religious interests, have adopted a secular approach. A natural secular outlook is apparent in societies which have changed from paganism to Islam or Christianity, for these are thought of as 'religions'. Of a politician in Gambia (90 per cent Muslim), Michael Crowder wrote, 'Yet Njie, a Catholic convert in a Muslim family, numbers amongst his followers many of the leading Muslim dignitaries, which is surprising since there is an exclusively Mohammedan party opposing him called the Gambia Muslim Congress. Muslim elders, if you ask them why they support a Christian like Njie, will reply: "Don't mix politics with religion."[15] ' This Muslim Congress Party was formed in 1952, but the appeal to common religious sentiments failed and it merged with the Democratic Party in 1960. H. A. Gailey comments:

> There are three reasons for this odd separation of religion from politics in the Gambia. Politics have so far been personality orientated and thus the popularity of the leader has been far more important than his religion or his political platform. Secondly, the extended family system overrides religious differences. One can change his beliefs and still retain his position within the group without loss of popularity or prestige. Thirdly, there is little connection between Gambian Muslims and any outside pan-Islamic movement which equates Islam with political goals.[16]

C. RELATIONS WITH THE ARAB WORLD

This is another sphere which it is not necessary to enlarge upon since relationships fluctuate with political expediency. We mentioned in the Introduction that until recently sub-Saharan Muslim Africa was not truly integrated into the Islamic world. The European conquest hardly changed the outlook for, though the administrations favoured Islam in many ways, they also regarded it as a potential threat to their rule, especially the French with their North African experience and campaigns against West African Muslim states. European rule might have been expected to facilitate communications with the Arab world, but in fact hardly changed the situation. What movement took place was chiefly on pilgrimage. The British did not encourage contacts with outer Muslim countries, and anyway many, like the Northern Nigerians, did not desire it. The main barrier was African Muslim mentality. The large numbers of pilgrims and the relatively few who studied at the Azhar or Qarawiyyīn were little changed by their experience.

However, during the last stage of European rule a change of outlook began to be felt, more especially among the neo-Muslim *évolué* class, and this has become more evident since independence, especially on the political level. Islam has come to be seen as providing a link with Arab states. A feature has been the pilgrimages undertaken by many heads of state and ministers which provided the opportunity to visit Arab states; in fact, this aspect became more important to them and the pilgrimage sometimes omitted as less significant in a world of changing values. Pan-African conferences are more important. Not merely have these few discovered that the secularized Arab takes little interest in religion, but they have also found it expedient in these organizations not to stress religious differencies. Common allegiance to Islam plays little part in political relationships, and they have been suspicious of Egyptian aims in this respect,[17] nor have they shown special sympathy with Arab issues.

4. Social and cultural change

A. TOWARDS THE SECULARIZATION OF EDUCATION

In the context of the Muslim mind European culture and Christianity were associated. Christian missions were the pioneers of modern education in Africa, and Muslims, with their feeling for the interrelation of religion and society, naturally reacted against its introduction. Already having a system of education, distinguishing them culturally from pagans they opposed its being supplemented by or substituted for an alien system, especially since this was associated or even identified with Christianity. Colonial authorities respected their prejudices by excluding Christian missions from Muslim areas.[18] The result was that the modern evolution of pagan areas was more rapid than in Muslim areas. Even when colonial governments sought to develop and extend their own secular education they met with the same entrenched prejudice.[19] Strong opposition to the education of girls was encountered from both men and women, conservatives and *évolués* alike.

However, though they could delay, they could not block the inevitability of change. The rate of progress varied between different Muslim areas.[20] The new men found themselves up against the opposition of both the privileged classes and the whole clerical body. The latter realized instinctively that Islamic education cannot be changed without losing its essential character. A school where the Qur'ān is taught as one subject among others is a secular school.

The necessities of the changing situation forced, not reform, but the complete substitution of Muslim by secular education, one whose basis and aims are directly opposed to those of Islam. Islam, instead of being the whole of education, is incorporated into the curriculum as a subject following the Western method, whilst what was formerly its core, the law, has become the concern of a few specialists.

But the parallel existence of two educational systems remains,[21] though with the old continually losing ground. In more sophisticated places the beginning is apparent of a decline in the number of Qur'ān schools, a tendency far advanced in the Arab world. We have stressed their importance, not merely in teaching Islamic ritual, but also in imparting rudiments of social law and especially the Islamic outlook on life. Similarly schools for *'ilm* or legal studies are declining; even in Mauritania the higher instruction given in Shinqit, Tagant and Assaba is attracting ever fewer pupils.

B. SOCIAL CHANGE

The Western impact upon Africa has assailed the social bases of traditional society by undermining traditional authority, creating new classes, modifying the status of women, introducing a new education and new ideals and aims. Social change among Muslims has been retarded compared with other African societies, but this is another aspect of change about which it is impossible to generalize. Contrast, for example, the position of women among neo-Muslims like the Yoruba with that of Somali, Hausa or Moorish women. Western influence is unequal in its impact upon different aspects of culture, and social change is slower than others except the strictly religious. In addition, account must be taken of the variable rates of change between different types and classes of traditional society, as well as regional differences. The new classes in process of formation for life in a new age are more flexible than old integrated communities living traditional life. We have mentioned how Islam had little effect upon social stratification.[22] The colonial governments also did not interfere, rather they bolstered it up by then neutral policy towards indigenous institutions. But African secular movements are modifying these barriers. Modern political parties seek a broadbased appeal, as opposed to parties based on local, sectional or religious interests.[23]

In Muslim communities women have lagged well behind men. Conversely, in respect of men's attitude to women, Muslim men, with few exceptions, still hold traditional attitudes. The nature of the impact has to be taken into account. The spread of new economic forces is forcing men to change their attitudes to work, but there is no comparable impact of new social forces to make them change their attitude to women. The adoption of new political or economic forms, therefore, varies in initiating tendencies towards social change. Polygamy may become economically impossible in certain urban social contexts, but that does not mean that the attitude towards polygamy has changed. In other words, change in social outlook ensues when the social context permits it.[24] Thus in the Arab world juridical change reflects rather than initiates social change. Family law lies at the heart of the *sharīʿa*, and when Arab governments change it, this shows the extent of the social change that has already taken place. Of course, no change in this sphere will be possible in Muslim Africa for a long while yet, though changes in other aspects of the *sharīʿa* have taken place. Colonial governments increased the status and authority of the *ʿulamā'*,[25] but the changing attitude of the new men towards traditional Islamic values makes their decline inevitable. In the Arab world they have been displaced by the new élite and in Africa the process is beginning.

A modern feature is the development of new societies and associations such as political parties and trade unions. The functions of the *ṭarīqas* in some parts like the Sudan Republic are being taken over by these secular organizations for the needs and aspirations to which they ministered are being diverted into new channels.[26]

5. Religious change

Though the whole of this chapter has been concerned with religious change in the wider sense, since when confronted by

Islam as a culture any change is religious, we need to look at more specifically religious aspects, and especially any which are symptomatic of a changing outlook.

If the colonial period was that in which Islam gained its greatest following in the history of sub-Saharan Africa, that which followed has been one when the power of Islam to influence both society and the individual has been steadily waning. Of course, the change stems from the previous period which introduced the tendencies now beginning to make inroads even into established Islamic circles.

We think of detractions from religion and tentatives towards a rethinking of religion for a new age. The first we may call quasi-religious diversions (here meaning a channel into which religious energies are being increasingly diverted), such as secular nationalism as a substitute for religion. The millenarian messianism of Mahdism, alive in Africa up to 1910, has been diverted from the idea of the restoration of a golden age of Islam into a modern political and social messianism aiming at grasping now the benefits of the dynamic culture which has invaded African life. As we have shown, this is a factor which can break the power of the old factions such as the élite by birth not merit and ability, and channel and bring together the new men in the new states, a factor that can override tribal and religious divisions.

The problem with which Muslims are faced is how to preserve the values within their inheritance and integrate them with the values of the new. We have shown how Islamic cultural values are being undermined by the challenge of new assessments such as the attraction of modern as against religious education. Even in traditional Muslim communities the new men involved in three cultures, African, Islamic and secular, are increasing; the degrees of influence affected by many factors varying according to region, tribe, occupation or class. Let us look first at traditional Islam under the new conditions.

During the earlier colonial phase frustrated Islamic assertion found a compensatory outlet, not only in an exaggerated legalism and in millenarianism, but in personality-centred revivals of *ṭarīqa* inspiration. Very strong in Mauritania and the Moorish Sahil it penetrated among Negroes. The most interesting development was the Murīdiyya whose founder (d. 1927) in the Qādirī tradition was at first an opponent of French control, but then changed to cooperation and directed his order in a remarkable revolution affecting every aspect of life which endures as a factor to be taken into account in Senegalese life. Whilst the Murīdiyya was practically restricted to Senegal the Tijāniyya has experienced a vast expansion. Within former French West Africa appeared a number of leaders who gathered groups of followers. The most controversial was the Ḥamāliyya founded by Ḥamāhu'llāh (d. 1942) regarded as a deviation owing to its use of an 'eleven-bead' rosary instead of the usual twelve, whose order is still a religious force, especially in Mali. Other Tijānī leaders were Mālik Si (d. 1922), among Wolof (Ḥāfiẓiyya), and Ibrāhīm Nyās of Kaolak, whose influence spread into Northern Nigeria. No corresponding leaders have appeared in Nigeria but the regular Tijāniyya has been spreading until it has become the dominant *ṭarīqa*. The Sanūsiyya influenced parts of central Sudan, mainly Kanem and Waday, but its presentday influence is limited to eastern Sahara. In eastern Sudan and Somalia the orders were active, but a characteristic of the changing religious climate in the Near Eastern Arab world has been the virtual disappearance of the *ṭarīqas* and their appeal among even Arabized Hamitic Africans is weakening.[27]

Reformist attitudes have made themselves felt in open attacks on pagan cults active in their midst, in opposition to the *ṭarīqas*, especially hagiolatry of the Murīdiyya type, and in criticism of hampering traditional attitudes. Attempts have been made to modernize traditional education, but such efforts were few and received little support. We have referred to the fact that there has to be a general change in mental climate before reforms can take place; and the clergy are readier to tolerate a parallel rival system rather than to reform their own. In consequence, the process of change has been gradual, restricted in operation, influencing limited aspects of life, and then not integrated but allowed to exist parallel.

The result is that many 'new men' in regions of entrenched Islam find themselves increasingly out of sympathy with Islam as mediated by the clerics, whether of the legalistic or maraboutic or medicinemen type. This reaction affects only a small number and does not touch the country folk. It is stronger in the newly independent former French territories than in Northern Nigeria. These young men, alienated from traditional education, can read the Qur'ān only in French or English translations. Attempts to translate it into African languages are still resisted though the absolute prohibition is being breached.[28] Some are trying to reconcile the new ideas they are acquiring with the religious thought and practice of Islam, but they are without guides and are very much at sea. A few have welcomed Aḥmadī books for these give them a foundation upon which to support Islam, some welcoming their anti-Christian aspects, while at the same time rejecting Aḥmadī claims. They are relatively little influenced by the Near East (Nilotic Sudan excepted) since they cannot read Arabic.[29] Negroes in Mauritania have reacted against Arabism because of racialist feelings inspired by Moorish predominance in the region. Others advocate the formulation of a law based on Western, Islamic and customary elements, but imbued with the Islamic spirit. These are just a few of many conflicting reactions which will progressively become more intense. Ease of communications and the exchange of ideas by radio and print, together with increased North African and Egyptian awareness of Muslim Africa, must result in change in African Islam in a more positive rather than the negative way so far exhibited.

NEO-AFRICAN ISLAM

In addition to the new mentality making its appearance in established Muslim communities another type of new men is found among people who have been adopting Islam during the last 100 years at a time when Western civilization was also penetrating. Secular civilization, including Christianity, has been slowly affecting the outlook of many Africans. The way this has affected Islam is that it has been spreading, less as a religious culture than as a religion in the Western sense. People affected in this way by simultaneous Western and Islamic penetration, which includes ordinary people, cultivators and townspeople, as well as the educated, have been absorbing elements from two outlooks on life at one and the same time; and in most spheres except the more strictly religious the West tends to predominate. Besides Wolof in Senegal and Yoruba in Western Nigeria it includes others in Guinea, Sierra Leone and other parts of former French territory.

These people, drawing upon the heritages of three cultures and seeking a working compromise, have therefore not adopted the conservative outlook of traditional Muslims. They have adopted Islam as a 'religion', together with such religio-social elements as are found in the transitional rites. Formerly, you could not adopt a religion for religion was not a separate part of culture. You were born into a society through whose whole fabric religion permeated. Today, however, Islam (or Christianity) is coming to be looked upon as a personal religious allegiance. Consequently, these new men with their divided allegiances are freer to come to terms with changing society and more open to new ideas and outlook.

Since these regions are also regions into which Christianity has penetrated the relationship of followers of the two religions is significant. In old Islamic areas where Christians tend to be represented by immigrants the attitude remains that of mistrust and even hostility, but wherever neo-Muslims and neo-Christians are in contact there is often an atmosphere of tolerance and understanding. Among such areas may be mentioned: Senegal (Wolof), parts of Sierra Leone, Guinea, Ivory Coast, and in south-west Nigeria among Yoruba, in all coastal towns and some in the interior. In coastal regions where Muslims and Christians are intermingled they are only distinguished by a few factors (that is, natives of the region, excluding immigrants like Hausa). Change of religion is not regarded as undermining the unity of the community. Family syncretism has been referred to previously; among Yoruba and Bamun (Foumban in West Cameroons), for example, the three religions may be represented in the same family. This, of course, is a secular conception of religion. On a wider canvas, in all the newly influenced areas like Tanzania the same situation is found, in that certain tribes are mixed from the religious point of view and this is not necessarily divisive. Muslims and Christians cooperate in building churches and mosques, and in some places they hold circumcision rites in common. In Kenya and Uganda Islam is weak in numbers and influence, often represented by non-Africans. Religious distinctions tend to be more pronounced in Uganda where Muslims are more sensitive than elsewhere owing to Uganda's peculiar history of religious conflict.

The most important social force in both the old and new Islamic communities is the small élite of new men, for they form the bridge between African society and secular civilization. Not only are they the mediators for the penetration of Western ideas, attitudes and institutions, but they have the task of reconciling and moulding the old and the new in changing Africa. The question is whether they can become a religious as well as a social and political force. When we reflect that apart from Islam and Christianity there are other contenders for the souls of Africans—nationalism, modern materialism and secularism—we have to recognize them as quasi-religious factors.

We have to distinguish between secularization and secularism. The first is that process we have been describing, the change from a religious to a secular culture in which all the different spheres of life are autonomous; whereas secularism is an ideology, an attitude to life that rejects spiritual values and the religious outlook. Secularization as a process is inevitable here as elsewhere in the world. This process changes the domain of religion; in other words, it restricts and narrows the spheres in which Islam can mould the lives of its adherents. For the traditional Muslim the spiritual cannot be separated from other aspects of life. African life has always had this total relatedness and we have tried to show that this outlook was not greatly disturbed by the adoption of Islam, the old and new were reintegrated in the fully formed Islamic society. But the effect of secularization is to break life into compartments, and for Muslims this means the channelling of Islam to becoming one factor among others. Secularization need not necessarily lead to secularism, but it opens the way for the adoption of a secularist attitude to life. There are those in Africa to whom Islam as a spiritual and moral force is becoming irrelevant to life, who at the same time retain full loyalty to Islam as the cultural environment to which they belong. Islamic culture like Western culture is being gradually weaned from its religious roots, and the gulf between the spiritual and secular spheres of life is widening. Islam, whilst continuing to influence deeply individual lives, will gradually cease to have the profound effect it formerly exercised over vast ranges of people. Here, as elsewhere, the future of Islam depends upon the forging of a new form of relatedness between religion and life different from anything known in the past.

Chapter 6

A decade of expanding horizons

In this chapter I am concerned to bring out the way both Arab and African outlooks have changed in respect of inter-Arab (Mediterranean and Asian) relationships, and in particular the mutual drawing together of the Asian and African worlds. The way in which the state of Israel was founded, which has acted as a catalyst, is also sketched in.

A second major theme relates religion in Africa to the world-wide revolution that is taking place in the relation of religion to personal and social life. In the past, religion was socially determined and directed. Allowance has to be made, not only for religion becoming a personal matter, but for the way religion has contracted from being the regulative principle of African life to becoming one among many diverse factors that make up men's lives in society. African religion is seen as 'natural' religion, arising from the working of universal Spirit within natural man, but monotheistic religions, such as Islam and Christianity, that have arisen from the working of universal Spirit outside man, are seen as 'unnatural'; in consequence they are found to be exclusivist and divisive.

1. African Muslims in a wider setting

Since the early days of the expansion of Islam Muslims have viewed black Africa (*Sūdān*) as another world from white Africa (*Bīḍān*). The Sahara formed a real divide. Today, this distinction is no longer valid. In fact, Africans and Arabs have asked me why I restricted this book to Africa south of the Sahara. The reason was that the book was intended to summarize the work I had already done in a number of studies on regional Islam in sub-Saharan Africa, whereas many studies had been undertaken on the religion of the peoples of the Maghribi and Egyptian zones.

It is true that Arabs and black Africans had developed mutual relationships since the time when Arabs first penetrated beyond the first Nile cataracts into Kushite Nubia, and Berbers dominating the Saharan trade routes carried Islam to trading communities among Sudan-belt blacks. But nothing can hide the fact that Arabs regarded black Africans as an inferior race, the very word '*abīd*, 'slaves', being their common name for black Africans.

New interests and sympathies have swept away these distinctions between Black and White Africans. There has been a complete change in Egyptian understanding of the word 'Arab' also. Formerly, Egyptians never thought of themselves as 'Arab'. To them the word signified 'bedouin'. They were simply 'Egyptians', defined and insulated by the banks of the Nile. Significantly, the freedom of Egypt brought the name 'Arab' into the name of their state, whether as signifying a union, 'The United Arab Republic', or in 1971 as 'The Arab Republic of Egypt'. Likewise, the peoples of the Maghrib also now call themselves 'Arabs' by reason of language, although they recognize that they, like the Egyptians and northern Sudanese, are only Arabs culturally, not ethnically. The term 'Arab' today signifies anyone who speaks Arabic as his mother-tongue. Some seventy per cent of Arabs so defined now live in Africa. This last decade has seen a real and definitive encounter and understanding between Arab and African nationalisms, above all their meeting together on an equal basis in the Organization of African Unity.

2. Towards the formation of the O.A.U.

Only in recent times have Arabs and Africans awoken to the realization that their lives, problems, aspirations, and destinies were interconnected. For example, African awareness of Arabs as friends who have been through similar crises of confrontation with a basically alien and irreligious Western world has forced them to take up a definite attitude towards Arab problems, of which that of Israel is the chief.

The vision of Jamāl 'Abd an-Nāṣir, leader of the Egyptian revolution of 23 July 1952, was the significant factor in initiating this change. The Egyptian anti-colonialist revolution which swept away an alien monarchy was a direct consequence of the implantation in Arab heartland of the Zionist state of Israel. Two years after the revolution 'Abd an-Nāṣir released his remarkable book, *Egypt's Liberation: The Philosophy of the Revolution*. Here he saw Egypt's destiny as a central factor in the Arab world, embracing not only

Arabic-speakers but by concentric circles the Islamic world and the whole African continent. Freedom for Arabs and Africans to guide their own destinies had a unique meaning for Egypt, for no other country had so long endured a succession of alien rulers since the Persians overthrew the last Pharaonic dynasty in 525 B.C.

'Abd an-Nāṣir's support for African nationalists south of the Sahara represents the initiation of an Arab role as allies of Africans in support of their liberation from colonial rule. Significant as a first move was the Egyptian revolutionary junta's abandonment of the slogan, 'the political unity of the Nile Valley' (1953).

The foundation of Afro-Arab neutralism may be seen as going back to the Bandung Conference of April 1955, to have been reinforced at the Afro-Asian Solidarity Conference in Cairo in December 1957, and to have culminated at the Accra Conference of April 1958, out of which was voiced the determination to work harmoniously together to create a permanent organization for liaison embracing the whole African continent. At this conference eight independent states took part: Ethiopia, Ghana, Liberia, Libya, Morocco, Sudan, Tunisia, and the U.A.R. (Egypt with Syria). This conference demonstrated the new turn African outlook had taken. The newly independent states affirmed their moral support for countries like Algeria that were still struggling to free themselves.

From this time Egypt was giving material and moral support for nationalist and dissident groups in Africa by welcoming exiles, offering support and scholarships for Africans, and supporting insurrectionists in various ways.

The attitudes of black Africans to Arabs have varied from indifference to hostility. Some Africans had prejudices to overcome. East African schoolchildren, for example, had been treated to the Arab record in the slave-trade, while the British had been depicted as entering Africa for purely humanitarian reasons. There were phases when African nationalist leaders mistrusted Arabs even when they were receiving encouragement and material help. But black Africans were going through a phase of readjustment as well as Arabs. On opposite sides of the continent Nkrumah of Ghana and Nyerere of East Africa saw themselves alongside the Algerians in being engaged together in a common struggle. Their pan-Africanism embraced the whole continent in confrontation with European powers. Their leaders saw Arabs as the vanguard of the anti-imperialist front.

In Egypt itself the genuine attempt that has been made to improve the lot of the *fallāḥīn* as well as that of the urban workers has not been without influence on black African relationships and understanding. In addition, it did not escape African eyes that Egypt enjoyed a measure of political stability in spite of its relatively meagre resources, even surviving a series of defeats by Israel. In this it contrasted with many other Arab and African newly-independent states. African reactions against Egyptian propaganda and forms of influence have varied, but the way had been prepared under the regimes of 'Abd an-Nāṣir and after his death (September 1970) the smooth succession of Anwār as-Sādāt. As direct Egyptian influence waned, African sympathy with Arab issues and aims has increased.

Arab nationalism has undergone many changes in its evolution, in particular the role of Israel which we shall consider shortly, more especially in its relation to the Arab role in Africa. But through the Arabs' experiences in achieving independence, the successive failures of Arab unions, internal changes, and inter-Arab movements, the feeling of Arab solidarity survives unimpaired.

In 1957 the Gold Coast became the first British dependency in tropical Africa to achieve independence, under the presidency of Kwame Nkrumah and the name of Ghana. Israel, hungry for support, had been for some time courting African nations that were nearing independence. Nkrumah's support of Israel at first might have seemed to set up a barrier between him and Arab aspirations. In 1960 in a speech at the General Assembly of the United Nations he had called on the Arabs 'to recognize realities' in respect of the Israeli occupation of part of Arab Palestine in spite of the manifest injustice of the way Israel was brought into existence. The Arabs retorted that White power in Southern Africa was also a reality, but Africans were not thereby obliged to recognize that power's policy in relation to its black subjects, and were justified in working to undermine such a regime in the United Nations. Interchanges between African nationalists showed that other Africans were discovering for themselves that Israel represented a remnant of the very type of colonialism that had resulted in the settlement of Biblical white aliens in southern Africa with whose regime Israel was directly connected.

3. The Arab role in the O.A.U.

The creation of the Organization of African Unity in 1963 provided the newly-independent states of Africa with a forum in which they could discuss common problems. These states were still marked by divisions of interests and aims about the nature of such an organization. In 1961 separate meetings were held, the moderates meeting in Brazzaville and Monrovia, the more radical at Casablanca, where Egypt (then the U.A.R.), Libya, Morocco, and the Algerian F.L.N. worked in concert with Ghana, Mali, and Guinea. But the overriding feeling of African unity was strong enough to allow the parties to come together at Addis Ababa in 1963 to establish formally the O.A.U.

The Arab role in the O.A.U. has varied. By 1973 the Arabs had discovered the hidden power that resided in the oil reserves within their barren lands. In the O.A.U. they found means by which they could exercise influence in the Third World of the underprivileged nations. At the same time, African nations saw in the O.A.U. a means by which they could engage Arab powers in their interests and draw from them economic concessions. But before reaching this stage we must look at the way in which Africans ranged themselves alongside the Arabs, once accomplices with Europeans in Africa's enslavement, in the Palestinian cause.

The cause of the Palestinians had the effect of stirring even the most conservative Arab elements in a radical direction, and Arab concern to enlist allies in their struggle with Israel was a factor in broadening Arab political horizons.

In its attempt to gain sympathy Israel had been zealously courting the newly-independent African states, presenting itself as a tiny country beset in an ocean of hostile Arabs, and had been giving them help and guidance in various ways, even military. But now Israel was presented to Africans as one further illustration of the perfidy of Western nations in ousting peasant farmers from their ancestral homes in favour of a particular type of protégé.

We have mentioned how Nkrumah had himself been seduced by Israeli propaganda, but now after the Arabs invited him to look at the comparison between Zionism and Afrikaner Biblicism, he was even ready to sign a communiqué prepared by the more radical African states at the January 1961 conference at Casablanca, in which Israel was described as a 'tool of neo-colonialism'. In June of the same year Modibo Keita of Mali, when in Cairo to sign a treaty of friendship, likewise described Israel in the same terms.

Now, at the increasing number of Third World conferences Africans found themselves drawing out the similarity between Zionism and South African racism in its apartheid form, and this led them to identify themselves with the Arab cause. The fact is that Israel is itself a quasi-caste state, having within its boundaries a large Arab population, the original inhabitants of the land of Palestine for more than 2000 years. In addition, Israeli policy was geared to operate a form of apartheid in which the indigenous Arabs were treated as second-class citizens. This was increased when the Israelis provoked the Six Days War in 1967 which left under Israeli military occupation the remaining section of Palestinian Arabs still in their own country. In this solidly Arab section, that the media designate 'the West Bank' (of the River Jordan), Israelis are pursuing a policy of dilution and eventual permanent control by the introduction of Jewish military settler colonies.[1]

In 1971 the O.A.U. commissioned a committee of ten heads of African states under the chairmanship of President Senghor of Senegal to study the prospects for peace. Four of them consulted the heads of Egypt and Syria, but were in effect rebuffed by Israel. They ended by recommending the implementation of the United Nations Resolution 242.

African states began breaking their relations with Israel in 1972. This has been linked with the oil crisis, but this did not occur until the end of 1973. Idi Amin of Uganda was the first to sever relations,[2] and his action was followed by Chad and Congo, and in 1973 by Mali, Niger, Senegal, and others. In spite of persistent efforts the Arab cause had so far been successfully smothered in the international forum by the United States. It was even prepared to risk setting off a nuclear war in October 1973 for the sake of Israel when it ordered a nuclear alert. But at this point oil power paved the way to bring out the advocacy of the *legitimacy* of the Palestinian cause in the world forum. The application of the Arab oil boycott against the United States in the course of the October 1973 war had dramatized the issues that oil power could evoke. These were highlighted at the conference of the O.A.U. held at Mogadishu in June 1974. A further diplomatic triumph in the international field was won in the same year when Yasir 'Arafat, leader of the Palestinian Liberation Organization, was allowed to address the General Assembly of the U.N., and in January 1976 the P.L.O. took part in the Security Council debate on the Middle East question.

Arabs were seen to be in the forefront of the Third World attempt to create a new international economic order. In this respect they were seen as working beyond their own national or pan-Arab interests in serving the underprivileged slaves to Western capitalism. In 1974 the Algerian president had taken the initiative in calling for a special debate at the General Assembly on raw materials, which took place in 1975. This also struck a new line to guide U.N. interests away from the dominant self-interest-centred superpowers. The Arab oil embargo had as a by-product the highlighting for Africans of the basic callousness of the Western world in the selfish exploitation of the world's natural resources.

Another international forum in which Arab states play a leading role is the Organization of Petroleum Exporting Countries (OPEC). This Organization may also be viewed as a political power block of Islamic influence, since two-thirds of its members, in respect of both number of states and quantity of oil production and revenue, were Muslim. If Saudi Arabia is seen as the stagnant heartland of Sunni Islam, Iran stands as the equivalent in Shī'ī Islam. Indonesia is the most populous Muslim state which has not tried its influence in Muslim councils, while the small Gulf states wield immense financial resources that can be tapped for projects far beyond the boundaries of the Arab world. In Africa, apart from the Arab states of Libya and Algeria, the OPEC has two black African members in Nigeria, with an immense Muslim population, and Gabon, whose President Omar Bongo has become a Muslim.

4. Conflicts misnamed 'religious'

In the past the domain of religion covered the whole of man's life in society; now it is an aspect of life seen as secular. But even in this secular age it has proved convenient, if misleading, to label 'religious' many of the conflicts that are taking place. In fact, many of these have little to do with religion, unless one sees religion as itself a material fact used by men for their own purposes, as in the conflicts now scarifying Northern Ireland and Lebanon.

Africa has been cited too as providing examples of religious conflict during the decade or so since this book was first published. Such have been, in southern Nigeria, Biafran Ibo Christians seeking autonomy from a supposed threat of domination by northern Muslims; or southern Sudanese, Christian impregnated, warring against having Islam forced upon them. Ethiopia is pictured as warring on two fronts against Muslim rebels. But with the dissolution of the colonialist empires, British, French, Belgian, Spanish, and Portuguese, Ethiopia alone is left, now an empire without an emperor, committed to 'furthering the aims of the Marxist revolution'. Its Christian 'Voice of the Gospel' has been changed to the 'Voice of the Marxist Revolution'. When any of these conflicts are analysed it is found that they have nothing to do with religion, certainly not in any spiritual sense.[3] Religion is exploited for secular ends.

Most of the African states attained independence within the boundaries that had been defined by the colonialist powers related to the method by which they had been acquired. Accordingly, most of them had no natural unity; their populations were frequently very heterogeneous. They have therefore embarked on enterprises of living together that are quite unique. Within them tribalism is the strongest factor in defining relationships, but also the new factor of religion. Somalia alone, its people united in language, ethnic characteristics and religion, formed a natural unity. In this particular instance the colonialist boundaries are not accepted.

Since independence, conflicts have arisen that have been labelled 'religious', not in relation to African natural religion, but to the intrusive religions of Islam and Christianity. It is only since the monotheistic type of religion invaded Africa that religion has become a cause of division and conflict between peoples and individuals. Religion has changed in Africa from being the regulative principle of life to becoming a theology or a law that man could use to forward secular urges.

The Chad, the Sudan, and Eritrea present contiguous territories of separatist conflicts that have been labelled religious. In Chad towards the end of 1960 the recently formed government of François Tombalbaye, labelled 'Christian' for want of another definition, had to face a 'Muslim' revolt in the northern part of its territory, supported by Libya and Sudan, against a 'Christian' threat. The death of Tombalbaye and the military take-over of April 1975 have left the main problem unresolved.

This was the opposite of the conflict that raged in the neighbouring Sudan (independent on 1.1.1956), which has at last reached a happy solution. Here the secessionists were black Nilotic and Negroid tribal peoples living in Sudan's southern territories, still mainly pagan, but among them many Christians who could draw on Christian support far beyond their confines. The revolt of 1955 arose because the Southerners felt they had been betrayed by the British. They had received no firm guarantee against being dominated by the northern Muslims.[4] The newly-independent Sudan government, obsessed by their Arab–Muslim axis, oblivious to any pan-African ideal and indifferent to the aims and troubles of emergent black Africa, had been prosecuting a pro-Islamic policy in its southern territories. In their enthusiasm they confused proselytism with the idea of power under the banner of Islam. Fearing separatist trends they saw Islam and the Arabic language as providing the best basis for the integration of a country ridiculously defined by Anglo-Egyptian history. In black African eyes the Sudan government's image was damaged by its inability to demonstrate, after it had won independence, the possibility of unity between Arab and Negro Africans. Arab pressure in the councils of the O.A.U. served to veil the question under 'a conspiracy of silence'. The state of war continued for some seventeen years, until in February 1972 representatives of the Khartoum government and of the militant Southerners met in Addis Ababa and worked out a peace settlement that would allow the Southerners a greater measure of autonomy.

Many Sudanese Muslims now feel that religion should have no part in politics, both within the Muslim community itself (looking back on the Mahdist–Khatmiyya rivalry) and between the northerners and southerners. In view of the infiltration of secularist tendencies and ideologies, they feel that Christians and Muslims have a common concern for fostering a religious outlook on life, whether labelled Muslim or Christian.

The Solomonid monarchy of Ethiopia, which had been given an imperialist role by Menelik II at the end of the nineteenth century, provides examples of so-called 'religious' conflicts. Eritrea, which had become self-governing, had been brought under the sovereignty of Haile Selassie because part of it was within the original Christian Abyssinia. The inhabitants, who were half-Muslim half-Christian, have for long years been fighting to govern themselves. The conflict, which still continues, must not be seen out of proportion. The same is true of the other conflict that has been taking place in the south-east of Ethiopian territory. Somalia, which became independent in 1960, made an attempt in 1976 to incorporate by force the Somalis in the Ogaden region of Ethiopia. This attempt has so far failed. The Solomonid monarchy is now no more, but the power that governs Ethiopia, though called Marxist, is just as determined to cling to territory as the previous imperialist regime.

Religion in these conflicts is simply a surface veneering over deeply seated ethnic urges. Much of it is related to the period of readjustment to independence. Amicable relations have been restored in the Sudan. Tanzania since independence (1961) has seen its Muslims unite with Christians in electing a Christian president in Julius Nyerere, who has two Muslims as vice-presidents, Rashidi Kawawa and Abeid Karume, who represents the revolutionary government of Zanzibar.[5] At the opposite side of the continent the people of the predominantly Muslim country of Senegal have likewise affirmed their continued support for their Christian leader, Leopold Senghor.

Since independence the Islamic factor has been gaining in influence in certain African states. Among these is Nigeria, where Islam by reason of Nigerian history was seen by both Muslims and Christians as a factor that urged its adherents to dominate, and in the same context of thought Nigerian Muslims saw their Western conquerors as Christian. The attempt of the Ibo of south-eastern Nigeria to break away from the Federation in May 1967 has been presented as a 'religious' conflict. It was in fact the result of a complex series of events which culminated in September 1966, when northern mobs had slaughtered as many as 10,000 Ibos living among them, while a million other Ibos fled back to the already densely populated Iboland. The Ibos feared that northern Muslims were intending to dominate the Federation in their own Islamic interests. Although this was manifestly an ethnic confrontation, religion was seen as a factor, and Colonel Ojukwu and other Ibo leaders did in fact give the conflict a religious tinge, and they received strong support from Christian missionary societies. In the conflict there were attacks on the few mosques and other Islamic centres in Ibo country, and immigrant Muslim settlers were forced to flee. The conflict lasted for two and a half years (July 1967 to January 1970) before the secessionists were forced to surrender and the Nigerian military government declared a general amnesty. But the defeat of the Ibo secessionists meant that Nigeria would remain Muslim-dominated by an illiberal form of Islam.

In the aftermath, with Ibo country under military occupation, there was a considerable amount of peaceful propagation of Islam. The northern Muslims who had fled from Iboland returned and revived the relatively few Muslim institutions that had existed there. Wherever soldiers were stationed mosques were opened. The Jama'at Naṣr al-Islām (Organization for the Defence of Islam), which had its headquarters in Kaduna in the north, launched a propagandist drive in Iboland. It opened branches in southern towns and reopened or founded Muslim schools. It undertook special proselytizing missions, and the secretary of the Jamā'a's central organization, Ibrahim Dasuqi, during his southern visitation of 1973, claimed to have converted over 500 Ibos. However, one gathers that the Ibo Christians are in no way disturbed, their position is strong, and they are prepared to live in peace with the relatively few Ibo Muslims among them.

5. A religious assessment

I have shown how the religion of African Muslims rests upon a double foundation of an African underlayer and an Islamic superstructure; how elements from both layers, though separated in relation to the spiritual principles that lay behind them, were in practice fused or synthetized. Once the legalist structure of Islam had solidified it could no longer incorporate new elements and synthetize them, but a sort of practical dualism operated, a parallelism which allowed Muslims to participate in both the legal system and a spiritual system. This protected the rigid legal core of Islam and enabled Islam as a theology, that is, as a revelation from a sphere outside the Spirit of Man, to retain its unique character. The Spirit that welled from the Spirit within Man himself knew that religion was not only 'revelation' but was also 'mystery'. In traditional Islamic life this recognition of the mystery of the Spirit is seen in the parallel existence of Islamic mysticism and its associated cult of saints outside the legalistic structure.

Thus it came about that the application of the legal structure of Islam was restricted to personal, social, and religious life within limits, while certain African elements were allowed to exist alongside, but the whole in practice was synthetized. The general picture that has emerged from the analysis given in the preceding chapters has been of the great diversity of African Islamic life. Communities absorbing an imported religion, which neither in its initial stages nor in its development as a social and cultural system derived anything from the African religious genius, were shown to be at various stages in its incorporation into African life. In other words, the naturalization of the alien religion was at many stages which correspond to stages in the historical spread of the religion.

But the religious picture at the present time is not simply one of the relationship of Islam and the African underlayer; the influence of Secularism as a religious catalyst has to be taken into account. The mutual action of legal Islam and of secularist institutions has resulted in the elimination of Sufism almost completely from the lives of Asian Arab Muslims. At the same time, a series of elements have brought into life a kind of secular parallelism that has diluted the religious theme. The whole relationship of religion to life is changing. Recently Islamized African adherents can no longer change to the *traditional* type of Islamic community, except where individuals are absorbed into an existing traditional community that delays the onset of change. This means that as religious adherence has been spreading quantitatively, Negro Islam is being modified qualitatively. The fact must be faced that neither Islam nor Christianity can penetrate into the bloodstream of their more recent converts as their natural religion functioned through birth into a community linked by religious ties, in such a way that it surfaces in their outlook and ways of life. These intrusive religions have treated African society as a largely passive 'object' of their missionary activity and have had little concern for the religious African as a 'subject'.

Today in any religious assessment account must be taken of the effect of the Spirit of Secular Man as it is embodied in religionless societies. Put in the simplest terms, men in the Western world *act* as though the Realm of the Spirit does not exist. They act—and consequently believe since action defines belief—that they are not *in* and *of* the Spirit. They do not see the Spirit as 'the Breath of Life'. Western civilization is based on Man's negative understanding of Man himself, and every import into African life carries this negative message.

Today, Islamic countries can in no way avoid pursuing the secularist way, however strenuously they uphold Islam, and even when its political advocates seem most militant. Even European countries still recognize Christianity as having historical significance in the moulding of their country's life and its culture, but Christianity no longer directs and moulds its people's way of life today. In England, to which I have just returned, remnants of the discarded religion survive but merely threads of its spirit. A clerical élite struggle with admirable persistence to maintain traditional ways of worship, but their cathedrals resound with the tramplings of non-worshipping hordes.

This revolution is directing and moulding the lives of all peoples today, but in varying and varied degrees. The newly-independent African states are new creations. Whether their people are predominantly Muslim or Christian, they react strongly against any suggestion that either religion should be proclaimed the state religion. They are secular states in whose outlook religion has no direct role, even in certain North African states that can claim to be officially Muslim. African governments have generally continued the policies followed by the colonialist regimes: they have succeeded in being neutral in relation to the religions of their peoples.

Associated with this are all the moves that are taking place towards the secularization of life: Western-type schools, technical education, industrialized groups, and the growth of urban centres. In modern diversified regimes, when societies are actually in the process of change, the religious outlook of the educated Muslim is bound to fall out of sympathy with many aspects of the traditional Muslim outlook.

The rise to influence of the Arab world, Arab leadership in Third World affairs in particular, must not be taken to indicate any renewal of Islam. The secularizing process is weaning away, or alienating, even severing, religions from their guiding Principle. Islam is weakening while serving Muslims to mark or underline a cultural and historical distinction that distinguishes their societies from those of the Western world.

Islam did not develop any pastoral system; unnecessary under a legalistic system. In practice, the spiritual office was exercised through the Sufi orders and saint-veneration—that 'parallel' aspect of Islamic life known in the Maghrib as 'maraboutism'. This was the means by which the Islam of the Spirit was exercised within men's hearts. But today in the Asian Arab world, the Sufi orders and the saints are neglected as redundant to Arab life. They are no longer of significance to the welfare of the family or the village. When the Palestinian peasants left their homes they left their soul behind them and have now adopted a new 'religion'. This weakening has been reinforced by the stress laid in some regimes on the legalistic tradition. The Saudi Arabian state perpetuates the Wahhabi tradition of a theocracy based on divine law. The Wahhabi tradition decreed that God's Law prohibited the spiritual tradition of Sufism and its practices, to the impoverishment of Muslim spirituality. The desire to interpret 'a purer Islam', as meaning the rigid enforcement of the Sharīʻa, rules out *ijtihād*, interpretation for a new age. They forget that the Sharī'a is itself interpretation.

The relations between the independent African states was not necessarily determined by Islam. Whereas Northern Nigeria by its stress on one-dimensional Islam isolates itself, Guinea opens itself to the future. We may note how Muslim states (Somalia, Sudan, and Guinea, with Tanzania and Zambia) were the strongest supporters of Milton Obote, a Protestant Christian, after he was ousted in January 1971 from the presidency of Uganda by Idi Amin, claiming to be a Muslim. More important, the Ghana–Guinea–Mali Union[6] had shown that other ideals—pan-African but above all *socialist* objectives—were stronger forces than Islam. The parties formed by Sékou Touré of Guinea, Kwame Nkroumah of Ghana, and Modibo Keita were committed to the liberation and unification of Africa. They were committed to programmes of socialist reconstruction and saw socialism as meaning pan-Africanism.

The people of Guinea are predominantly Muslim, but Guinea as a socialist state rejects anything that smells racist. It even rejects the concept of *négritude*, the idealization of the Africans' own heritage. Accordingly, it refused to take part in the Festival of Negro Arts held at Dakar in 1966 and a subsequent similar one held in Lagos. Sékou Touré said[7] that to talk of Africa in terms of colour or of religion was to divide the continent: 'Let us rather have an *African* cultural festival.' He particularly condemned maraboutism, hereditary holiness and leadership, and its charlatanism and exploitation of the masses. Socialism is a more powerful 'religious' force for the people. Islam smacks of reactionism, of religious imperialism: 'We must free ourselves from ourselves, from our old customs and old conceptions of life . . . Self-liberation is synonymous with self-development.'

I have shown elsewhere[8] how the decline in the influence and practice of the Sufi orders has been less marked in what I have distinguished as the 'Hamitic' regions of Africa, in particular the Maghrib and Nilotic Sudan, than in the Asian Arab world. But the whole complex of maraboutism, to use the term popularized by the French for the real religion of the people of the Maghrib, is manifestly declining. Although this mainly derives from the changes that are taking place in people's lives, they have also had against them pressures from Islamic fundamentalism and from movements like the *salafī* and the Ikhwān al-Muslimīn. Changes in social values mark a corresponding decline in the numbers and influence of *zāwiyas*. Restrictions continue to be placed on the leaders, especially when they become involved in political matters.

The eclipse of the Sanusiyya *ṭarīqa*, after its shaikh, Muhammad Idrīs, accepted as legitimate to represent the traditional role of a theocracy uniting the sacred and secular functions in himself as head of the State of Libya, is sufficiently well known. Libya was the first African colonial territory to be given independence (1951), but in September 1969 a group of radical officers inspired by the example of 'Abd an-Nāṣir abolished the monarchy and proclaimed a republic. The leader, Mu'ammar al-Qaddafi was animated more by Islamic fundamentalism than by any radical ideology and saw himself as agent in a back-to-the-Qur'ān revolution. An advocate of Arab unity, he also saw Libya as part of Africa, and quickly dispensed aid to both Maghribi countries (Tunisia and Mauritania) and to black African (Niger and Uganda).

The irrational desire for a purer Islam has evoked a self-consciousness about manifestations in popular practice that might be seen as primitive. In the Sudan, for example, it was decreed in April 1970 that saint-veneration should be prohibited, and all that was associated with it. The communal *dhikr* should be restricted to recitations of Qur'ānic phrases, to the repetition of attributive names of God, and to praisings of the Prophet. Such decrees are not taken seriously by the devotees, but all the same the Sufi orders are declining rapidly in the Sudan, though this must be attributed to changes in the rhythm and patterns of everyday life.

In Afro-Islamic culture, when Islamic law collides with strong family-centred systems it is quite simply ignored. The British regarded it as their duty, as custodians of Northern Nigeria, not merely to regard the pagan Hausa as Muslim because the usurper Fulani rulers were Muslim, but even to enforce Islamic law upon them and genuine Muslims alike against the will of the people. This practice has been continued, and various commissions of jurists have sought ways in which Islamic law can be codified in such a way that it could be applied in an independent state.

Arab states saw the prestige and promotion of Islam as directly related to their aid programmes. While the masses may have seen the rout of the colonial powers as a defeat of Christianity, the leaders were well aware that religion had been rejected by western countries as an instrument of policy; moreover, by their characterization of westerners as atheists they saw their vulnerability, though the more far-sighted saw the distinct possibility of Islam also being swallowed up by indifference.

Muslims realized that the strongest feature of Islam is the Law. In their aid programmes, Egypt, Libya, and Saudi Arabia have had the spread and strengthening of Islam in view. They have been confronted by many problems. The teachers they provided have frequently found it difficult to adapt themselves. They could not speak either English or the local languages. African Muslims even are not prepared to learn spoken Arabic, and only the few are prepared to learn the law-book Arabic their *malams* taught, simply because they regard Arabic as offering no future in a modern African state. The Arab countries have offered scholarships for study in their own countries. They have provided Arabic text-books and support for local *madrasas*; the Saudis for instance have recently taken over the finances of the Arabic Institute at Ibadan.

There are no sectarian divisions in African Islam. What divisions are found among Muslims have been in allegiance to *ṭarīqa* organizations. What heretics are found in Africa, like the Qadiyani Aḥmadīs in West and East Africa (see above p. 80), no longer have the colonial power to defend them. In particular situations, Christians have had to face pressure. In Uganda, where Muslims were still no more than five per cent in 1971, Muslims found an advocate in Idi Amin, and accounts circulate of pressure being used to force Ugandans to join Islam. A Muslim Supreme Council was formed to strengthen the prestige of the religion, but the killing of the Anglican archbishop, Janani Luwum, in February 1978 proved disastrous to Uganda's image in African eyes.

The Saudi Government has helped Nigerians by supplying teachers in Arabic and Islamic subjects. Not only have problems of communication arisen, but also problems of legal interpretation, since the Saudi teachers belonged to the Ḥanafī *madhhab* and the Nigerians were Mālikī. One particular problem that arose was over the Tijani enthusiasm for succeeding ritual *ṣalāt* by a session of invocations of the Prophet, who is thought to be actually present seated on a white cloth in their midst. The Saudis have condemned this practice as a disallowed innovation (*bid'a*).

Islam, seen as a legal code of divine origin, to be obeyed unquestioningly, may be a simple dichotomy of the letter and the spirit. '*Ālims* rule that simple assent is enough. The Wahhābi ruling is that mysticism is alien to the law and ethos of Islam.

Islam as a system of law is itself a secular system, but a God-given reference necessitates belief in God. The letter of the ritual *ṣalāt* may be formal, detached from the spiritual *ṣalāt*. The danger of the weakening of the Sufi spirit is the loss of the spiritual dimensions of the Sharī'a.

African Muslims look to Egypt rather than to Saudi Arabia. They respect Saudi Arabia as the guardian of the holy places, a bulwark of the holy Law, and welcome it as a source of financial help in forwarding Islamic projects, but they look more hopefully to Egypt as an example of a Muslim republican country that has adapted itself to the modern world. They admire it as a model of how an Islamic state can adapt itself and live as an equal partner in a secular world. They see the Sharī'a as an element in the law of the secular state instead of being the subject, the Law itself. The Azhar University, which formerly would not admit *taṣawwuf* within its walls, has had to adopt a parallel secular policy of admitting the new world, diversifying its curriculum and making modifications in its teaching.

Today the forces of fundamentalist Islam are asserting their power against the disruptive and anti-religious forces of Western secularism. The Shī'a revolution in Iran in February 1979 is simply a reassertion of the former primacy of Islam marked by a token rejection of Western influence. But to counter Westernism, Islam has only the method that has served it in the past—the separatist way of parallelism—as, for example, it is asserted in Saudi Arabia. Even then it will be remembered that throughout history the rulers of Islamic states have avoided the strict following of the full reaches of the Sharī'a, particularly 'criminal law'. Its revival in certain states is a new phenomenon. But so contrary is Islamic legal fundamentalism to the global trend of modern life that its revived power to survive is limited and may be quickly overturned by a change of regime.

The power to survive of Islamic fundamentalism must not be exaggerated, for it is clearly contrary to the trend of man's life today, and it must not be taken as a guide to future trends. There seems little possibility of traditional Islam meeting the spiritual needs of African Muslims moving into a new era. Only a reformed Islam, that is, the original revealed Islam, not legalist (one-dimensional), but reinterpreted and informed by a Sufism related to the life and spiritual needs of present-day man (that is, two-dimensional man), could counter a one-dimensional secular trend of life and its secular ideologies.

Appendix A

Parallel comparisons between Egyptian and Maghribi life

When Africans have asked me why I restricted this study to Africa south of the Sahara it was obvious that I was not making a crude distinction between 'white' and 'black' Africans as such, since I had already made such a distinction between Hamite and Negro, and the Africans of the Maghrib and Egypt are also embraced within the range of Hamites. I had been concerned with marking the distinctions characterizing the different ways in which Hamites and Negroes had assimilated or adapted themselves to Islamic usages.

The first two cultural regions into which I had divided Africa, from the point of view of the influence of Islam, Egypt and the Maghrib,[1] are those into which Islam spread from an early date and where it became so deeply implanted as to influence all subsequent history and every aspect of life. The two regions are, however, clearly differentiated. This derives from the fact that their basic pre-Islamic cultures were quite different, and each followed distinctive trends of historical development.

Islam spread in the Hamitic regions of Africa where Christianity had prepared the way. Monophysite Christianity had already become an Egyptian national trait when Islam made its appearance within the mantles of Arab warriors, and as such a national religion has never been undermined by the movement of Christians into the Islamic fold. In the Maghrib the picture was quite different. Latin Christianity became the surface religion of the people of the urban and settlement centres. It had also spread into the Berber highlands rapidly between A.D. 250 and 280, where it became a local Berber national trait in opposition to Latin Christianity, and this is where the Donatist heresy thrived.

The destinies of all these peoples changed when Muslim Arabs gained political control of the Nile Valley and the Maghrib. The Christians of Africa were cut off not only from the rest of the Christian world, but also from the independent Christian states of Nilotic Maqurra and 'Alwa and the mountainous Christian outpost of Abyssinia.

Egypt formed a world in itself, and though brought out of cultural isolation and subject to profound cultural change through adherence to monotheistic religions, it had always displayed unique political and social characteristics. Even today it is a country of two religious cultures: Coptic Christianity and normative Sunni Islam. Egypt was fully within the world of Islam from the early days of its expansion, whence I wrote above (p. 2) that its religion 'was Islamically undifferentiated, belonging wholly to Arab Islam.' All the same the underlying factors have meant that Egyptian Islamic life is distinguished from that of Arabs in Asia. The specifically Egyptian features are seen especially in the practices and institutions of the land-workers, the *fallāḥīn*.

The Maghrib formed another ethnic, historical, and cultural entity. Berbers have given it a definite individuality. Basically, it belongs to the Mediterranean complex, but now through the adherence of the majority of its inhabitants to Islam and their adoption of Arabic, it is seen as forming the western wing of the Arab world, balanced between its Asian and African sectors. The majority of its Berber inhabitants have Arabized, though significant minorities, especially in Morocco, have preserved their language. The levels of life are more varied than in Egypt. This derives from the different levels of subsistence economy, especially the continuance of nomadic life, and Berber resistance to the disruption of their traditional mode of life, both reacting against a legalist defined religion. Their Islam embraces a distinctive religious outlook embraced in the term 'maraboutism', a Berber reaction that also penetrated deeply into the Arab tribes and into the cities too. The nomads, Berbers and Arab migrants alike, maintain customary life with all its sanctions. The distinctive Berber interpretation of Islam was carried across the Sahara into parts of Western Sudan.

The following table on pages 145 and 146 form a representative selection of contrasting distinctions.

Appendix A

A. Pre-Islamic Factors

MAGHRIB

Basic Berber culture, peasant and nomadic

Diversity of material life: cultivators of plains and mountain dwellers, nomad and oasis-dwellers, towns-people

Mediterranean influences, Carthaginian and Roman

Christian influence restricted

EGYPT

Riverain culture (Kushite-negroid) based on predictability of Nile flood

Urban and peasant life alike unified by Nile Valley

Highly developed civilization

Relatively minor role of nomads (Beja)

Religious change to Christianity Monophysitism and Separatism

Strong Greek influences

Flowering of native Christian culture: Coptic ritual, art and literature

B. Historical Factors

After advent of Islam, urban civilization underwent a reorientation with founding of urban centres like Qairawan and Fez

Regional and occupational culture

As urban culture becomes Islamic, Christianity disappears

Early political sectarianism, Kharijite and Shīʿī movements

Political disunity, isolationism

Little creative role in Islamic culture, except in architecture and exact sciences

Contacts with Asia marginal

Political disunity

Late French influence marking another distinction

Urban culture thoroughly Islamic, indistinguishable in essentials from Asian Arab world

Village culture basically unchanged

Parallelism, e.g. Islamic calendar alongside Nilotic calendar

Egyptian Christianity: flourishing, Christian festivals marking life phases

Egyptian Islamic development latish, though arts and sciences flourished, especially under Fatimids

Political unity under alien rulers

Shīʿī sectarianism unable to take root among peasantry

Contacts with Asia continuous

Political unity under Ottoman regime

European influence from early 19th century

C. Cultural and Religious Factors

Language: distinctive dialects of Arabic and retarded script-marking lines of demarkation from main Arab World

Persistence of Berber as spoken language

Mālikī in *madhhab*, isolated Ibāḍī groups. Customary law ruling all communities

Distinctive Maghribi maraboutism

Hereditary Sufi orders

Distinctive material characteristics: dress, *burnus* type of hooded cloak

Architectural styles: contrast Kutubiyya minaret with minarets in Egypt. Berber Substratum: age-old customs and associated beliefs

Coptic disappears except as a liturgical language

Coptic substratum

Egyptian Arabic dialects, Eastern Arabic script

Shaf'i in *madhhab*, not displaced by Ottoman introduction of Ḥanafi as official code

Ṭariqas of Eastern type

Saint veneration: Aḥmad al-Badawī of Tanta: characteristic great saint

Uniform peasant dress (*jallabiyya*)

Cult of the Dead (*qarāfas*)

Notes

Chapter 1

1 Apart from Morocco, the proportion of Berber-speakers is 23 per cent in Tripolitania, 1 per cent in Tunisia, and in Algeria in the provinces of Constantine 27 per cent, of Algiers 34 per cent, and of Oran 1 per cent.

2 The ancient south-Saharan state is written as Gana in this book to distinguish it from the modern Ghana, the former colonial dependency of the Gold Coast situated in the forest zone.

The adoption of this name upon achieving independence in 1957 to provide a mythological tradition for the new state derives from speculations that the Akan stock to which the Ashanti and Fanti belong was connected with the ancient kingdom of Gana or Awkat.

3 Al-Bakri, *Description de l'Afrique Septentrionale*, ed. de Slane, 2nd ed, 1911, p. 178.

4 Takrūr is the general term by which western Sudan was known to the Arab world since the first and most frequent pilgrims had been Takrūrīs or Tokolor.

5 See 'Umar's own account of his training under Muḥammad Ghālī in his *Rimāḥ Ḥizb ar-Raḥīm* on the margin of 'Alī Ḥarāzim, *Jawāhir al-Ma'ānī*, Cairo 1929, pp. 190–4.

6 Ya'qūbī, *Kitāb al-Buldān*, p. 345.

7 Al-Bakrī, *op. cit.*, p. 11.

8 Although Maqrīzī gives Dunama Dabalemi (*c.* 1210–50) as 'the first of their chiefs to adopt Islam' (see J. S. Trimingham, *Islam in West Africa*, p. 115), it is clear that Islam had been spreading since the 11th century and Ibn Sa'īd's account (1240) shows it to be well established among the ruling class.

9 Ibn Khaldūn, i. 428; tr. ii. 346–7; but the title probably relates to Ibn Khaldūn's time.

10 Pulo shaikhs from the west are referred to in the Kano Chronicle as visiting Kano and Bornu around 1452–62, presumably on pilgrimage. Formerly, pilgrims had taken the Saharan and North African route, but it seems that from 1400, after the establishment of Islam in the Nilotic state of Maqurra (around 1317), parties of pilgrims began to take the trans-Sudan route to Red Sea ports.

11 Muḥammad Belo, *Infāq al-Maisūr*, p. 10.

12 In Futa Toro the Tokolor were strong Muslims and the *jihād* was directed against pagan rulers, and did not result in the imposition of a foreign dynasty. But it should be pointed out that even in the

theocratic states there was a difference between the theoretical attitude towards *kāfirūn* (pagan Muslims) and *mushrikūn* (polytheists) and the actual policy of the ruling authority. Even in Masina complete religious uniformity was not achieved, except among the Fulbe. In Futa Jalon no such task was attempted, except so far as it remained the ideal policy to be achieved some day, but the zeal of the reformer became lukewarm in his successors.

13 An outstanding analysis of the functioning of a Fulani-Hausa state is given in M. G. Smith's *Government in Zazzau: 1800–1950*, 1960.

14 Nothing is known about the subsequent history of 'Alwa, and although Arab writers (in particular Ibn Salīm al-Aswānī and Ibn Ḥawqal, both writing about the same time) give some account of 'Alwa during the time of its prosperity, accounts practically cease after the state of Maqurra came to an end (1317) and the traditional material on the rise of the Funj and 'Abdallāb and the fall of Soba is unreliable. 'Alwa may have disintegrated even by the time of the embassy of Ador, *makk* of al-Abwāb, to Qalawūn in 685/1286; cf. anonymous life of Qalawūn, Bibl. Nat. Paris, Arab. Suppl. 810 (Cat. 1704), fol. 292–3, which lists many small makships but does not mention Soba or 'Alwa.

15 On this question see two articles by P. M. Holt, 'A Sudanese historical legend: the Funj Conquest of Sūba', *B.S.A.O.S.*, xxiii (1960), 1–12; *ibid.* 'Funj Origins: a Critique and New Evidence', *J. Afr. Hist.*, iv (1963), 39–55.

16 Al-'Umarī, *Masālik al-Abṣār*, tr. Gaudefroy-Demombynes, 1927, pp. 48–9.

17 Scrolls in Coptic and Arabic recently discovered at Ibrīm record the consecration of a bishop of Ibrīm and Faras in Cairo in 1372; *Illus. London News*, 11 July 1964, pp. 50–3.

18 See *Oriente Moderno*, xviii (1938), 56.

19 *Ṭabaqāt* of Wad Ḍaifallāh, ed. Mandīl, pp. 4, 155.

20 The Bani Shangul region of western Ethiopia between the Blue Nile and the Sudan border, occupied by various Negro tribes known collectively as Shanqela among whom there has been some diffusion of Islam, we do not regard as constituting a fifth region since it is more associable culturally and Islamically with the Sudan whence Islam came.

21 According to Mas'ūdī (*Murūj*, iii. 5–6) the Zanj, a type of Kushite (he classes them among *Aḥābish*), spread southwards along the coast, 'extending their settlements (*masākin*) up to Sofāla'.

22 If Unqūja is the island of Zanzibar, then Islam had gained most of the inhabitants, and Yāqūt (iv. 366) refers to the people of Tumbatu Is. as Muslim.

Chapter 2

1 I have treated the history of Islam in this way in a chapter of *Islam in Africa*, edited by J. Kritzeck and W. Lewis, Van Nostrand Reinhold, 1969.

2 The spread of Islam during the colonial phase will be considered in the last chapter.

3 But primarily affecting towns like the older trading settlements of Ujiji on Lake Tanganyika and Tabora on the trade route there. Thus R. G. Abrahams writes of Kahama township (pop. 1497) of western province of Tanzania: 'Out of 150 people on whom material was available 116 claimed to be Muslims or roughly 71 per cent. This large number of people sharing the same religion also seems to me to be a strong co-ordinating factor and once more in contrast to the surrounding country where if any outside religion is practised it is Christianity'; *Social Change in Modern Africa*, ed. A. Southall, 1961, p. 249.

4 We may mention the Sanhāja responding to the driving zealotism of Ibn Yāsīn, Fulbe rallying to the call of 'Uthmān dan Fodio with its promise of booty, or the relationship of the Khalīfa of the East Sudan Mahdī and Arab cattle nomads. Nomads in wars of religion proved an unstable element, tending to disperse after a successful raid with their looted animals.

5 The role of the Sufi orders in the spread of Islam in West and Central Sudan has been consistently overrated. Popular Sufism was important in Mauritania, Nilotic Sudan and north-east Africa, but elsewhere the role of the clergy is what counts. The clergy certainly professed an order, but the form of the traditional orders with their hierarchized system and elaborate ritual, which might have been expected to appeal to Sudanese Negroes by offering them a substitute for their mystery cult societies, was not part of the equipment of West Sudan clergy.

6 People with political systems based on age sets, such as the Galla *gada* system, are resistant to Islam as long as they maintain their traditional mode of life. Galla changed when they changed their environment, and in recent times when peculiar conditions were involved; see P. T. W. Baxter, 'Acceptance and rejection of Islam among the Boran of the Northern Frontier District of Kenya', in *Islam in Tropical Africa*, ed. I. M. Lewis, 1966, pp. 233–52. Other Kushite nomads of north-east Africa did not have this system and all adopted Islam without difficulty.

7 Except among the Bantu of East Africa and similar societies. This seems due to the following factors deriving from the nature of Bantu society which did not obtain in general in the Sudan belt: (*a*) Islam spread as an individual religious allegiance and ancestral conciliation was not displaced; and (*b*) Islam did not penetrate until

the second half of the nineteenth century and therefore did not become established, for there were no truly indigenous clergy.

8 'Dans tel village bozo des environs de Ségou, où se dressent quatre minarets, où le culte est régulièrement célébré, on peut voir au bord de l'eau la pierre du Yégou, à laquelle sont présentés les circoncis, le bosquet de la retrait, les lieux des sacrifices, les masques de la société des adolescents;' M. Griaule, 'Les religions noires', *L'Encyclopédie coloniale: A.O.F.*, i. 141.

9 The militant nineteenth-century conquerors destroyed the old ruling lines and substituted Islam as the basis for ruling power, but those indigenous chiefs who survived in Northern Nigeria and who adopted Islam after the British occupation retained the old ceremonies and symbols as the real basis of authority alongside Islamic ceremonies of turbaning and Friday prayer.

10 Women and prayer tend to be related to attendance at Qur'ānic schools; see below p. 130, 11. Sudan-belt Muslims do not allow women to enter mosques, but frequently provide an adjoining enclosure for their devotions.

Chapter 3

1 The creator-god has no definite relation to the reality of African life. African life in its traditional form is defined by ritual and little or no ritual connects man and the sky-god. Ritual is concerned primarily with the interdependence of clan members (ancestor cult), or of villagers (nature cults), or of age grades, or initiates in a mystery cult, with the various spirit realms; but the sky-god has no power or functions, and if so is It the source of power at all? If God has Its being in some realm of the spirit distinct from and external to the processes and relationships of men then, like God in the Western world, It is non-existent and scarcely worthy of consideration as a vital aspect of African religion.

2 See below p. 76. Both Aḥmad at-Tijānī and Aḥmad ibn Idrīs stressed that the aim of the *dhikr* was union with the spirit of the Prophet, rather than union with God, thus altering the basis of the mystical life. Consequently they called their Way, *aṭ-ṭarīqat al-Muḥammadiyya* or *al-Aḥmadiyya*, the latter term referring, not to their personal names, but that of the Prophet.

3 After the Ottoman conquest of Egypt in 1517 the Ḥanafī school of that empire became the official code. Similarly, it was introduced into the Nilotic Sudan after the Turko-Egyptian conquest of 1820 but the people continued to follow the Mālikī code. Indian orthodox Muslims in East Africa are Ḥanafī.

4 The Shāfi'ī code was first introduced by an Egyptian, Muḥammad b. 'Alī b. Qadam, early in the Funj regime and the notice on him in

the *Ṭabaqāt* of Wad Ḍaif Allāh (ed. Ibrāhīm Ṣidaiq, 1930, p. 169) gives a list of his pupils.

5 The mosque throughout the whole Sudan belt from the Atlantic to the Red Sea is not primarily a building but an open space where a congregation can gather for ritual prayer, for a *masjid* is simply 'a place for prostration'. The Prophet himself conducted the prayer in the courtyard of his house. The mosque square in Omdurman where the Mahdī and his Khalīfa gathered their thousands is a typical Sudanese mosque. This was designed to embrace the whole male population, but for the ordinary prayers every community has its modest mosque. In villages, town sections and nomad encampments a mosque is a small plot generally delineated by stones, branches, or a low mud wall. In the northern part of Nilotic Sudan and parts of the western Sahil mosques are generally buildings of mud. All towns of the Sudan belt had formerly mud mosques in a typical Sudanese style, but these are now being gradually replaced by concrete structures. These mud mosques served to protect the regulars from the sun, but they were generally small, even the west and central Sudan-type of large mosques did not hold many owing to the thickness of the interior pillars. But there are all kinds of other structures based on local techniques, from the simple *rākūba* (a square-shaped shelter of millet stalks) to the round reed hut, sometimes of great size, of the Fulbe in western Guinea. Invariably, whatever the size, the Friday prayer is held in the open space always left before the mosque. East Africa is the exception. There mosque buildings proliferate for it is unthinkable to pray without a roof over the head and the smallest group has generally a wattle and daub building which on the coast is indistinguishable from the houses of the people.

6 Early European travellers noticed these wandering clerics. Jobson writes of them around the River Gambia, 'carrying an outward burthen of religious blessings' (that is, amulets). 'One chief reason to encourage their travell, we have learned, which is, that they have free recourse through all places, so that howsoever the Kings and Countries are at warres, and up in armes, the one against the other, yet still the Mary-bucke is a priviledged person, and many follow his trade, or course of travelling, without any let or interruption of either side;' R. Jobson, *The Golden Trade*, London, 1623, p. 64. Mary-bucke is presumably Mande *mori-ba*, 'cleric'.

7 Trimingham, *Islam in the Sudan*, p. 118.

8 Trimingham, *Islam in West Africa*, p. 160.

9 Certain clans specialized in teaching and centres like Walāta, Tijikja, Tishīt and Wadān acquired a reputation for learning. All this has now changed through both human and physical changes. The once famous Shinqīt in Mauritanian Adrar (founded 1262) has been just

about swallowed up in the *erg* of Warān. However, in the Sahil, clerical clans are still active in teaching.

10 *Fuqahā'*, plural of *faqīh*, is not in fact used in the spoken language, but *fuqarā'*, plural of *faqīr* is used instead; see J. S. Trimingham, *Islam in the Sudan*, p. 140, *n.* 2.

11 Women's obligatory duties are limited to the recitation of the *shahāda* and, if possible, the *ḥajj*, which the Prophet said is the equivalent for women of the *jihād*. They are not compelled to pray in the mosque or at the *muṣallā* on the two *'īds*, or to fast or pay *zakāt*.

12 Al-'Umarī (*op. cit.* p. 53) records its institution in the capital of Mali by Mansa Mūsā (1312–37) and Ibn Baṭṭūṭa describes the *'īd* prayer and ruler ceremonial as he saw it in Mali in 1352.

13 The conditions governing *ṣalāt al-jum'a* make this duty impossible in the countryside so most people could not observe it unless near a town.

14 Apart from coastal town states, Zanzibar was the only Muslim state, and being officially Ibāḍī before the revolution of 1964 it was peculiar in not having an official Friday-prayer *khuṭba*.

15 See Qur'ānic verses mentioning *tazakka* as purification with the sense of 'to be a Muslim' (92/18, 87/14, 53/34, 79/10, 80/3). *Ṣadaqa* also had the same ethical significance, 'Take of their wealth a *ṣadaqa* which purifies them and renders them unblemished' (ix. 104).

16 In earlier states taxation might sometimes be called *zakāt*. In the Funj state of Sennar on the Blue Nile tribal and *ṭarīqa* leaders competed for receiving *zakāt* and this led to friction between them.

17 According to tradition the Prophet prescribed *zakāt al-fiṭr* in A.D. 624 when he abolished the 'Ashūrā fast and substituted that of Ramaḍān.

18 In Nilotic Sudan this is called *karāma* if an animal is sacrificed.

19 West Sudan came to be known as *Bilād at-Takrūr* in consequence of Senegalese Takrūrīs (Tokolor) being the earliest and most persistent pilgrims.

20 Many were accompanied by large bodies of slaves for sale to cover their expenses, for not all had access to the gold of the Mali kings. For example, Maqrīzī writes that 'In 752 (1351–2) at the moment when the caravan was about to depart for Mecca arrived pilgrims from Takrūr who brought with them a number of slaves, and who had a king at their head.'

21 The local authorities of Abéché (Chad) estimate that 80,000 pilgrims pass through each year; A. le Rouvreur, *Sahéliens et Sahariens du Tchad*, 1962, p. 367.

22 See *Ṭabaqāt* of Wad Ḍaifallāh, ed. Mandil, p. 31: account of al-Muḍawwī.

23 Those who read Sufi treatises knew about the spiritual *jihād*. Even

al-Ḥājj 'Umar, the most ruthless of the *jihād* leaders, in his Sufi treatise, contrasted the warfare of the soul (*jihād an-nafs*) and warfare against unbelievers (*jihād al-kuffār*). His book was written in 1845 long before he served his apprenticeship in the *jihād* of the sword under Muḥammad Belo in Hausaland, but he confesses even then that the spiritual *jihād* is only for an élite; *Rimāḥ Ḥizb ar-Raḥīm*, Cairo 1348/1929, ii. 218. A notable point in the career of Aḥmad Bamba occurred in 1907 when he exchanged the aim of his life mission from opposition to the French and recommended the spiritual *jihād* to his followers.

24 The solar calendar of the Swahili east coast is unusual in that it is of Persian origin; New Year's Day is called *Naorozi* (Persian *Nawrūz*) and in Swahili *Siku ya Mwaka*, 'Day of the Year'. However, the ritual that has cohered to this day is Bantu.

25 Precisely the same thing happened when the Prophet, at the time of his Pilgrimage of Farewell, instituted a year of twelve lunar months for the *ḥajj* and other religious dates. This destroyed the former ritual cycle. The Qur'ān in *sūra* ix. 36–7 clearly links the abolition of the intercalary month (*nasī'*) with the attack on polytheism.

26 It was observed in Timbuktu under the Askiya regime. Maḥmūd al-Kāti mentions a recital of the *'Ishrīniyyāt* and the *Takhmīs* of Ibn Muhīb (*Fattāsh*, pp. 124/226). The rule of the pashas increased its popularity; see the account of the celebration in 1733 (*Tadhkirat an-Nisyān*, pp. 153/247).

27 *Mawālid*, sing. *mawlid*, are panegyrics in verse and rhymed prose in honour of the birth and life of the Prophet. Their recitation is not confined to this festival, but forms part of the regular recitals of the religious orders. The most popular *mawlid* among Qādirīs (mainly those in Nilotic Sudan, Egypt and East Africa) is that of al-Barzanjī. On the East coast it is taught in Qur'ān schools and its recital plays a great role in coastal life. Some orders have their own *mawlids*. The Mirghaniyya recite one composed by their founder, Muḥammad 'Uthmān al-Mirghanī. A description of an evening's recital is given in Trimingham, *Islam in the Sudan*, pp. 215–17.

28 Popular works include that of ad-Dardīr (d. 1786) and Najm ad-dīn al-Ghaiṭī (d. 1573), whilst the Mirghaniyya has its own, composed by the founder.

29 We distinguish morality from ethics (*'ilm al-akhlāq*) which, in Islam as elsewhere, is a theoretical pursuit of the philosopher and is one of the Islamic sciences which did not penetrate into Africa.

30 On the Day of Judgment each person will be held responsible for his deeds, 'The fate of every man have we bound around his neck . . ., neither shall any laden soul be charged with the burden of another'; *sūra* xvii. 13, 15; vi. 34.

31 In Nilotic Sudan the peril is called *mushāhara*, derived from *shahr*, 'month', i.e. moon. On these occasions (seventh month of pregnancy, at circumcision and marriage) the *jirtiq* is assumed at a special investiture. The *jirtiq* consists of a red silken cord on which are threaded green or blue bead(s), the vertebra of a fish and a tassel suspended from a bracelet. A *karāma* or almsgiving generally accompanies its assumption. Such protective rites are known as *sibr*.

32 A custom which seems to be peculiar to Swahili is the performance of the '*aqīqa* over a dead infant; see Trimingham, *Islam in East Africa*, pp. 127–8.

33 See J. Boulnois and B. Hama, *Empire de Gao*, 1954, pp. 81–2. Similarly with many other peoples. Among Wodabe (nomadic Fulbe) in Bornu, 'a child is not regarded as a person until it has been named; a child in its first week is called "it", and there is no distinction between a stillborn child and one which died before being named'; D. J. Stenning, *Savannah Nomads*, 1959, p. 118.

34 Circumcision has social elements if performed at or near the age of puberty, thereby introducing the newly circumcised into the grade of adults when he is expected to pray and fast. In fact, these Islamic duties are not closely tied to circumcision for African Muslims circumcize at various ages, some on the seventh or fortieth day after birth and others even after puberty.

35 See H. Cory, 'Jando', *J. R. Anthrop. Inst.*, lxxvii. (1947), 159–68; lxxviii. (1948), 81–94. For participation in *jando* as an aid to Islamization see Trimingham, *Islam in East Africa*, p. 132 f. This is an individual initiation in spite of its group features and communal character.

36 See H. Minor, *The Primitive City of Timbuktu*, 1953, p. 159.

37 This fear of the 'eye' may be regarded as belonging to Arab and Hamitic Islam, but not in the same sense to Negro Islam, though they have their own equivalent dangers to guard against.

38 *Lailat al-ḥinnā' al-kabīra*, a feature of Arab-Hamitic marriage ceremonial from Morocco to Nilotic Sudan, has been adopted by Songhay and Hausa.

39 The word *walīma* has been adopted by many peoples for the feasts involving sacrificial *ṣadaqa* at naming, marriage and upon completion of a *khatma* of the Qur'ān.

40 In Egypt the popular belief is that the departed soul returns to the tomb each Friday and can be communicated with (*talqīn*) by grasping the *shāhid* ('witness' stone) and pronouncing the *salām* 'on him'.

41 In Negro Islam the most effective manifestation of such a charismatic leader was in Aḥmad Bamba and his Murīdiyya *ṭarīqa* in Senegal. Pilgrimage to the tombs of the founder and his successors at Toube (Baol) is a feature, and on his festival a vast concourse gathers. Yet it is not the traditional saint cult. Similarly with the

Ḥāfiẓī Tijānīs (also mainly Wolof) who visit the tombs of Mālik Si and other leaders at Tivawan in Cayor.

42 See above pp. 9–10.

43 See above pp. 24–25.

44 Belo, *Infāq al-maisūr*, ed. C. E. J. Whitting, 1951, p. 185. 'Uthmān regarded himself at one time as the forerunner at least, since he sent Belo in 1805 to proclaim to the men of Kano 'the good news about the approaching advent of the Mahdī'; *ibid.* p. 105.

45 One Jibrīla Geni, a Pulo of Katagum, declared himself mahdī in Gombe in 1888, defeated and expelled its emir and was able to defy the Fulani rulers until defeated by the British in 1902 (see S. J. Hogben, *Muhammadan Emirates of Nigeria*, 1930, pp. 175–6, 181–2). Between 1900 and 1906 a dozen mahdīs appeared in Sokoto province alone. In 1907 mahdīs appeared at Bima in Bauche and Marāwa in Adamawa, then under German control (*R.M.M.* iv. (1908), 144, 443). P. F. Lacroix ('L'Islam Peul de l'Adamawa', *Islam in Tropical Africa*, ed. I. M. Lewis, 1966, p. 405) says that there were six manifestations from Yola division to Cameroon: the first being *modibbo* 'Abdullāhi in Yola (*c.* 1890) and the last Aḥmadu of Tourningal (Ngaoundere) in 1952.

46 See above pp. 25–26.

47 Since the coming of the Nabī 'Īsā was awaited with expectancy, 'Īsās and in some cases *mahdīs*, appeared with persistent regularity even in the Khalīfa's time and especially during the early days of condominium rule. A list of such risings is given in H. A. MacMichael's *The Anglo-Egyptian Sudan*, 1934, pp. 98–9, 176–9.

48 The *jihād* of Muḥammad 'Abdullah Hasan of Somalia (1899–1920), prosecuted within the context of the Sālihiyya *tarīqa*, was not a true millennialistic movement for he never claimed to be the Mahdī, but must be seen within the general complex of African Muslim reaction to European encroachment; see I. M. Lewis, *The Modern History of Somaliland*, 1965, chap. 4.

49 In Nilotic Sudan the fekis claim to have special relations with *jinn*. Abdullah al-Tayib writes, *Sudan Notes and Records* xlv. (1964) 14: 'Very often khalwa fekkis would not touch serious mental cases because (according to them) they have covenants with the *jann* not to interfere with their victims.'

50 The cult of the dead has been strong in the Arab world and above all in Egypt where, of course, it goes back to Pharaonic times. The Egyptian *qarāfa*, city of the dead, is visited by women on Fridays and festival days 'to hear fekis recite the Qur'ān and to offer alms of unleavened bread, sesame cake and fruits for the soul of the deceased'; Ahmad Amīn, *Qāmūs al-'ādāt wa 't-taqālīd*, Cairo 1953, p. 322.

51 See above pp. 63, 73.

52 This refers to Muslims inland, not the long-Islamized Swahili who, however, have special commemorations, the most important taking place during the first nine days of Dhū 'l-ḥijja preceding *'īd al-aḍḥā* (on the tenth) when rice offerings are made in honour of the dead.

53 It will be pointed out that these cults survive and wield power in areas of recent Islamization, but the whole force of organized Islam is against them.

54 Whence Islam's crusade against 'idolatry' whilst leaving other forms of animism intact. Similarly with the saint cult in much of Hamitic Muslim Africa. The fact that the saint cult corresponds roughly to spirit-worship accounts at least in part for its absence in Negro Africa, along with other manifestations of *baraka*. The Mande *dasiri* are not ancestors, but symbols of the community; for example, the founder of a village becomes a 'power' like a saint, only instead of a tomb it has a concrete temporary abode, like conical earthen erections or a natural object such as a tree or a cave. At these material points worship of the surrealist spirit can be localized and concentrated.

55 Whether the wearing of an amulet supplied by a Muslim has the significance frequently assigned to it in opening the first breach by which Islam penetrates may be questioned. Nowadays, in areas of mixed religious allegiance like Sierra Leone one finds people wearing pagan, Muslim and Christian amulets regardless of the religion professed.

Chapter 4

1 We have mentioned previously (pp. 43, 82) the rapid decline and then elimination of the ancestor cult.

2 See above pp. 41–43.

3 It will be interesting to see in what ways they are changed by their transplantation to a different environment in consequence of the flooding of their land through the building of the High Dam.

4 See Ibn Khaldūn, *'Ibar*, Bulaq, A.H. 1284, v. 429. Stress has been laid on the fact that in eastern Sudan a migrant Arab group marrying into a ruling Hamitic matrilineage has, through their principle of succession, secured dynastic rights to chieftaincy. In fact, this frequently resulted in the absorption of the Arabs. The Arab's son by a Beja mother was brought up as a Beja not as an Arab and only started a new lineage according to Arab reckoning. Mas'ūdī (*Murūj*, iii. 33) reports that in consequence of these marriage alliances the Beja became stronger. However, this process did lead to dynastic Islamization, especially in central Sudan. Legend ascribes the foundation of the Kaira dynasty of Darfur to the arrival of a Muslim who married the daughter of the Tunjur ruler, and their son, Sulaimān Solong, succeeded to the headship of the state. Succession

then changed to the paternal line. Similarly with Tegali in the Nuba Mountains; on which see R. A. Stevenson in *Islam in Tropical Africa*, ed. I. M. Lewis, 1966, p. 214.

5 The eastern Beja resisted this process, the more exposed gradually succumbing, but those of the Red Sea Hills blocking any such process of change to this day, maintaining their language, to-Bedawie, tribal organization (though adopting an Arab lineage system), and customs. Obviously no Arab tribes who crossed the Red Sea stayed in 'Afar or Somali country otherwise they would have been Arabized, but Somali absorbed individual Arabs who provided them with new tribal beginnings and whose name they adopted as the tribal eponym. Similarly Negro peoples were not Arabized (though Arab tribes were Nigritized) and the linguistic influence of the Baqqāra living in central Sudan belt from Kordofan and Darfur to Lake Chad, has not been strong. Arabic is frequently widely understood among Negro tribes in Baqqāra areas, but does not seem likely to substitute itself for their languages.

6 The expression *humanité moléculaire* is used by R. Capot-Rey in *Le Sahara française*, 1953, p. 162.

7 The cultivable parts of the Saharan intermediary zone were formerly inhabited by Negroes, but they were subjected or pushed south through the expansion of nomadic tribes. Blacks who still inhabit the Sahara belong to the Moorish cultural zone. A quarter of the Kunta, a Moorish religious tribe, a third of the Tuareg of Air and a half of the Ullimmeden Tuareg is composed of slaves. The black nomads of central Sahara, the Teda or Tubu, are not hierarchized in this way, and although the strongest Islamic influence among them has been the Sanūsiyya they belong rather to the central Sudan religious sphere.

8 In notes supplementing Mary Smith's transmission of the fascinating autobiography of a Hausa woman, *Baba of Karo*, 1954, p. 281.

9 K. M. Barbour, *The Republic of the Sudan*, 1961, p. 102.

10 The old type of state still exists even when all the people are Muslim. The sultan of Waday maintains the traditional regal ancestor-propitiation ritual. Each year he goes just before the rains to the ruined former capital of Wara, where are the tombs of his ancestors, to sacrifice camels and cattle in their honour, to pray for the prosperity of the country, and ask for rain. The fekis take part in the ceremony with prayer and Qur'ān recitation. See Mme M.-J. Tubiana. *Survivances préislamiques en pays Zaghawa*, 1964, pp. 176–178.

11 *Qāḍīs* were found in traditional Sudan states which maintained Maghribi trading relations as a feature of their allegiance to Islam, but they remained an extraneous element, and in Mali probably only dealt with cases involving foreign traders. A *qāḍī* system was set up

in the Arabized-Hamitic state of Wad 'Ajīb tributary to Sennar in the time of *Makk* Dakīn (1570–87; see *Tabaqāt* of Wad Ḍaifallāh, ed. Ṣidaiq, pp. 90, 114), but customary and executive law ruled until the administration of the Mahdī. Similarly the 'Shirazi' communities of Zanzibar and Pemba had no *qāḍīs*. The Ibādī rulers set them up in Zanzibar town and after the system was introduced into the countryside by Sultan Barghash (1870–88) greater modifications in customary law took place.

12 I. M. Lewis, *Marriage and the Family in Northern Somaliland*, 1962, p. 37.

13 In assimilability Arabs contrast with Egyptians. The Egyptians have always had open communications with Negro and Kushitic Africa. But the Egyptians were riverain cultivators rooted tenaciously in their homeland. They were never colonizers except in Nubia where the remains of an Egyptian-inspired civilization are dotted along the Nile banks. On the contrary, they were colonized. But of the various rulers of Egypt none had deep effect upon the *fallāḥīn* except the Arab ruling class whose religion changed their whole religious and cultural outlook. As for Arab nomads, the Egyptian deserts are so arid and inhospitable that they soon passed on to more favourable lands.

Chapter 5

1 One illustration may be given. Everywhere is found the decline and shortening of the initiation 'bush' which formerly might last for several months. J. Rouche writes, 'To Bambara . . . whose traditional beliefs are very strongly impregnated with metaphysical conceptions, Islam comes as a simplifying religion whose rites replace animist rites that have become too complicated to carry out since the European occupation'; J. Rouche, 'Migrations au Ghana', *J. Soc. Africanistes*, xxvi (1956), 168.

2 For 1000 years the Buduma islanders of Lake Chad (numbering 25,000) remained untouched by the Islam of Kanem and Bornu. 'In 1910', writes A. le Rouvreur, 'only some rare notables had embraced Islam. Now all the Buduma without exception are Muslims. The religion was brought by Kanembu and Kanuri fakis who took Buduma wives and settled among them' (Le Rouvreur, *Sahéliens et Sahariens du Tchad*, 1962, p 236).

3 Notice the decline in animists in Ibadan:

	Muslim	*Christian*	*African Religion*
1913	35%	1%	64%
1952	60%	32%	8%

4 The population of Bamako, now capital of Mali, numbered between eight and nine hundred at the time of the French occupation in 1883;

now it is over 130,000. Founded in the midst of pagan Bambara it attracted traders, acquired the characteristics of a Muslim settlement, and then came within the sphere of the Tokolor conquerors. As a Muslim base among people who had been strongly resistant to Islam its influence increased in the atmosphere of modern change.

5 On the influence of Islam among the Mossi see B. Bichon, 'Les Musulmans de la subdivision de Kombissiry', *Notes et études sur l'Islam en Afrique Noire*, 1962, pp. 75–102; and E. P. Skinner, 'Islam in Mossi Society', in *Islam in Tropical Africa*, ed. I. M. Lewis, 1966, pp. 350–70.

6 For example, in the Nuba hills and the region south of the Jezira, both regions of small tribes. The process began in the days of the Funj state with the conversion of the Tegali Nuba.

7 I say 'unlikely' owing to Islam being manifested in the persons of alien 'Arabs', culturally too different for mutual understanding to be possible. Compare with west and central Sudan where the Islamic mediators were culturally close to those they sought to influence.

8 J. A. K. Leslie, *A Survey of Dar es Salaam*, 1963, pp. 11–12.

9 L. V. Thomas, 'L'animisme, religion caduque', *Bull. I.F.A.N.*, xxvii., ser. B, 1965, pp. 12–13.

10 J. S. Trimingham, *Islam in West Africa*, p. 201.

11 The minority in Niger are Hausa pagans and their eventual Islamization is inevitable.

12 Senegal is not quite in the same category as Mauritania, Niger and Somalia since conditions are different. Though religious leaders have been a strong political influence, there has been a deep penetration of secular civilization among certain classes, and also a small (5 per cent) but significant Christian minority. Article 1 of its constitution states that the state is 'secular, democratic, and social'. The only groups among whom animism is of any significance are the Dyola of Basse-Casamance, the Serer of Sine and the Basari of eastern Senegal. Of the Dyola 60 per cent are Muslim, 13 per cent Christian, and the rest animist; see L. V. Thomas, 'L'animisme, religion caduque' (*Bull. I.F.A.N.*, xxvii., sér. B, 1965, 12), who writes: 'Under the double influence of Christianity and Islam, on the one hand, and of modern socio-political structures, on the other, traditional Negro-African religion has entered upon a phase of disintegration.'

13 Like all generalizations this needs qualifying. Whereas in Northern Nigeria, where the British fostered the Fulani ruling classes, the privileged were lukewarm to the appeal of nationalism, particularly since it came from despised southerners, the French destroyed or bureaucratized Muslim political authority and in the Nilotic Sudan where the British took over a region where it had already been destroyed, the leaders, both clerical and lay, often supported

nationalism as at least not directly opposed to Islamic aims. The clerical class, of course, did not realize the implications of secular nationalism for the position of Islam in the state.

14 Mauritania and Somalia are the only states where the majority of the population are nomads. Of Mauritania's 700,000 inhabitants, 500,000 are nomadic whites (*bīḍān*) and of the remainder half are sedentary blacks (*sūdān*). Somalia is the only state in Africa south of the Sahara which possesses cultural-ethnic loyalty and belonging as a basis for nationalism.

15 M. Crowder, *Pagans and Politicians*, 1959, pp. 34–5.

16 H. A. Gailey, *A History of the Gambia*, 1964, p. 201.

17 President 'Abd an-Nāṣir's book *Falsafat ath-Thawra* (1954) pays considerable attention to Africa within the context of Egyptian Islam, stressing that Egypt is part of Africa as well as of the Arab world, and can fulfil a role as a bridge between them. It is the duty of Egyptians to champion the cause of African peoples. The pursuit of this policy after the colonialist period meant supporting dissident Africans against their own authorities. 'Abd an-Nāṣir sought at one time to use Islam as an instrument of policy but later changed and does not appeal especially to Africans on the ground of a common bond in Islam.

18 During the early period of their rule colonial authorities, in an attempt to satisfy Muslim prejudice, tried to see if it were possible to reform the existing system of Qur'ān schools and train their teachers in other disciplines, but found it impracticable.

19 In French territories Roman Catholic orders ran schools until 1903 when Church and State were separated in France and a federal administration formed in West Africa. The administration adopted a neutral policy in regard to religion, but since they also discouraged Christian missions among pagans they left the field wide open for Muslims. The federal administration set up its own schools, but these were French schools and Muslims feared to send their children to them. Later a changing attitude became apparent. 'The mere functioning of the French educational system alongside the Koranic school has revealed to the Federation's Muslims the anachronistic character of the latter and has also caused it to decline in both popularity and quality. Throughout the Federation, even in the Mauritanian stronghold of orthodoxy, Muslim parents are becoming increasingly dissatisfied with a type of religious instruction that stresses memory rather than understanding and does little to prepare its pupils for life under present-day conditions'; V. Thompson and R. Adloff, *French West Africa*, 1957, p. 530.

20 States which were wholly Muslim such as Somalia on the Indian Ocean and Mauritania on the Atlantic seaboard experienced the greatest problems, even after independence, which, for the new men,

meant freedom from internal conservatism as well as colonial rule. The difficulty experienced by Mauritanians even to adjust themselves to modern Arabic is referred to elsewhere (see below p. 141, n. 29), whilst they are having trouble over the question of the Arabization of the administration and educational system since a fifth of the people is non-Arabic-speaking. The Somalis too are experiencing difficulties in deciding between Arabic and a secular script as a medium for writing their language.

21 Even in the Maghrib. Yet ultraconservative institutions such as the Qarawiyyīn in Fez have not been spared the need to break with traditional patterns of teaching method and curriculum. Modernization of the Qarawiyyīn has only begun since independence (1956), and was forced upon the still reluctant *'ulamā'* by the government, the Istiqlāl Party and the trade unions (see R. Landau, 'The Karaouine at Fez', *Muslim World*, 1958, pp. 104–12).

22 See above p. 94.

23 See R. S. Morgenthau, *Political Parties in French-speaking West Africa*, 1964, pp. 287 ff.

24 Wolof use the word *dā'ira*, a *ṭarīqa* 'circle', for a benevolent society.

25 Colonial governments strengthened the authority of Islamic law and extended its range of application, and consequently the power of clerics, thus affecting the traditional working compromise between parallel institutions. There was often strong pressure to get a 'purer', that is, more legalistic, Islam. Though recognizing its application within certain spheres the administrations qualified this by a clause 'excepting those points where customary law applies'. At the same time, they applied their own law, especially in the sphere of criminal law (here Islamic law was only recognized in Nigeria), and, since it was they who decided what spheres should be governed by customary, Islamic, or Western law, the ruling factor was the colonial power.

Professor J. N. D. Anderson has recognized how, by way of reaction, indirect rule in the Fulani states of Northern Nigeria increased the liability of the inhabitants to the imposition of Islamic law. The emirates tended to assume an 'almost fictitious orthodoxy and rigidity in the face of any unwelcome demands or innovations, while the Protecting Power has almost invariably respected this attitude for the willing cooperation of the Muslim rulers' (*Islamic law in Africa*, 1954, p. 219).

26 So a panel of jurists which met in Northern Nigeria in 1958 was able to propose reforms in the application of Islamic law because the mental climate was changing. 'Its eyes had been opened, through the delegation which had visited Libya, Pakistan and the Sudan, to the backward state of the region by comparison with the greater part of the Muslim world' (J. N. D. Anderson, 'Conflict of Laws in

Northern Nigeria—A New Start', *International and Comparative Law Quarterly*, viii (1959), 442–56).

27 They are still a vital element in the Nilotic Sudan, but Sudanese tell me there has been a great change in both influence and range of membership since I completed my *Islam in the Sudan*, actually in 1944 though the book was not published until 1949. G. Draque writes of Morocco, 'Le declin des zaouïa commença dès le XVIIIe siècle. Il est maintenant total, sinon définitif' (*L'Afrique et l'Asie*, No. 53 (1961), 42).

28 The Aḥmadiyya took the initiative in translating the Qur'ān into African languages, and their example, or rather the fact that the new men made use of their translations, stimulated an orthodox translation into Swahili which began appearing in small sections in 1956. One cannot help feeling that the miserable way (poor paper and bad printing) in which this translation is produced reflects the feeling that 'virtue' has left the Qur'ān once it is translated.

In Northern Nigeria Hausa have frequently pressed for a translation against strong opposition. They even had difficulty in publishing a Hausa life of the Prophet. However, a number have persevered in the work of translation against the opposition of their elders and have published school pamphlets which have included Qur'ānic excerpts accompanied by their Hausa translations.

The secularized Muslims are not inhibited from translation by fear of authority but are hindered by their lack of knowledge of Arabic. A Yoruba group are said to have translated the whole Qur'ān but it has been criticized as inaccurate and has not yet been published.

29 A complete lack of interest in modern Arabic literature and thought is shown. This is shared by the Arabic-speaking Moors of Mauritania who have hardly begun to participate in the new Arab world, though not by the people of Nilotic Sudan. This lack of appreciation is accounted for by the fact that Arabic is closely bound up with traditional African Islamic culture, the whole emphasis being on Arabic as the word of God in the Qur'ān and as the key to divine law. The traditionalists have no use for Arabic in any other way (some have expressed revulsion at its secular use), whilst the *évolués*, having turned their back on traditional Islamic values, have no use for Arabic at all, since French and English are the keys to the new values they covet. With the Arabs of North Africa and the Near East, among whom the process of secularization is far advanced, the position is entirely different. Arabic is their language and not exclusively tied up with Islam.

Chapter 6

1 I am writing this shortly after the results of the Camp David Conference had alienated the Arab world, moderates and extremists alike, by the way in which the most vital Arab questions were ignored: the fate of Jerusalem, no term fixed to Israeli occupation of Arab lands, and failing to put a stop to Israeli colonization of the West Bank of Palestine.

At the same time, Ian Murray, writing in *The Times* (20.10.78) about the fourth congress of the Polisario Front fighting Morocco and Mauritania for control of the western Sahara, points out that 'refugee camps often find a real purpose and become a military camp, where men teach boys to fight for causes, and so perpetuate the very struggle which brought the refugee camp into being.' Then he shows the awareness of refugees for each other though separated by vast distances. 'Camp David,' he ends, 'was virtually a swear word at the Polisario congress.'

2 At the invitation of Milton Obote the Israelis had come to Uganda as advisers. Idi Amin was then second in command of Uganda's armed forces. With the help of the Israeli advisers he overthrew Obote by a military coup early in 1971, and he broke off relations with Israel in March 1972. In August of the same year he announced action to be taken to expel the entire Asian population of Uganda.

3 In one instance at least religion was not forced into a human social situation to provide a scapegoat. This was the expulsion of the 'Asian' communities from the east African states of Uganda, Kenya, and Tanzania. These were *Asians*, culturally different from Africans, seen as exploiters of Africans, who were themselves religiously diversified: Hindus of many groups and Muslim sectarians (Shīʿī Ithnaʿasharis, Ismaʿilis, Mustaʿlis or Bohoras, and Nizaris). In other words, they were people bound together into strongly-knitted social groups, entirely different in their ways of life from Africans. See above, pp. 79–80.

4 'We find on evidence that the real trouble in the South is political and not religious; neither the slave-trade nor the differences in religion played a part in the disturbances that took place in Equatoria . . . Christians, pagans, as well as Muslims, took part: in fact, some of the leaders of anti-Northern propaganda are Southern Muslims.' *Report of the Commission of Enquiry into the Disturbances in the Southern Sudan during August 1955*, Khartoum, 1956, p. 6.

5 The revolution in Zanzibar of 1964, which has been seen as inspired by Marxist ideology, was ignited by the desire of the island's black African population to free themselves from the hand of the Arab oligarchy fostered by the British, and from Arab dominance in so many areas of the island's life and economy. Other Arabs, with the exception of Algeria and Egypt, took no interest in the plight of the

Arabs slaughtered or expelled from the islands in the uprising. It should be remarked that Marxist theory is only partly relevant to African life. The union with Tanzania is logical, since Nyerere's *ujamaa* has worked well in relating modern socialism to traditional African collective ideals.

6 In de Gaulle's referendum, Guinée voted 'Non' and proclaimed its independence: 2.10.58. The Ghana–Guinea Union (November 1958) was joined in December 1960 by Mali. 'Union' was seen then as a first step in a confederation.

7 Sékou Touré is himself a descendant of Samory Touré (*c.* 1830–1900). Samory, of a Dyula family, was not born a Muslim but found Islam a unifying force. He should not be compared to the legists prosecuting a *jihād* like the *almamys* of Futa Jalon in Guinea, Al-ḥājj 'Umar and 'Uthmān dan Fodio, but is rightly judged an African (not a Muslim) nationalist. He founded a Mandinka empire that offered the most effective resistance the European invaders of West Africa had yet encountered. Finally, defeated by the French in 1898, his body is now enshrined in a tomb in the centre of Conakry.

Sékou Touré founded the Parti Démocratique de Guinée in May 1947 as a popular movement against colonialism and Islamic 'feudalism', and it became the party of the Socialist Republic of Guinea. Sékou Touré claims it to be 'a revolutionary party-state which endeavours to exclude from the political, economic, and social life of the country any arbitrary hierarchy.' Islam is seen as a personal allegiance that must be excluded from national life.

8 J. S. Trimingham, *The Sufi Orders in Islam*, Oxford 1971, pp. 255–9.

Appendix A

1 When the invading Muslim Arabs had gained control of the principal centres in North Africa, their advance into Africa came to a halt by reason of the desert. They saw the cultivable stretches bordering on the Mediterranean as an island, and so they called it *Jazīrat al-Maghrib*, 'the Island of the West'. But the Maghrib embraced distinctive regional differences and in consequence the Arabs distinguished between *al-Maghrib al-Aqsā*', 'the Farthest West' (Morocco), beyond which they confronted a narrow strait dividing Africa from Europe, which was independent of the Caliphate except for a brief period (A.D. 710–39), *al-Maghrib al-āwṣaṭ*, 'the Middle West' (Algeria), and *Ifrīqiyā* (the Roman term, now Tunisia).

Bibliography

'ABD AN-NĀṢIR, JAMĀL. *Falsafat ath-Thawra*, Cairo 1954

AMĪN, AḤMAD. *Qāmūs al-'Ādāt wa't-taqālīd*, Cairo 1953

AMIN, S. *The Maghrib in the Modern World*, 1970

ANDERSON, J. N. D. 'Conflict of laws in Northern Nigeria', *International and Comparative Law Quarterly*, viii (1959), 442–56

—— *Islamic Law in Africa*, London, H.M.S.O. 1954

AYROUT, H. H. *The Fellahin*, tr. Cairo, 1945

BA, AMADOU HAMPATÉ and DAGET, J. *L'empire peul du Macina: 1818–1853*, I.F.A.N., Bamako, 1962

BAKRI, AL-. *Description de l'Afrique septentrionale*, ed. de Slane, 2nd edn, Paris, Paul Geuthner 1911

BARBOUR, K. M. *The Republic of the Sudan*, London, University of London Press 1961

BARBOUR, N. (ed.) *A Survey of North West Africa (the Maghrib)*, ed. 2, 1962

BAULIN, JACQUES. *The Arab Role in Africa*, Penguin African Library, 1962

BEHRMANN, LUCY C. *Muslim Brotherhoods and Politics in Senegal*, Cambridge, Harvard University Press, 1970

BEL, A. *La Religion musulmane en Berbèrie*, Paris, 1936

BICHON, B. 'Les musulmans de la subdivision de Kombissiry', *Notes et études sur l'Islam en Afrique Noire*, pp. 75–102

BIRKS, J. S. *Across the Savannas to Mecca: The Overland Pilgrimage Route from West Africa*, London, 1978

BLACKMAN, W. S. *The Fellahin of Upper Egypt*, London, 1927

BOULNOIS, J. and HAMA, B. *Empire de Gao*, Paris, Librairie d'Amérique et d'Orient 1954

Cambridge History of Africa, III (1977), IV (1975), V (1976)

CAPOT-REY, R. *Le Sahara française*, Paris 1953

CHAILLEY, BOURBON, BICHON, AMON D'ABY, QUESNOT. *Notes et études sur l'Islam en Afrique Noire*, Paris 1962

CORY, H. 'Jando', *Journ. R. Anthrop. Inst.* lxxvii (1947), 159–68; lxxviii 81–94.

COUR, A. *L'Établissement des dynasties des chérifs au Maroc*, Paris, 1904

CROWDER, M. *Pagans and Politicians*, London, Hutchinson 1959

—— *French Assimilation Policy in Senegal*, Oxford University Press, 1962

DOUTTÉ, E. *Magie et religion dans l'Afrique du Nord*, Paris, 1909

L'Encyclopédie Coloniale, A.O.F., Paris 1949

EVANS-PRITCHARD, E. E. *The Sanusi of Cyrenaica*, Oxford, 1949

FROELICH, J. C. *Les Musulmans d'Afrique noir*, Paris, 1962

GAILEY, H. A. *A History of the Gambia*, London, Routledge 1964

GELLNER, E. *Arabs and Berbers*, 1973

—— *Saints of the Atlas*, London, 1973

GRAY, RICHARD. *A History of the Southern Sudan: 1839–1889*, London, 1961

HASAN, YUSUF FADL. *The Arabs and the Eastern Sudan*, Edinburgh, 1966

HOGBEN, S. J. *Muhammadan Emirates of Nigeria*, London, Oxford University Press 1930; revised edition: *The Emirates of Northern Nigeria* (with A. H. M. Kirk-Greene), 1966

HOLT, P. M. 'A Sudanese Historical Legend: The Funj Conquest of Suba', *Bull. Sch. Or. and Afr. Studies*, xxiii (1960), 1–12

—— 'Funj origins: a critique and new evidence', *J. African History* iv (1963), 39–55

—— *The Mahdist State in the Sudan: 1881–1898*, Oxford, 1958

—— *A Modern History of the Sudan*, London, 1961

IBN KHALDUN. *'Ibar*. ed. Bulaq, A. H. 1284

IBN SALIM AL-ASWANI, quoted by Maqrīzī, *Khiṭaṭ*, ed. G. Wiet. III, ii, Cairo 1922

JOBSON, R. *The Golden Trade*, London 1623, repr. 1904

JOHNSTON, H. A. S. *The Fulani Empire of Sokoto*, Oxford, 1967

JULIEN, C-A. *L'Afrique du Nord en marche*, Paris, 1953

—— *Histoire de l'Afrique du Nord*, 2nd edn, Paris, 1952–3

KING, N. Q. *Christian and Muslim in Africa*, New York, 1971

KLEIN, M. A. *Islam and Imperialism in Senegal: Siné-Saloum, 1847–1914*, Stanford University Press, 1968

KNAPPERT, JAN. *Swahili Islamic Poetry*, Leiden, 2 vols, 1970

KRITZECK, J. and W. H. LEWIS (eds). *Islam in Africa*, New York, 1969

LACOUTURE, J. and S. *Le Maroc à l'épreuve*, Paris, 1958

LANDAU, R. 'The Karaouine at Fez', *Muslim World*, xlviii (1958), 104–12

LAST, MURRAY. *The Sokoto Caliphate*, London, 1967

LE ROUVREUR, A. *Sahéliens et Sahariens du Tchad*, Paris 1962

LESLIE, J. A. K. *A Survey of Dar es Salaam*, London, Oxford University Press, 1963

LEVTZION, N. *Muslims and Chiefs in West Africa:* A Study of Islam in the Middle Volta Basin in the Pre-Colonial Period, Oxford, 1968

LEWIS, I. M. *Marriage and the Family in Northern Somaliland*, London, Kegan Paul 1962

—— *The Modern History of Somaliland*, London, Weidenfeld and Nicolson 1965
——, ed., *Islam in Tropical Africa*, London, Oxford University Press 1966
—— *A Pastoral Democracy*, London, 1961
MACMICHAEL, H. A. *The Anglo-Egyptian Sudan*, London, Faber 1934
MAḤMŪD AL-KĀTI *Tā'rīkh al-Fattāsh*, ed. and trans. O. Houdas and M. Delafosse, Paris 1913–14; repr. 1964
MAQRĪZĪ *Sulūk*, tr. Bouriant (Mission Arch. au Caire, xvii)
—— *Khiṭaṭ*, ed. G. Wiet, Cairo 1922
MAS'ŪDĪ, AL- *Murūj adh-dhahab*, ed. and tr. Barbier de Meynard and Pavet de Courteille, Paris 1861–77; revised edn, Ch. Pellat, Beirut 1966
MCCALL, D. F. and N. R. BENNETT (eds). *Aspects of West African Islam*, Boston University, 1971
MINOR, H. *The Primitive City of Timbuktu*, Princeton 1953
MONTEIL, VINCENT. *L'Islam noir*, Paris, 1964
MORGENTHAU, R. S. *Political Parties in French-Speaking West Africa*, London, Oxford University Press 1964
MUḤAMMAD BELO *Infāq al-Maisūr*, ed. C. E. J. Whitting, London 1951
PADEN, J. N. *Religion and Political Culture in Kano*, University of California, 1973
PRINS, A. H. J. *The Swahili-Speaking Peoples of Zanzibar and the East African Coast*, London, 1961
ROUCH, J. 'Migrations au Ghana', *J. Soc. Africanistes*, xxvi (1956)
—— *Contribution à l'histoire des Songhay*, Dakar, 1953
—— *Les Songhay*, Paris, 1954
SMITH, MARY *Baba of Karo*, London, Faber 1954
SMITH, M. G. *Government in Zazzau: 1800–1950*, London, Oxford University Press 1960
SI, CHEIKH TIDIANE. *La confrérie sénégalaise des Mourides: Un essai sur l'Islam au Sénégal*, Paris, 1969
SOUTHALL, A., ed. *Social Change in Modern Africa*, London, Oxford University Press 1961
STENNING, D. J. *Savannah Nomads*, London, Oxford University Press 1959
Tadhkirat an-Nisyān, trans. O. Houdas, Paris 1901
THOMAS, L. V. 'L'animisme, religion caduque', *Bull. Inst. Franç. d'Afrique Noire*, xxvii, ser. B (1965)
THOMPSON, V. and ADLOFF, R. *French West Africa*, Stanford, Calif., Stanford University Press, 1957
TOURNEAU, R. DE. *Évolution politique de l'Afrique du nord musulmane, 1920–1961*, Paris, 1962

TRIMINGHAM, J. S. *Islam in the Sudan*, London, Oxford University Press 1949
—— *Islam in Ethiopia*, London, Oxford University Press 1952
—— *Islam in West Africa*, London, Oxford University Press 1959
—— *A History of Islam in West Africa*, London, Oxford University Press 1962
—— *Islam in East Africa*, London, Oxford University Press 1964
—— 'Islam in Sub-Saharan Africa till the 19th Century', in *The Muslim World: A Historical Survey*, Part III, Leiden, 1969, pp. 153–179.
—— 'The Arab Geographers and the East African Coast', in *East Africa and the Orient*, ed. H. N. Chittick and R. I. Rotberg, New York, 1975, pp. 115–146, 272–83.
TUBIANA, M.-J. *Survivances préislamiques en pays Zaghawa*, Paris 1964
'UMAR IBN SA'ĪD TAL AL-FŪTĪ *Rimāḥ Ḥizb ar-Raḥīm 'alā Nuḥūr Ḥizb ar-Rajīm*, on margin of 'Alī Ḥarāzim, *Jawāhir al-Ma'ānī*, Cairo 1348/1929
'UMARĪ, IBN FAḌL ALLĀH AL-. *Masālik al-Abṣār: L'Afrique moins l'Egypte*, trans. Gaudefroy-Demombynes, Paris 1927
WAD ḌAIF ALLAH. *Ṭabaqāt Awliyā' as-Sūdān*, ed. Mandīl, Cairo 1930; ed. Ibrahim Sidaiq, Cairo 1930. New edition edited by Yusuf Fadl Hasan, Khartoum University, 1971
WESTERMARCK, E. *Ritual and Belief in Morocco*, 2 vols, 1926
YA'QŪBĪ, AL-. *Kitāb al-Buldān*, B. G. A. vii, Leiden, Brill, 1892
YĀQŪT. *Mu'jam al-Buldān*, ed. F. Wüstenfeld, Leipzig 1866–73
ZIADEH, NICOLA. *Sanūsīyah*, Leiden, 1958
ZOGHBY, S. M. (ed). *Islam in Sub-Saharan Africa*, a bibliographical study, Library of Congress, Washington, 1978

Index

Amin, Idi, 131, 139, 141
amulets, 57, 60, 84
ancestor cult, 43, 45–6, 49, 55, 73, 75, 82
angels, belief in, 53, 55
animism, Islamic, 42, 49
animist societies, 36, 41, 105
Anṣār group, 115, 116
Anwār as-Sādāt, President, 129
apartheid, 131
'*Aqīqa*, 46, 51, 69
Arab bedouin, 40
Arab civilization and culture, 3, 37, 57
Arab conquests, 7, 8, 22, 34
Arabia, 26, 31, 76, 86, 94
Arabic Institute, Ibadan, 141
Arabic language, 50, 67, 141
  and Arabization, 99–102
  loss of, 23, 106, 123
  in Maghrib, 8, 144
  and nationality, 127
  in Sudan and Swahili, 25–6, 61 115, 133
Arabic literary culture, 3, 7, 57, 68
Arabic script, 31 101–2, 106
Arabization, 30, 99–102
  of Berbers, 8–9, 33, 38, 91, 100
  of Nilotic Sudan, 23–4, 86, 88, 90, 99–100
Arabs, 31, 69
  in Maghrib, 10
  migrations of, 8, 20–4 *passim*, 34, 88, 91, 99–100
  in Nilotic Sudan, 22–3, 68, 71, 91
  role of, in Africa, 99–102, 126–8
Arab world, modern, 111, 138
  African contact with, 117–18
  education in, 119
  sharī'a in, 120
'Arafat, Yasir, 131
Arḍ al-Wāqwāq, 30
arts and sciences, 58
asceticism, 75
Ashanti tribes, 38
Ashiqqa Party, 116
'Ashūra, 63, 66
Asian Muslims, 79–80, 112
'Asīr, 76
Assaba, 119
Awdaghast (Saharan oasis), 10
Axum, kingdom of, 7, 26–7
al-Azhar, 3, 118, 142

Bagirmi, 20, 22
Baibars I, Rukn ad-Dīn, 23
Bait Asgede tribe, 29
Bait Juk tribe, 29
Bait al-Māl, 63
al-Bakrī, 11, 17
Bali, Kushite state, 27
Bamako, 104
Bambara states and tribes, 14–15, 16, 37, 97, 104–5
Bamun tribes, 124
Banādir towns, 29
Bandung Conference 1955, 128
Bani Hilāl, 8, 100
Banjagara, 17
Bantu culture and language, 30, 32, 101
Bantu tribes, 3, 31–3 *passim*, 38
  Muslim, 32, 40, 45, 49, 82, 90, 108, 113
Banu Kanz, 23
Baqqāra, cattle nomads, 65
Barābara tribe, 30, 88
baraka, 10, 40, 74–5
Barbour, K. M., 95
Bariba, 104
al-Barzanjī, 56
Bauchi, 19–20
Beja tribes, 22–3, 26, 29–30, 38, 40, 65
  Arabization of, 88
  assimilation of Arabs by, 100–1
Belen tribe, 29
belief, 53–5, 62
Berbers, 40, 64, 127, 144
  Arabization of, 8–9, 34, 38, 91, 100
  of Moroccan mountains, 89
  Saharan, 10–11, 60
Bilād at-Takrūr, 14; *see also* Takrūr
Bilād az-Zanj, 30
Bohoras, *see* Musta'līs
Bongo, President Omar, 132
bori cult, 47, 67, 83
Bornu, 17–20 *passim*, 61, 66, 78

Index

Hilāl tribes, *see* Bani Hilāl
Hobat, Ethiopian state, 27
Hoggar, 87
holé cult, 67, 83
holy men, 24, 39, 74
Hume, *mai* of Kanem, 17

'ibādāt, *see* ritual
Ibāḍism, 31, 58, 80
Ibn Abī Zaid, 62
Ibn al-'Arabī, 9
Ibn Baṭṭūṭa, 14, 40
Ibn Khaldūn, 18
Ibn Sa'īd, 30
Ibo tribes, 38, 132, 135–6
Ibrāhīm Mūsā, 15
Ibrāhīm Nyās, 122
Ibrāhīm ar-Rashīdī, 76
Ibrāhīm Sori, 15
'īd al-adhā, 67
'id al-fitr, 66, 67
idol worship, 82–3
'id prayers, 62, 67, 85
al-Idrīsī, 30
Idrīsiyya, 76
Ifāt, 27
Igellad (Tuareg tribe), 87
Ihyā' (al-Ghazali), 68
ijma' (consensus), 67–8
Ikhwān al-Muslimīn, 139
ilhām, 53
Ilorin state, 20
imam, 15, 16, 59–60, 80, 97
India, 31
individualistic aspects, *see* Islam
inheritance systems, Islamic, 50, 51, 88, 92
  and widow inheritance, 87, 92
Inislimen (Tuareg cleric class), 93
initiation cults and rites, 51, 70–1, 83
initiation schools, 59
Indonesia, 132
Iran, 132, 142
'Isā, Nabī, 79
'Ishrīniyyāt (al-Fazāzī), 66
Islam,
  accommodating African institutional elements, 15, 19, 34, 37, 41–2, 44–6
  in Central Sudan, 17–22
  and civilization in Africa, 1
  as class religion, 11, 17, 30, 34, 39, 45, 51, 64, 77, 93–4, 96–7
  conversion to, *see* conversion to Islam
  and cultural change in Africa, 2, 36, 44, 47, 56, 137
  culture zones, of, 2–3, Ch. 1
  in East Africa, 30–3
  effect of, on religion and society, 36, 48–52, 56, Ch. 4, 133
  in Egypt, 7, 9, 34
  in Ethiopia, 27, 29–30
  fundamentalist, 141–3
  individualistic aspects of, 41, 88
  legalistic aspect of, 3, 34, 46, 47, 51, 80, 136, 138, 141–2
  in Maghrib, 8–10, 34, 37
  militant, 34; *see also jihād*
  missionaries in, 24–5, 26
  and nationalism, 113–16
  in Nilotic Sudan, 22–6, 38, 64, 68, 107
  pillars of, 56–7, 62–7, 68
  and political parties, 116–17
  religious institutions of, 62–5
  results of adoption of, 44–8
  and secular culture, 110–13, 138
  and social structure, 39–42, 47, 56, 86–91; *see also* social change
  spread of, Ch. 1, 34–42, 86
  as state religion, 19, 29, 34, 51, 96; *see also* theocratic states
  unifying features of, 56–74
  universalism of, 85, 104, 107, 114
  and urban life, 3, 89, 94, 104, 112
  and Western civilization, 107–10
  in Western Sudan, 10–17
Islamic animistic practices, 42, 49
Islamic culture, 41, 43, 125
Islamic institutions, 46, 50, 57, 96–7
Islamic law (shari'a), 49–52 *passim*, 56, 57–8, 111
  application of, 98–9
  and customary law, 46, 92, 95, 98
  and European administration, 103, 140